Vigilant Faith

Vigilant Faith

Studies in Religion and Culture
John D. Barbour and Gary L. Ebersole, Editors

Passionate Agnosticism
in a Secular World

Daniel Boscaljon

UNIVERSITY OF VIRGINIA PRESS   *Charlottesville and London*

University of Virginia Press
© 2013 by the Rector and Visitors of the University of Virginia
All rights reserved
Printed in the United States of America on acid-free paper

First published 2013

9 8 7 6 5 4 3 2 1

LIBRARY OF CONGRESS CATALOGING-IN-PUBLICATION DATA

Boscaljon, Daniel.
  Vigilant faith : passionate agnosticism in a secular world / Daniel Boscaljon.
      pages   cm. — (Studies in religion and culture)
  Includes bibliographical references and index.
  ISBN 978-0-8139-3463-1 (cloth : alk. paper) — ISBN 978-0-8139-3464-8 (pbk. : alk.
paper) — ISBN 978-0-8139-3465-5 (e-book)
  1. Faith. 2. Skepticism. I. Title.
  BT771.3.B65 2013
  234'.23—dc22

                                                                2012049803

For Laura and David,
 who had faith in me from the beginning

If the title "The Religious Meaning of Atheism" is not nonsensical, it implies that atheism is not limited in meaning to the mere negation and destruction of religion but that, rather, it opens up the horizon for something else, for a type of faith that might be called, in a way that we shall further elucidate, a postreligious faith or a faith for the postreligious age.

—PAUL RICOEUR, "Religion, Atheism, Faith"

Contents

Preface

My interest in faith was sparked in the midwestern pews of evangelical America and whetted through exposure to existential philosophy and post-modern theology. Those interested in fate could describe as inevitable my frustrations with what posed as answers and my subsequent embrace of a faithful and passionate agnosticism as an alternative to impossible knowledge claims. Over time, I found that I was writing the book that I wished that I could have read long ago, discussing faith and uncertainty as valuable on their own terms. The resulting book is a work of faith formed and informed by my passions, my reason, and my volition. Peculiarly, perhaps perversely, probably naïvely, I believe in the possibility that I have written something true.

Books generally rise to the level of the community that surrounds their authors, and I remain incredibly grateful for those who have supported and challenged my work. Because the gestation of this text was slow, I wish to thank a number of people from over the years. David Klemm, who pushed me away from what was easy and maintained confidence in my abilities, was an invaluable resource and ally. Laura Inglis and Peter Steinfeld first introduced me to Kierkegaard, Tillich, and Heidegger and allowed me to make mistakes. David Wittenberg, David Jasper, and Lori Branch permitted me to develop my insights about faith in strange ways that nonetheless bore fruit, and Andrew Hass, Mattias Martinson, and Darren Middleton provided me with good feedback as this project developed. I credit the vigilance of J. Sage Elwell, Janeta Tansey and Forrest Clingerman for helping me work through early ideas and drafts, sharpening my best points and eliminating the weakest: their pains were essential. Michael Baltutis, Peter Yoder, Nathan Eric Dickman, Ben Jenkins, and Shawnacy Perez helped me determine the proper boundaries of a vigilant faith between religion and skepticism. Cathie Brettschneider saw the promise of early drafts and has championed the process of seeing this to completion. Finally, I thank my parents for having instilled confidence in me, and Becky and Madeleine for their continued support and patience.

Opening the Domain of Presymbolic Faith

> Our fathers were our models for God. And, if our fathers bailed, what
> does that tell us about God?
>
> —TYLER DURDEN, *Fight Club*

Our current existential terror has taken the form of brokenness;
tragically, we remain unable to name this terror and thereby defend ourselves against it. Bob Dylan prophesied the onset of this struggle in 1989
and fittingly re-released his song "Everything Is Broken" in 2008. The song
catalogs the disintegration of the world through the dissolution of things:
"Broken lines, broken strings, broken threads, broken springs / Broken
idols, broken heads, people sleeping in broken beds."[1] As the song continues, Dylan attends to how tools (cutters, saws) and humans (bodies, bones,
voices) are broken and testify to the loss of what had once held things together. Simultaneously a warning and a dirge, both versions of Dylan's
song impress listeners with an impending crisis of brokenness. Unlike the
encounters of emptiness found in the wake of World War II, brokenness
leaves us with pieces of a whole that seems impossibly large, tangible reminders of loss that intensifies our plight. Having confronted Nietzsche's
Madman, who testifies to the death of God in the twentieth century, we now
must define and challenge the terror unique to us.

People have confronted the horror of dwelling in a broken world with
limited degrees of success. Most distract themselves from brokenness
through a variety of mass-produced objects, upgrading and consuming
without thought. This pursuit of new things, literally replacing what is bro-

ken with what is improved, converts an existential problem into a mechanical one and thereby displaces the issue. Other people seek solace in psalms and sermons, using tradition to retrieve a past time. Doing so denies the experience of brokenness by treating the solution for a past problem as applicable despite differences. A third strategy redefines defeat as victory: positing wholeness as myth, these find freedom in the fall of fantasy and the elimination of illusion. Their strident denials of the idea of the holy have balanced out the equally fundamentalist voices who insist, with certainty, that nothing has changed. These reactions, of course, occur in a real world full of more pressing needs and worries—unemployment, war, illness, food, shelter—that obviate any sort of focus on the problem at all.

Distraction, refusal, and celebration are very human modes of dealing with change, and Kierkegaard ably characterized them as "despair," the "sickness unto death" he saw plaguing Christendom in the nineteenth century. His cure for nineteenth-century despair was faith, resting transparently in the hand of God, a definition that Kierkegaard intended as a corrective for the impoverished definitions of faith that haunted Lutheran Copenhagen. Because our ability to recognize faith's virtue has continued to dwindle, my task is to offer a revitalized definition of faith capable of confronting our existential brokenness at its source. But before demonstrating how vigilant faith uniquely restores us from brokenness, I will define the cause of brokenness in our times and determine how a vigilant faith differs from other theologies of faith.

Secularism

Charles Taylor's work on secularism clarifies problems with the original Weberian position while simultaneously articulating why using the term "secular" still meaningfully defines how life in the twenty-first century differs from life five hundred years earlier. Arguing against definitions of secularism that assume something has been lost, Taylor identifies three forms of secularism. The first two, the emergence of secularized public spaces and the decline of belief and practice, are familiar; Taylor's innovation comes in identifying secularism as a state in which "naiveté is unavailable to anyone, believer or unbeliever alike," which implies "a new context in which all search and questioning about the moral and spiritual must proceed." Taylor ultimately roots the secular age in the development of an "exclusive humanism" rooted in the "identity of disengaged reason, disenchantment and instrumental control" (136). Although preceding versions of vigilant faiths were lived in the past, a vigilant faith becomes increasingly important and widely available in the secular age that Taylor describes.

One reason the terror of brokenness so powerfully grasps us is the influence of secularism on our understanding of what faith means. One symptom manifests etymologically; as Wilfred Cantwell Smith showed, the meaning of "believe" has shifted drastically over the past four hundred years. The verb (derived from *belieben*, or beloved) initially denoted devotion without a necessary direct object. Belief first shifted when people grounded their faith in a person to whom they were devoted and then altered from a focus on a person's character to that person's word. The penultimate shift occurred in the advent of moral-sense philosophy, when Locke used faith as a synonym for belief, defining it as accepting a proposition as true based on argument and in spite of knowledge. The final step converted believing into a merely mental act centered on a proposition, resulting in a sense of faith where believing implies an absence of knowledge and not a fullness of it, transforming all faith into bad faith.[3] Problematically, in a time when our things testify to brokenness, we deny our potential to remain devoted without a direct object and lose a ground of faith. Our current crisis of faith emerges in the conjunction of expanded sites for faith in the world and its simultaneous conceptual and even linguistic diminution.

A second effect of secularism on faith manifests in the recent popularity of the New Atheists, whose reiteration of old arguments for a wide audience has garnered critical scorn. The importance of their books as a symptom arises neither in their strident tone (of, say, Sam Harris's 2004 *The End of Faith*) nor in their best-seller status, but instead in how the popularity of such books exposes our widespread theological ignorance. Faith is devalued not only etymologically but also in terms of our working understanding of its potential. This constitutes a symptom of secularization inasmuch as such arguments produce neither the indifference one might feel toward a fanatic proclaiming that "the earth is flat" nor the ire from a more widespread audience than critics and scholars. By waging what a reading audience feels is either a "threatening" or a "successful" attack on obsolete conceptions of faith and God, New Atheists reveal the need for a rehabilitated sense of faith capable of thinking through their arguments with perhaps even more rigor than they use.

Secularism clearly has influenced the development of philosophical theology—which, unlike confessional theology, explores knowledge of God without relying on revelation. The profusion of varieties of philosophical theology in "postmodern," "postsecular," and "postreligious" forms reveals several efforts to take secularism as useful for the study and practice of religion. Each of these provides a perspective on theology's relevance in a secular world: as a general category, postmodern theologies take a critical attitude toward the two foundations of theology, revelation (*theos*), and reason (*logos*). In particular, postsecular theologies tend to emphasize the fallibility of secular rationality in order to promote the importance of trusting in revelation, while postreligious theologies explore the relevance of theological topics assuming the viability of critiques of revelation.

Thus, although the postreligious and the postsecular provide different perspectives on the secular age, each responds to the assumptions and values of the postmodern, secular era Taylor describes. Beyond the specific relationship to the question of secularism, varieties of postmodern theology have also questioned Enlightenment assumptions about race, gender, sexuality, and class. Feminist, postcolonial, and liberation theologies have explored the practical implications of human thought, expanding the importance of theology beyond the ivory tower and the steeple. These projects mirror the questions and frame the concerns of the twenty-first century and have allowed theology to retain its relevance to contemporary life. As a whole, these projects, using theological tools as a way to fight for better forms of justice, work to overcome systemic issues that cruelly exacerbate the problem of brokenness for those excluded from the goods of society.

Postmodern theologies characterized as postsecular and postreligious (instead of postcolonial, for instance) have recently become more focused on articulating better definitions of God—perhaps as compensation for the growing influence of secularism. These thinkers largely attempt to harness the potential offered by philosophical insights into questions of being and truth. Although this work interests theologians, the incohesive nature of the various models deprives those who search for God of knowing what they seek, exacerbating the sense of brokenness.

Examples abound. Mark C. Taylor's *After God* features a postmodern model of God, presented as a figure constructed to cover an infinite abyss that contrasts with finite gods, *neither* finite *nor* infinite (345–47). Creston Davis presents two depictions of God in *The Monstrosity of Christ*, a debate between John Milbank and Slavoj Žižek. Milbank ably conveys the Radical Orthodox mode of offering an alternative modernity by reviewing Scholastic thinkers through postmodern frames and argues for a paradoxical conception of a participatory God that saturates everyday reality in a nondialectical fashion, allowing finite goods to be simultaneously (and paradoxically) *both* finite *and* infinite (164–67). Žižek denies both the literal and metaphorical sense of "God," emphasizing the finite remainder by claiming that "God" is the "inhuman core that sustains being-human" (240). Richard Kearney announces his postreligious desires in the title of his *Anatheism: Returning to God after God*, a book that provides alternatives to theism that blend postreligious and postsecular theological strands masterfully. Kearney's work opens a space to question God in a multireligious sense that seeks after an inexhaustible God who is always "more" (180).

Each of these visions of God are accompanied with some analysis of what this God might mean to human experience and how it alters the ontological and ethical parameters for living in the twenty-first century. But even as these authors wrestle to unite the fragments of memory and anticipation that signal a broken world, incorporating atheist and secular criticisms of a theistic god, the god of wholeness remains sundered, absent, beyond our grasp. At best, secularized models of God that exchange the name of God for a human concept (as John Caputo interchanges "God" with "love" in his *On Religion*) grant temporary access to weak gods unable to overcome the situation of brokenness. I therefore bracket my own speculation about God and turn instead to determine how we might honor the question of God's possibilities in faith. The direction of my turn—toward the domain of prebelief—precedes and obviates distinctions of postreligious and postsecular, although I stay within the parameters of a postmodern philosophical theology.

Skepticism

Even a nuanced and sophisticated model of God cannot wholly restore a broken world, because, increasingly, we are haunted by a skepticism that results in our discrediting God. Our skepticism is not constrained to religion, however, but persists unconsciously in all of our interactions—it is both native and naïve, a reflex, a mechanism that protects its user from being duped. It is native inasmuch as we skeptically reject appearances without cultivating this ability, and it is naïve because we do not enact it consciously or reflexively: we reject in a simplistic and blind manner, looking behind what is given to avoid being taken unaware. Unlike Greek skepticism, naïve skepticism does not require constructive work—one does not have to make an equipollent argument in order to suspend the possibility of knowledge. Instead, skeptics assume that nothing can be certain, nothing can be trusted, and thus protect themselves from the possibility that what appears to be good may in fact be less than desirable. Prevented from dwelling in the openness of the first naïveté, skeptics engage in continual criticism, frequently attended with the sarcasm that now passes as ironic detachment. Although Paul Tillich and Søren Kierkegaard integrated doubt and faith, skepticism significantly diverges from doubt and demands its own treatment.

Skepticism, unlike doubt, emerges from an initial attitude toward the world that filters perceptions. The terror experienced as doubt occurs when the once familiar becomes regarded as uncanny: thrust from a comfortable feeling of being at home in the world, I cannot trust the viability of my world, my self, my freedom. Such doubt, however, follows an initial movement of having accepted the world and self as fundamentally trustworthy—doubt is an aberrant state whose disbelief is relative to a particular matter. Skepticism attacks the roots of knowing in general: it removes the possibility of being assailed by existential doubt because it eliminates the motivation for specific questions. By refusing openness to the givenness of the world, I obviate the threats of existential doubt and malaise and the possibility of existential disappointment, caused when the object of my trust proves unworthy of my initial evaluation. Problematically, using skepticism as a means to avoid doubt and disappointment invariably leads to an end similar to what was shunned—isolation and despair.

The all-encompassing nature of native skepticism, as opposed to doubt, produces isolation. This occurs primarily as one eliminates the benefit of the doubt relative to others. Theologians since Augustine have noted the importance of faith in the possibility of forming human relationships, and this faith allows my lack of knowledge about others to come to their credit. A distanced skepticism and initial mistrust of others' intentions prevents me from joining with others in a state of friendship. Although I may be able to live in a world with others—paying bills, watching sports, eating food— my wondering why another may desire conversation hinders my enjoyment of these goods. Because native skepticism precedes my intentional interactions with the world, it becomes impossible to understand the resulting appearance of brokenness: a cold and friendless world populated by those prone to causing pain.

A second reason that skeptics cannot enjoy the good of communities comes from the relationship of community and symbol. A symbol encapsulates the heart of the community, including its idiosyncratic vocabulary, hermeneutic biases, and expectations for the future—symbols gain power over time as long as they remain central, accruing particular histories that deepen the communities that they gather. Symbols are instrumental in the formation of any given community, not merely religious ones: sports teams, political groupings, and national identities all revolve around key symbols that provide contexts in which individuals see themselves as part of a larger whole. My lack of faith causes my inability to fully participate within a community or allow it to influence my identity, the hesitation I feel in committing to a group, and my pervasive desire for differentiation.

Examples of the centrality of symbols for communities proliferate. On a political register, the connection appears through flags: each country's flag carries a unique significance, and understanding and respecting this history invites me into a matrix of terms and assumptions about the worth of this ideological order. Recently, the Constitution has been the central rhetorical rallying point for the Tea Party; its symbolic importance for candidates often overrides any tangible or concrete concerns. On a religious level, the symbol presents a threshold, condensing the central realization or transformation that one has prior to finding oneself at home within a community. A symbol makes no sense outside the context of believers: being moved relative to the symbol is the necessary precondition for the possibility of understanding the nature of the group. Native skepticism interrupts my initial encounter with symbols, however, and pushes me into a state of differentiation, as, skeptical, I lack the suspended disbelief necessary to allow the symbol to unlock my self or the deeper dimensions in which it participates. This state of being differs from a doubt that questions the good provided by the symbol *after* the symbol has already provided this function.

The movement toward skepticism's protective possibilities in America began in the late nineteenth century during the transition into urban environments. Early movies used skepticism as a feature differentiating the sophisticated city dweller from the gullible country rube. The unnatural order of the cities, liberated by technology from constraints on time and space, was a welcome haven to increasingly large numbers of individuals. Technology also diminished the number of people required to grow food to feed the city, causing cities to become a destination, even for those who once saw its unnatural foundation as denoting a vicious or godless wasteland. Although the crowds that became universal attributes of city life might have offered new possibilities for camaraderie, they instead became objects of fear: philosophers preached against the leveling effects of the herd even as individuals struggled to maintain a sense of self in a world that denied individuality and therefore real community. Skepticism shielded city dwellers but required habituation and practice.

The shock of the new city has obviously waned, especially as even rural environments have become increasingly urbanized and set apart from nature. Skepticism has survived, remaining useful as a protective shield against the force of marketing. Marketers promote goods with claims that raise our suspicions, and most have had a formative experience when merchandise did not present the happiness that advertisers associated with it. This shield is only rarely inappropriate, as advertising techniques sell everything from church services to art showings to presidential candidates. We have become increasingly inured in our skeptical mind-set and more comfortable as our lack of faith protects us from disappointment: not having ever believed the message of the minister or the performance of the politician, when tabloids and talk shows reveal a hero's hypocrisy, I can shrug indifferently at what already seems like old news. Relying on doubt would allow such news to catch me off guard; skepticism keeps me safe. No longer the province of philosophy, skepticism allows us to forestall our complicity in our failings.

Naïve skepticism differs from a philosophical skepticism in more ways than mere rigor. Unlike Descartes, for example, for whom skepticism prompted a written meditation, modern skepticism is so native as to be impossible *not* to use. It has become more common to approach all things skeptically, holding the self in reserve, but we have thereby lost the ability to find joy in a first or fresh experience. Anything that presents itself as something of value causes alarm; we withdraw from such things, hesitating, and a moment of potential grace in this way is mediated, broken, and lost. The resulting emptiness creates a hunger for some sort of connection, a cyclical desire causing wary people to interpret the appearance of newness as another diversion—or worse, a confidence game intended to take what they most cherish. Naïve skeptics are productive and industrious and live in a state of permanent and self-imposed disconnection that eradicates the hope of attaining the goods of tradition we desire. The resulting despair differs from that caused by existential doubt—although despair also follows doubt, the despair of skepticism is produced internally instead of attacking individuals externally.

Because skepticism produces despair as well as protection, continued use is costly: skeptics look within the self or within communities and find only broken fragments pointing toward failed wholeness. Some choose to hold themselves apart from what promises to grant internal wholeness—politics, religion, art—worried that it will cost their souls instead of providing restoration. Idols, after all, have a well-known thirst for human vitality. The flourishing of knitting circles and book clubs, gym memberships and church small groups testify to the increasing drive to find meaning and connections with others. The desperation with which humans seek this out and the unsatisfying results show that the use of skepticism is the cure that kills as it is used.

Naïve skepticism disables the faith process by precluding the possibility of mediation in faith. All symbols appear to be broken because naïve skeptics lack the introductory belief required to open them. Skepticism, which is negatively individuating, forbids me from participating through the symbol directly. Lacking the faith that would lead to a second movement of doubt, I see how symbols affect others while I withhold my trust. I witness the honest appreciation of the country's values that emerge when others view a flag but am alienated by their earnest display of patriotism. Watching a minister breaking bread and sharing wine, I can only say, "This is not for me." The symbol unlocks a space in others—but not in me. My own emptiness is redoubled and magnified: although the self-negating element of the symbol is exposed, it leads nowhere. Symbols break because skepticism propels me past the openness of a first naïveté and into a hermeneutic of suspicion. The symbol reflects my internal emptiness and does not allow me to participate in its infinite depths.

My alienation leads to another problem: in addition to the problem of a self-generated barrier to faith and the absence of community born out of native distrust, I am also denied access to the depths of human culture and existence. Skepticism prevents me from experiencing my self as a whole or as part of a human or spiritual community and, as a result, sentences me to an isolated and self-enclosing despair. In sum, the crisis of faith in the twenty-first century involves neither the belief that provides understanding nor the understanding that provides the basis for faith (to cite Anselm's model): understanding and believing are difficult for native skeptics. Integrating the brokenness that haunts the twenty-first century requires theologians to presuppose conditions of secularism and skepticism.

The Need for Faith

Theological projects that focus on the "object" of faith instead of the believer inevitably fail to accommodate skepticism, especially a naïve skepticism that precludes an openness to symbolic mediation. Historically, humans have thought about God and faith in tandem; theology about the object of belief and an individual's subjective response developed together. Detailed and nuanced theological descriptions of God feed our human longing to know the infinite and to feel that it knows us: they structure our religious experiences and offer a vocabulary capable of describing them. This is the genius behind the original hermeneutical problem, which holds the movements of believing and understanding in an edifying tension: we believe in order to understand, and we understand in order to believe.

In the middle of the twentieth century, theologians and philosophers interested in religion began explicitly considering the status of theology—particularly questions of God and faith—relative to the growing trend of atheism and secularism. They accomplished this work in a fog of overlapping cultural concerns: the shadow of world wars, the rise of historical criticism, the implications of nationalism, and the expansion of industrialization. A desire to show the human capacity to find meaning and connection in a world seemingly devoid of both connect authors as diverse in background as Buber, Frankl, and Berdyaev with others like Bonhoeffer, Tillich, Ricoeur, and Bultmann. These authors took seriously the critiques of God presented by Freud and Nietzsche and the implicit denial of God that erupted historically in the form of World War II.

A second key moment in twentieth-century thinking came in the onset of postmodern criticism generated in the aftermath of post-1968 France. These thinkers shared a background in postwar European culture and an intellectual history framed by Nietzsche and Freud (through Lacan, at this point) and were interested in the question of the possibility of meaning. Like the earlier group, these French thinkers explicitly desired to describe a world that had broken away from what had anchored it and the consequences of this for human beings. This second project broke from the first. The French thinkers shared a Marxist affinity for investigating the effect that assumptions about reason had on creating social structures and institutions, while the earlier group spent more time contemplating deeper and better ways to describe the plight of human existence in terms of God and world. In other words, although a structural affinity connects the questions at the center of each group's concern, the shift in emphasis correlates with a loss of theological depth.

As discussed above, twenty-first-century attempts to recover the theological through the secular have generated complex and nuanced visions of God that have not restored a sense of wholeness, and, even if successful, these theologies underestimate the trauma of skepticism. Rather than continuing along these lines, then, I will recover the studies of faith written during the postwar period that have lain fallow as current theologians have pursued questions of God. Today's philosophers of religion and philosophical theologians have not pursued the possibilities that Bultmann, Tillich, and Ricoeur opened for exploring the possibility of a posttheistic faith capable of surviving the rigors of demythologization, the terrors of nonbeing, and the criticisms of atheist philosophies. Although different challenges confront us in the twenty-first century—including the disintegration of nature, the despair of meaningfulness, and the rise of fundamentalist tendencies within religions (including atheism)—the course opened by this earlier wave of theologians remains an important and overlooked means of addressing the human situation today. In other words, the question of what remains of faith if one grants the full force of Nietzsche's and Freud's atheism persists as a theological starting point relevant to contemporary issues but overlooked by contemporary scholars.

Responses to this situation varied in the middle of the twentieth century. Bultmann's task of demythologization anticipated an increasingly hostile audience, showing the truth of the biblical narrative that persisted in spite of its mythological language and roots. Tillich also emphasized the existential benefits of theology; taking Bultmann's insights a step farther, Tillich focused on how faith could be generated symbolically through the biblical narratives and the God above the God of theism that participated in each narrative and symbol (but was not exhausted by it). Ricoeur posited that Heidegger's existentialism was a significant resource for those interested in a posttheistic faith; additionally, he believed that striving for a faith after atheism was an important task both for philosophers interested in religion and for theologians. This movement reached its most radical extreme in the writings of Thomas J. J. Altizer, who reread Hegel and the Christian tradition in order to proclaim the death of God and a new gospel of Christian atheism.

Postmodern theologies have explored more rigorous understandings of secularized Christianity, or what John Caputo calls "religion without religion." Continental philosophers have enriched the debate, as thinkers from Nancy to Žižek have weighed in on the meaning of religion in a secularized society and the possibilities of an atheist theology. With few exceptions—Jean-Luc Nancy's *Dis-Enclosure* and Kearney's *Anatheism* among them—contemporary projects remain focused on questions of God and overlook the practical element of faith.

My work follows the tradition of atheistic—or perhaps, following Kearney, anatheistic—theology. Conforming to a secularized mind-set, an atheistic bias is a necessary (and intended) consequence of placing faith in skeptical human consciousness: bracketing God and embracing a godless world is a means to the end of relating to the God above the God of theism (to borrow Tillich's term), not an end in itself. This keeps my definition of faith from spinning into a nihilistic deconstructive spiral that lacks a place to rest. I retrieve the concern for the systematic and practical function of faith for individuals and communities as a way of supplying an element lacking in today's theological conversation, not because of nostalgia for a "better" form of theology.

Theology and Faith

One might argue that Paul Tillich's systematic treatment of faith has caused subsequent scholars to avoid the subject. His definition of faith as "ultimate concern" in *Dynamics of Faith* remains adequate: it builds on Heidegger's conception of *care* and thus is suitably philosophical; it is simultaneously religious in orientation given its "Protestant principle," which warns against the allure of idols. Because "ultimate concern" provides a model of faith that incorporates the doubt necessary to appease critical thinkers as well as the religious experience more suited to traditional approaches to faith, it has persisted as a viable model.

Tillich's continuing influence on current theological discussions supports this view. Although contemporary philosophical theology has focused on secularization (which manifests as theological interrogations of politics and religion), recent works suggest elements of Tillich's teachings. First, the emphasis on religion, literature, and the arts—in which theologians interpret secular artistic products as reflections of theological questions or as foundations for theological statements—is indebted to Tillich's work in developing a theology of culture. Secondly, current theological models of God preserve Tillich's influence: Kearney's transcendent and paradoxical God belongs within this tradition, as does Mark C. Taylor's God, figured as a neither-nor that reflects Tillich's insight while revising what a God above the God of theism might mean. My point is not to offer a complete intellectual genealogy but instead to show that Tillich's thinking remains relevant even though the specific issues that arguably were of central concern—the role of faith in human existence and ways to incorporate a relationship with the nontheistic God beyond symbols—have been neglected. Expanding Tillich's work on faith provides a critical supplement to the current theological discussion, driving thinking back toward the boundaries of the pragmatic.

Although most theologians acknowledge the explanatory value and influence of Tillich's definition of faith as ultimate concern and description of

God as the ground and abyss of Being (or power of Being-itself), the rise of secularism and skepticism requires revisiting and expanding Tillich's model. I do this by promoting a model of faith rooted in Tillich's structure and discussing its consequences and permutations in light of faith's recent currency in continental philosophy.

The language of modeling clarifies the relationship between Tillich's work and my own. According to David Klemm and William Klink, we construct models to explain new phenomena—they explain why things happen. A theistic model of faith explains how humans have subjective conviction despite objective uncertainty by incorporating external entities (God, or a symbol of God). Theistic explanations emphasize our passivity relative to a divine symbol, which calls us to new levels of self-understanding.[5] Grounding faith in human consciousness allows me to emphasize human activity, deviating from traditional explications of faith by attending to human responsibility. By connecting theological definitions of absolute faith with contemporary philosophical models, I bridge the gap left by contemporary authors such as Nancy and Kearney, who do not often reflect on earlier models of faith.

Finally, and most important, the practical and ethical dimension of this book expands the domain of faith to incorporate those whose skeptical inclinations hinder them from having symbolic religious encounters. Vigilant faith offers a viable alternative to a symbolically mediated conception of faith, correlating to traditional models in its import without being exhausted by them.

The Value of the Domain of Prebelief

The growing presence of secularism and skepticism makes it necessary to define faith in a way that preexists movements of believers into symbolic communities (i.e., one of the many smaller communities that exist within a broader, shared social and linguistic horizon). However, far from an impoverished shadow, this type of faith ultimately manifests as an exemplary form of faith. I will refer to this domain, which incorporates both the skeptical and the atheistic into its presymbolic structure, as prebelief. Faith formed in presymbolic prebelief is atheistic (because it precedes an encounter with a specific manifestation of the divine), and it is individualistic (because it is maintained apart from a community). Because prebelief brackets larger potential wholes, it shares certain structural affinities with the "absolute faith" referenced by Kierkegaard and Tillich. This parallel allows me to measure the adequacy of faith in the domain of prebelief against the absolute faith they articulate.

Two elements distinguish the definition of prebelief from absolute faith. First, because the domain of prebelief is open to extreme forms of skepticism, it expands the viability and life of faith beyond parameters of absolute faith defined by Kierkegaard and Tillich. The domain of prebelief also precedes the experience of brokenness because it arises prior to a confrontation with symbols. Avoiding symbols allows the domain of prebelief to remain consistent with the atheistic mind-set of the secular age but requires following three main criteria. First, the origin and dynamic of faith must be anthropocentric, forcing humans to accept responsibility for their faith by bracketing the question of God's existence (one cannot have both an answer and have faith). Additionally, the definition of faith cannot violate the precepts of skepticism but instead must integrate skepticism within its structure. Tillich successfully accomplished a version of this in his classic *The Courage to Be;* here Tillich argued that faith could exist as faith if and only if it arose in spite of doubt. Because doubt is more limited than skepticism (although they are positively correlated), accounting for skepticism accomplishes the work of Tillich's model while going beyond it. Finally, the domain of prebelief requires that its faith remain open to the possibility of a future knowledge. Theologians—particularly Aquinas and Kierkegaard—have identified the correlation between faith and despair: despair comes because of a lack of faith in God, and faith mitigates the despair by allowing God to constitute the self. Although atheism allows despair (contextualized by failing to believe in God's providence), a skeptical faith resolves despair without relying on God. A skeptical faith requires remembering the temporary and provisional nature of a prebelief faith, remaining mindful of the possibility of knowledge even while denying its presence, in faith, at any given moment.

Incorporating vigilance also differentiates faith as prebelief from absolute faith. Vigilance manifests as a necessary precondition for the possibility of skeptical consciousness and thus becomes necessary for both consciousness and faith. The importance of vigilance grows throughout the book, as I argue that it is structurally analogous to the function of courage in Tillich's definition of faith in *The Courage to Be.* The important difference is that Tillich argued that we need courage to *overcome* doubt and thereafter attain faith; my model positively sublates skepticism into the structure of faith, allowing us in vigilance to remain simultaneously faithful and skeptical. In other words, I argue that vigilance allows us to understand that faith and skepticism correlate positively, not negatively. That all humans have the capacity to be and remain vigilant does not violate the requirement that faith stay grounded in the human. Additionally, vigilance gives a practical dimension to my model of faith: I can keep watch over myself, over the things in the world, and for signs of the coming of God. Although theologians, mystics, and philosophers have recognized vigilance as an important trait, its specific benefit for faith or consciousness remains underdeveloped. I correct this oversight in what follows.

My model of faith is Christian inasmuch as the theological definitions of faith I am most interested in arise from a confessional Christian—and Protestant—tradition. It deviates from this tradition to the extent that I explore the nature of that faith that precedes an interaction with a religious symbol, a faith useful to people for whom traditional Christian symbols seem broken. This is familiar ground for theologians and philosophers conversant with "postreligious" or "postsecular" versions of Christianity, although emphasizing faith introduces a substantive theological grounding to a terrain most frequently traversed by philosophers who have theological interests.

I ultimately produce a definition of faith that functions like a second naïveté, able to encompass a rigorous skepticism and generate a faith that relates absolutely to the absolute—but remains capable of returning to relative symbols of faith and relate relatively to them. As a philosophical theologian intent upon opening the prebelief domain of faith, I refrain from beginning with revelation: confessing the truth of a particular symbol would remove my prebelief. Returning to religion enables me to appreciate both the beauty and the limitations of traditional symbols, but this second encounter, which gains in understanding what it sacrifices in trusting, necessarily diminishes the possibility of confessing a truth based in the knowledge of trusting. In faith, I maintain a respectful and appreciative distance from religion.

Prebelief, Skeptical Faith, and Vigilant Faith

Because skepticism and secularism destroy our ability to form meaningful connections with greater wholes, leading to an experience of brokenness, it has become necessary to generate a definition of faith capable of standing against despair. Earlier models of faith, which integrated doubt within their structure, cannot provide solace for naïve or native skeptics; further, models of faith predicated on an object (God) fail to address the condition of secularism. Opening the domain of prebelief and expanding the faith that exists prior to selecting a symbol as true thereby provides a way to faith for those alienated from its comforts.

Those not burdened with native skepticism and those who misunderstand faith as a small step en route to knowledge tend to overlook the domain of prebelief. Intentionally occupying this domain requires a skeptical faith that works to avoid knowledge, that desires to remain divested of certainty: skeptical faith sufficiently resolves the brokenness that assails skeptics currently. Vigilant faith is a subset of skeptical faith, requiring a positive work that goes beyond the requirement of necessity. Opening up the domain of prebelief thus provides an alternative to the work of Žižek, Milbank, Caputo, and Taylor, who focus on redefining God. It also extends the possibilities of faith beyond what Kierkegaard and Tillich were willing to permit.

I divide my book into three parts of two chapters each, and each chapter builds on the ones preceding it. In line with traditional systematic theologians (such as Tillich), my chapters present a vision that expands as it moves forward. After skeptical and vigilant faith are defined as alternatives within the domain of prebelief in part 1, each subsequent chapter provides an aesthetic example that orients and concretizes the work of that chapter. These examples—literature, cinema, poetry, and scripture—show the diverse resources available to one with vigilant faith and demonstrate the importance of vigilantly reading the cultural goods that populate our world.

In line with my goal of bridging nineteenth- and twentieth-century works on faith with those written in the present, I begin by describing absolute faith as conceived by Kierkegaard and then as conceived by Tillich. Not only do these works offer models of faith, but they also provide a baseline to determine what constitutes a definition of faith. With this baseline in mind, the second chapter recontextualizes possibilities of faith by foregrounding its atheistic potential, defining faith wholly in terms of a human (and not divine) groundwork. To do this, I articulate the structural compatibility connecting absolute faith with a rigorous form of skepticism and then describe the forms of human faith originating from passion, reason, and volition. Altogether, part 1 outlines the model of skeptical faith and shows it to be a conceptual possibility.

Skeptical faith allows rigorous and naïve skeptics to undergo faith, but it is an uninteresting kind of faith that falters quickly. Part 2 outlines why vigilance needs to supplement skepticism and how it does so. Building on the analysis of skeptical consciousness offered in chapter 2, chapter 3 describes how a reflexive, vigilant consciousness allows faith to maintain its dynamic state—a state that pushes faith forward into the future by ensuring that I adequately scrutinize my self, testing my skepticism. The form of faith described in chapter 3 is rational in nature, universal (and thus open to any individual) but also empty and contentless. To maximize the ability of faith to move dynamically and push individuals to remain in faith into the future, I add to the contentless state (which drives humans to continue to search) the need to hesitate before affirming or denying (and thus knowing) a proposition to which one has assented. Hesitation is a key term, as it allows my atheist theology to avoid the peril of a continually deferred theology—in other words, I posit the possibility of there being *a* truth but describe how faith staves off this moment in order to remain faith (and not transform into knowledge or opinion).

In addition to watching over how it watches, the second key characteristic of a skeptical faith is that it keeps watch over the world at large. Chapter 4 discusses Heidegger's theory of revelation, working through his notion of displacement as it relates to art and tracking this argument through Heidegger's later work when all things foster revelations. Focusing on vigilant skeptics, I argue for the viability of *anonymous hierophanies* as an atheistic theological way of understanding the relationship of things and the divine. An anonymous hierophany expands Mircea Eliade's original insight by making hierophanies applicable to a postindustrial urban landscape, specifically emphasizing how common refuse can mediate revelations of the divine. This chapter concludes by showing how a vigilant faith that watches all things for their capacity to reveal the divine (but hesitating before claiming any one as God, definitively) meets Tillich's standards for an object of faith without appealing to the structure of a symbol.

Part 3 explores the works of a vigilant faith, articulating how it differs from the merely skeptical variety. Chapter 5 articulates how vigilance works as an end in itself and not just a means to faith. I build on Heidegger's late essays to reveal how vigilance forces us to live to our full potential. Finally, in chapter 6 I explore the ramifications of faith relative to the external world, looking to the history of a trusting faith as a way to qualify the life that a vigilant faith should produce. This shows the twofold relevance of vigilance to the theological writings of Jean-Luc Nancy and Richard Kearney. First, I describe how a vigilant faith allows prayer to and worship of the God above the God of theism, even though this God is in no way evoked or mediated by a central, defining symbol. Secondly, I discuss how the virtues of a vigilant faith—patience, hospitality, and re-creation—form an ethic suitable for the twenty-first century.

Because each chapter analyzes particular aspects of a skeptical faith, I conclude the book with a synthesis, which tracks how a presymbolic faith moves through a narrative of lived experience. This recontextualizes the different strands of faith into something that more closely resembles the human flow of time and reveals the power and importance of expanding the model of faith to include a presymbolic, absolute dimension. Some readers may prefer to start with the conclusion to gain a sight of the project as a whole before moving through its individual elements. Although my argument may not persuade fundamentalists of either Christian or atheistic persuasions, I do hope that the combination of theological analysis and explication of vigilance is persuasive to those interested in postmodern theology or who find themselves suffering from the malaise of a naïve skepticism that awaits a more rigorous and vigilant application.

The models of skeptical and vigilant faith are as arduous as they are idealized, but they nonetheless have value to contemporary continental philosophy and theology. In practical terms, a thorough analysis of this kind of faith will do much to expand the current, posttheistic definitions of God by providing the human component that makes such conceptions relevant to human beings on an individual and existential level. Second, showing how humans can integrate skepticism into a model of faith will restore the importance of faith to current theology, thereby recovering faith from the anti-intellectual biases of religious and atheist fundamentalists. Finally, to the extent that I accurately describe an idealized model of faith, vigilant faith provides a standardized vocabulary capable of determining good faith from bad.

Part I
Skeptical Faith

The Model of Absolute Faith

They say they want the Kingdom
But they don't want God in it

—JOHNNY CASH AND U2, "The Wanderer"

Religion satisfies both the human drive to forge communities using ritual and history and our longing to transcend them. Traditions point
backward toward our pasts and reveal possibilities for better futures, ar-
ranging time in a fashion that grants comfort and consolation. The tension
inherent in what academics identify as a "religion without religion" arises in
religious contexts that grasp the mere form of comfort and simultaneously
forsake the content mythology provides. Absent this mythology, we lose
the foundation for ritual and community. Theologians debate the nature
of God because it seems that faith has little to say in this situation, but this
unwarranted assumption obscures faith's potential as its own ground for
resurrecting religion in a secular society.

Focusing on pretheistic faith as a human possibility avoids what has become a trope of postmodern theology. While the focus on "religion without
religion" or "God without God" provides a succinct dialectical definition,
its sound-bite formula obscures the intellectual rigor that supports it. Put
otherwise, searching for a faith that precedes God (or a faith without God,
a faith before God) brackets questions of God and religion and thereby
emphasizes the *experience* of faith at a human level. Contemporary theologians have seemingly forgotten faith's function as the foundational center
of human flourishing and community: they step past the too often fleeting
moment of faith and discuss what can be known.

I therefore will return to theologians from the past, not nostalgically, but as a way to sketch an alternate path into our present situation. Situating a skeptical faith within the Christian tradition that it both precedes and presupposes requires that I articulate a model by which a definition of faith can be described and tested. This chapter therefore begins with a discussion of modeling, followed by a presentation of a general model of faith, and concludes with a model of absolute faith generated from the writings of Søren Kierkegaard and Paul Tillich.

Three Initial Definitions of Faith

Models function as explanatory mechanisms that allow us to understand conceptual relationships as we move through our hours and lives. Each model is rooted in a particular domain and has a particular scope that it explains, and because models are a working hypothesis, they remain open to criticism and further development. New models build on earlier ones, incorporating what worked from the older model even as they expand the domain by incorporating what were anomalies in former systems.[1] Thus, although my overall goal in this book is to offer a new model of faith, I will first define the dominant model of faith in our secular world and will follow with a comparison of two competing models of absolute faith, offered by Søren Kierkegaard and Paul Tillich.

As I mentioned in the introduction, current models of faith cannot account for those who desire belief but experience brokenness, those unable to connect with a symbol or to join a community grounded in a particular symbol. The obstacle is the fault of naïve skepticism, a mind-set that fears being deceived and therefore remains closed to communities and symbols that integrate larger wholes. Because the Tillichian model of faith is circumscribed by the question of symbols, the term "faith" seems inappropriate for those who find themselves in this situation; however, an improved model of faith—structured on a rigorous skepticism—will open faith to those who cannot make themselves believe in symbols. Further, I argue that this sense of faith, and the absolute relationship with God that it enables, is a more accurate manifestation of faith than what the relative symbolic structure provides.

One difficulty that attends creating a model of faith is that such a model must account for three distinct ways in which the word "faith" is used. Following Tillich's insight, three domains of thinking have recognized the importance of faith: theology, philosophy, and religion.[2] These three domains are grounded in a division between rival modes of thinking within the human being: we think through trusting or through understanding.[3] Philosophy uses the human capacity for understanding, religion requires our trusting, and theology rests in the identity and difference connecting the two. Accordingly, a model of faith must both define a faith that these three domains have in common and be based on a philosophical anthropology that acknowledges the possibility for these three different expressions of faith.

Before comparing how faith exists in each of the domains, I will assert a definition of faith that reveals the points of identity and difference among the three domains. First, philosophy understands faith as a possibility of thinking. The clearest definition of this sort appears in the *Critique of Pure Reason*, where Kant defines faith as the combination of subjective conviction and objective uncertainty. This contrasts with his definition of "opinion" (brought about by a lack of subjective conviction and objective uncertainty) and "knowledge" (having subjective conviction with objective certainty). In this way, Kant accounts for the peculiarity of humans, who are impassioned about what cannot be proven. This definition protects the domain of faith from unbelievers, who trivialize faith as being bad knowledge or uninformed opinion, and from believers, who treat their subjective conviction as though it provided adequate justification for abusing those who differ. Kant's use of conviction and certainty to divide modes of human thinking offers a neutral foundation for a discussion of faith that does not require any acknowledgment of a particular revelation. Because it originates as a form of thinking, this faith is open to those unable to generate the initial movement of trusting. Yet despite Kant's well-known familiarity with and respect for Christianity, his arguments—including his definition of faith—emphasize the human capacity for understanding. For Kant, trust does not arise from creed but from respecting the limits of human knowing.

A second and more familiar definition of faith emerges relative to religion; here faith, fulfilling a different kind of human need, is equated to trusting. Revealed religions are predicated on the human capacity for trusting, and the institutions, texts, and practices that compose revealed traditions grow out from this initial movement of trust. Humans yearn for an outside force to summon and grasp them, enveloping and defining them as complete and distinct entities. Like love or hope, this trusting faith has little to do with reason. Whereas reason allows us to maintain a distance from the object of our thoughts, trusting occurs before we realize it, implicitly and fully. Unlike the empty abstractions allowed by reason, religion promotes our coming together in mutual dependence to share together in contingent truths before which we are helpless. The strength of this definition of faith comes in its passionate embrace of a truth that has nothing to do with objective history or fact.

Viewed theologically, faith merges understanding with trusting, even though, in practice, one side is favored. The theological component has been long lived in Christianity, starting with the author of Hebrews, who defines faith as the "substance of things hoped for, the evidence of things not seen" (Heb. 11:1, KJV). Two key terms emerge from this definition. First, "substance," or *hupostasis*, makes a strong claim for faith: while *elpizo* (hope) points us to the future, faith does the work of creating that which underlies a hope before its realization (which partially leads Aquinas to credit faith as the first virtue in a temporal sense).[5] This portion of the definition thus emphasizes the requirement for trusting, as the foundation for one's desired future reality follows one's investment in it. Secondly, the Greek term *elenchus*, which the King James Version renders as "evidence" and the New American Standard Bible as "conviction," also refers to the Socratic style of dialectical argumentation. The author of Hebrews counted rational argumentation and the use of the understanding as ingredients in identifying what we cannot see. Faith functions as both *elenchus* and as *hupostasis*, as evidence for now and the substance for the future. This double function of *pistis* (faith)—as that which creates and grounds itself—remains true to the emphasis that Aristotle placed on it in the *Rhetoric*.[6] Both cases illustrate how *pistis* works within the Kantian tension of conviction and uncertainty.

Anselm ably illustrates how later theological definitions maintain a place for both trusting and understanding in a definition of faith. Reason plays a critical function, keeping one's conception of God from being purely in the imagination (which would encourage the unfettered generation of something idolatrous from one's whims of fancy). That reason possesses an object to critique reveals the primacy of trusting: the existence of God is assumed, and reason allows us to know this God better. This sets up a dynamic in faith in which trusting drives the understanding to clarify the object of faith and supply a greater sense of conviction about that which remains unseen.[7] Excepting only some of the negative or apophatic theologians, most theological understandings of faith follow Anselm in allowing understanding to follow a preexistent trust. Just as in Hebrews, the understanding aids one's subjective conviction, which is rooted primarily (both temporally and in terms of importance) in trusting. The question of God remains one necessarily outside or beyond objective certainty.

Models of faith rooted in biblical religion and philosophy use different words to describe how humans incorporate one of the primary paths to knowledge, but each assumes a one-dimensional understanding of the human capacity for faith: trusting *or* understanding. This tendency follows from a discomfort with the unknown that grows alongside an increase in our convictions. Our language operates accordingly—we "know" things proven to us philosophically or provided to us through revelation: in both word and deed, we forget the objective uncertainty that would obscure our assurance were we to reflect on it further. Our forgetfulness reveals that we experience faith as necessary but not desirable—we perceive faith as a means to an end and not as an end in itself.

Theology that promotes faith as a virtue emphasizes the desirability of faith as an end in itself. It does so by explicitly attempting to combine both elements of human knowing—trusting and understanding—as necessary for moving forward. Instead of a stagnant knowing, which can rest contentedly with having a fact (an attitude that resembles the desire of a tourist to "have" a souvenir, a thing that serves as a localizing reminder of an event), the state of faith grows, develops, and expands over time. Put otherwise: if trusting allows a knowledge that deepens over time (offering a more powerful vision or more examples of what one had at the beginning) and understanding allows a knowledge that can become more nuanced or rigorous (finding a greater variety of examples with which a concept can be explained), theology pits the strength of one against the other to produce a continuous constructive critique.

Theology also incorporates a structural dynamism—new possibilities for defining faith manifest in tandem with more rigorous developments in philosophical models of truth. Augustine begins this trend by successfully demonstrating the homologies between Plato's idea of the Good and the Christian idea of God. At root was the assumption that there was no need for the two types of truth to conflict. The next radical break came in the wake of Kant, whose reflexive critique of reason made necessary a new understanding of truth and enlarged the theological boundaries of faith. Heidegger's definition of truth in the twentieth century unleashed the third major wave of theology, whose "postmodern" turn understood truth as the event of concealing/revealing. Each new description of truth was useful in forming a new way for faith to underscore tensions between subjective conviction (of different kinds of truth) and objective certainty.

Trusting and Understanding as Sources of Faith

Even though theologians tend to emphasize trusting over understanding as a starting point for their thinking about faith, theological definitions of faith have the potential to do more. Philosophers frequently find faith at the furthest limits of our rational understanding, and ministers preach that we find it at the beginning of our learning to trust. Emphasizing the tension produced with theological definitions of faith reveals that faith is coextensive with—and nothing other than—the tension itself, produced between the two paradigms as one accepts the criticism that each sets against the other. Prioritizing this tension as an end in itself, embracing the flaws that both trusting and understanding point out in the rival paradigm, reveals the failure of our given (or preferred) way of enjoying the world. A possibility beyond trusting and understanding becomes available, reawakening us to a deeper relationship with our world. Accepting that we cannot understand, control, or secure our world kindles a sense of awe and wonder within us, as the mundane things that we would ordinarily overlook now reveal themselves to us as they do to children; unlike children, however, we hesitate before blindly accepting each new thing as a miracle lest we overlook the understanding's critique of trusting. Embracing the fact that the status quo cannot be trusted leads to a rejection of Panglossian optimism: rather than trusting that this is the best of all possible worlds, we are called to labor to improve the world. This convergence of awe and responsibility opens up a way to live and experience faith theologically.

Humans use faith in common, nonrigorous discourse in ways that do not distinguish the two paradigms of understanding and trusting. Problematically, this implies that faith-as-trusting is a weak substitute for understanding although, in truth, each fulfills a separate but important human capacity. Such illegitimate overlaps reduce faith to a stance that refuses what is objectively certain, stubbornly clinging to antiquated notions (like insisting that the earth is flat). Failing to differentiate trusting and understanding collapses all faith into bad faith, or self-deception.

Although bad faith is one form of having a subjective conviction in spite of objective uncertainty, it is the weakest and least desirable form of faith. Good faith allows us to maintain an increased awareness of what we do not know instead of an artificially enhanced conviction about what is unknowable. This type of good faith requires clarity and rigor, valuing how trusting and understanding differently enable faith.

Assuming that humans have two different modes of thinking—understanding and trusting—that are differently important for human well-being offers an adequate basis for a complex understanding of faith's multiple permutations: it accounts for the various disciplines that incorporate faith at some level—religion, philosophy, and theology. Kant's faith, defined as the conflict between subjective conviction and objective uncertainty, identifies what the three domains have in common (tension) and how they differ (the source of subjective conviction). All three disciplines independently offer different types of faith, and each reveals the fundamental human capacity for finding subjective conviction without objective certainty.

Each discipline allows a valid sense of faith; however, because religion and philosophy have the goal of providing knowledge, faith is seen as an unavoidable and unfortunate necessity that is best overcome. The trivialization of faith and the corresponding hyperinflation of the need for knowledge come as consequences. While knowledge clearly is useful, the drive for absolute knowledge often pits religion and philosophy at odds. Religion often is guilty of emphasizing the knowing possible through trusting in a way that wholly excludes understanding. Similarly, the discipline of philosophy derides trusting as weakening the pure knowledge offered by the understanding. The polarizing tendencies artificially remove the uncertainty that haunts and produces faith by collapsing the system into one element at the expense of the other; as a result, faith disappears because of a lack of tension. Although clearly not all religions require an absence of thinking and some philosophy accounts for the need to trust, too often we limit ourselves to bad faith that poses as knowledge.

The personal practice of faith allows trusting and understanding to merge in a productive, dynamic tension and thus on face has the best chance of maintaining faith as faith, as an end in itself and as a means to the end of knowledge. Although traditional theological conceptions of faith have persisted within the structure of a particular revealed religious domain, and even though this element has historically taken priority, these are contingent and not necessary to a theological understanding of faith. Especially in the context of an atheist theology, there is no requirement that any one traditional or historical revelation provide the foundation for faith. At a personal level, the subjective experience of a theological faith requires only a willingness to hold one's trusting at odds with one's understanding—one is required neither to be in a particular religious community nor to have training in philosophy.

As this is a work of philosophical theology, however, my goal is to account for philosophy, theology, and religion in order to present a model of faith that seeks itself as its own end, actively perpetuating the tension defined by Kant. Writing in the context of a posttheistic theological climate, I will not presume the practice of a particular religion in outlining the nature of trusting, although, relative to the theological tradition, I will filter much of what I say about trusting through various Christian understandings of

God. Similarly, I will rely upon the tradition of understanding developed in Western, especially continental, philosophy. This context frames how I expand the academic theological conception of faith by showing how a presymbolic experience constitutes faith beyond what most Tillichian and post-Tillichian conceptions of faith would allow.

The closest models of theological faith to what I hope to express are those developed by Kierkegaard and Tillich, whose theologies center on Kantian tensions. Both of these models introduce the absolute, although each theologian arrives at a point of absolute, nonmediated faith differently. In order to identify what is most useful from these two rival conceptions, I will analyze each in terms of how it provides a *ground* of faith, interprets the *object* of faith, preserves a *dynamic* of faith, and conceptualizes the *work* of faith. These four terms will serve as a heuristic capable of identifying similarities and differences among competing models of faith. Kierkegaard and Tillich, who each developed a sense of absolute faith, will generate a baseline against which my eventual description of a skeptical faith can be checked. In other words, a successful model of skeptical faith will account for what already exists as a model of absolute faith but will expand the domain of faith in order to open new possibilities for naïve and native skeptics who find the initial movement of belief instinctually problematic.

The Structure of Faith

Although my goal is to detail a model of skeptical faith that incorporates the individual experience of faith prior to symbolic mediation, the structure of faith I propose is more general. Focusing on basic components of faith allows this structure to analyze theological concerns present in historical definitions of faith. After defining the structure, I justify its functionality by analyzing the versions of absolute faith described by Kierkegaard and Tillich. I then use the structure as the organizational mechanism through which I will construct a new version of absolute faith capable of incorporating radical skepticism.

I define the *ground* of faith, the first of four necessary elements in a structure of faith, in terms of how faith navigates the theological space that moves between philosophy and religion (at a systematic level), or between understanding and trusting (at a personal-existential level). Because faith itself is concerned with issues of knowledge and trust, the way theologians articulate (or assume) theological ground significantly influences definitions of faith. The three dominant grounds of faith have come through interactions with Platonic, Kantian, and Heideggerean models of truth. Building on the philosophical models, a model of faith choosing the Heideggerean ground (as I will do in defining skeptical faith) should be able to account for theological models predicated on Kantian or Platonic conceptions. Although a definition of faith may only employ and not argue for a particular theological ground, an adequate or coherent definition requires clearly defined ground.

The *object* of faith is the second structural element. This is created theologically by connecting the philosophical model of truth with a symbol revered within the revealed religious tradition and thereby personalizes the abstract ground of truth. Personalization connects a particular aspect of the conception of truth with the particular existential needs of the community and individual and allows the beginning of a relationship between the individuals or communities and truth. The object of faith, embodied in the symbol, takes precedence over the ground of faith for the individual or corporate practice of religion, because worship requires that the initial moment of trusting precede the possibilities opened by theology. Within the Christian theological tradition, God and Christ have served as the two dominant objects of faith. Because the relation to an object of faith is primarily practical, individuals often speak of having faith "in" the object.

The third element of a model of faith is its *dynamic*. The dynamic of faith moves in two directions simultaneously. On a horizontal level, the dynamic of faith looks at how faith maintains itself *as* faith, in time, avoiding situations of a premature entry into knowledge. To use the language of Hebrews, this is the substantive (*hupostasis*) dynamic in which faith creates the ground for its prolongation into the future. Individuals accomplish this theologically and religiously by understanding faith as a process whose conclusion they continuously defer. This pattern manifests in Christianity as the need to delay the realization of one's faith, encapsulated in the notion that the Kingdom of God remains ever "at hand," near, but never here.

This aspect of the dynamic of faith is generally disregarded in order to focus on the second dynamic of faith: vertically understood, the dynamic of faith allows an individual to experience an increased integration with the infinite. This builds on the dialectical nature of faith (*elenchus*), whose negative work forces one into a deeper and clearer conception of the nature of faith. Theologically, this is accomplished through the integration of a negative element into the structure of faith—what Tillich did through his integration of doubt, for example. When one doubts at a reflexive level, one's faith remains something active and not simply just held or carried forward in time, like a possession.

The frame around this process at a religious level varies depending on the ground and object of faith. For example, theologians who choose God as the central object of faith tend to refer to the vertical dynamic as the process of redemption or salvation, whereby the spirit of God increasingly fills the individual. Whether understood as the unity of the self with God or as the integration of the self with the self as an existential movement, the dynamic of faith provides a bulwark against the crushing sense of brokenness and estrangement experienced as the counterpart to our longing for the infinite.

The final component is the *work* of faith, focusing on how individuals and communities attempt to realize the unveiling (or full manifestation) of truth on earth. The work of faith moves in the direction opposite the dynamic of faith, seeking to imprint the infinite truth received in the initial encounter with the object of faith onto the finite world that one inhabits. The question of what works one ought to do has changed over time, and the tendency has been an expansive one: although most definitions include a concern for one's own soul, theologians have gradually expanded the work of faith to include other humans and—most recently—the surrounding natural environment.

A Preliminary Definition of Faith

Faith is an arduous undertaking, especially if one desires it as an end in itself and approaches it without the comfort or guidance of a symbol. Because humans find it desirable to have a subjective conviction about what is objectively certain, the time of faith is uncomfortable. Being bereft of knowledge bewilders us, and it is not surprising that we attempt to keep ourselves from this state by finding communities in which others confirm our beliefs and thus provide an approximation of objective certainty. This type of reinforcement allows us to identify multiple groups in which we participate and through which we are able to define ourselves and give ourselves meaning.

Humans tend to think of faith as something that one holds or has—we speak of knowledge and opinions in this way, trying out opinions and possessing or losing facts. Although faith exists between opinion and knowledge, its tension makes it different in kind from its companions. Faith is a state the way health is a state: we can be in better health or worse health. Although we can use possessive terms (one has good health or has lost his or her health), these phrases seem awkward; so it also is with faith. In the Christian scriptures, Jesus describes faith as a state—a character is defined by his or her relative *quantity* of faith. This distinction manifests in the choice to call someone "Ye *of* little faith" instead of ruing, "You *have* little faith." The relative state of faith, indicated by quantity, reveals how faith qualifies a person's essential nature. While this may seem like a trivial distinction, it is one consistently employed throughout the Christian scriptures: faith depicts someone's relative state of being and is not spoken of in terms of a zero-sum external possession.

Granting that faith is appropriately understood as a special state of being or way of interacting with the world even beyond the specificity of the Christian religion presupposes that I cannot suddenly find myself in a state of faith—it requires an impetus capable of displacing me from my normal modes of being. Determining the nature of this catalyst requires delineating what types of events are sufficient to move people from their given or normal state of knowledge or opinion and into a state of faith. Such events are *revelations*, generally taken in the positive sense as passively received by the human being, who necessarily relates to the revelation in the mode of trusting. In addition, however, we can think of negative revelations, which we actively acquire after engaging in critical thinking. What is revealed in both cases appears to be inexplicable; because the event of revelation manifests to individuals, one does not know whether it correlates with the experiences of others. Displaced from my normal patterns of thought, I feel alone, afraid, alienated—but consoled with the promise of a new understanding.

Revelations importantly occur in the domain that I have been describing as presymbolic, or pretheistic: the beginning of even a symbolic faith would need to occur in this domain because, otherwise, revelations requiring symbolic knowledge would be presented to those who did not require this knowledge. The event of revelation is upsetting precisely because it reaches to us in our presymbolic domain: the content of the revelation is that which exceeds the confines of the presymbolic vocabulary. Although we may be adequate speakers of one or several languages, words we know cannot capture the revelation. Revelations introduce us to the limitations of what we have and expose the inadequacy of what we find comfortable. Additionally, revelatory events, characterized by wholeness (providing the *hupostasis,* or substance, that underlies the experience of faith) allow the feeling of brokenness to be overcome.

Negative and positive revelations challenge one's presymbolic understandings differently. Positive revelations provide a content that overflows the symbolic capacity of one's basic linguistic symbolic world. A similar problem erupts any time we attempt to take an idea or concept, half-formed, and put it into language: the words we choose, no matter how much care we put into them, seem inadequate to the grandeur of the original vision. The awe-inspiring nature of a theistic revelation, the disclosure of a new world that recontextualizes the relationships we assume, magnifies this experience exponentially. In other words, in addition to having the usual problem with translating an idea into words, revelations disclose the poverty of our language: the ghosts of sound and bones of letters we possess render stillborn our attempts to communicate. Symbolic communities (more restricted in sense than the general language community) are valuable because they provide central symbols and an idiosyncratic vocabulary. These gifts allow everyone to simultaneously recognize the nobility of the vision and to share in the knowledge that allows one's chosen words to mean more than normal. It is in this way that a symbolic community grants the feeling of being at home; although the symbol and community remain incomplete manifestations of the new world that has been revealed, they nonetheless offer the solace of a group of others also willing to attach the new meanings to the things and objects that surround them at the everyday level.

A negative revelation, arising as one understands the inadequacy of reason and the understanding, is also difficult to put into language. Our reaction to such failings is generally a feeling of humor, a passion that expresses our own frustration with reason's hold; this is why (at least in Freud's estimation) slips of the tongue prompt chuckles. The event that reveals reason's failings allows us a new understanding of the nature of how we live in our world, and these become symbolic reminders of our limitations. The nature of this event is less powerful than a positive revelation, however, although we are more in control of causing it. Structurally, then, both positive and negative revelations force a recognition of the poverty of one's present world (either relative to a new world that has been disclosed or relative to one's own capabilities). Both types of revelation inspire a faith caused by an event, and both events push individuals away from traditional uses of language. It is important to note that we do not experience the actual event of revelation with faith: as with all experiences, we receive revelations in undergoing them, without a critical distance that allows for uncertainty. Like unveilation, revelations are moments that define the boundaries of faith but are not included in the purview or domain of faith itself.

Time passes, and the experience of even a life-changing event shifts from something we actively undergo to a memory of something that we have undergone in the past. This translation from experience to memory requires the intervention of language, and we fall back on our inadequate words to define that which we had lived without understanding. The words recall to us the truth we had been able to live, experience, or appreciate despite not *knowing* it. Fortunately, the words still possess a power to generate a reminder of this truth within us, although it functions more like an echo than it does like a re-creation of the first event itself. Surrounded by the mundane setting of our shared general community, this linguistic statement—a belief—is what remains.

Beliefs are linguistic translations of a revelation or hypothesis that sustain and prolong the state of faith or allow one to more accurately determine when the event of unveiling has occurred. Most commonly, we use the term "belief" to solidify in language a truth that a smaller community knows even though it is not a shared or assumed understanding relative to the world at large. The assumption that a smaller community can confer objective certainty is confusing inasmuch as it undermines the distinction between faith and knowledge: the belief is *known* within its context and only claims the status of faith (or objective uncertainty) relative to outsiders. Although the vision represented by the statement of belief is not shared in general, communities relieve adherents of the need to relate to the belief in an attitude of faith.

On an individual basis, however—one involving a presymbolic faith—it remains possible to speak of faith in regard to a statement of belief. Faith, here, remains relative to the proposition of belief; it persists as an important yet unknown quantity insofar as one keeps the truth value of the proposition in the realm of possibility. In faith, believing (as opposed to knowing) requires assenting to the possible truth of a proposition and maintaining this truth as possible by understanding reasons to both affirm and deny it. As an example, hearkening to a belief that God created the world in six days places an individual in one of three possible communities that rise out of the larger culture by virtue of understanding the belief as one worthy of contemplation. The smaller community that affirms this proposition does so in terms of knowledge relative to the community (as it becomes something the whole community regards as objectively certain), although it remains objectively uncertain relative to the larger world.

The smaller community that negates this proposition does so with the same mixture of faith and knowledge. Those within the community claim with objective certainty that there is no God or that it took God millennia to create the world, even though, relative to the larger community, there is no way that one can offer anything more compelling than an assertion. In other words, the negation of a proposition only makes sense relative to a community that has also hearkened to the proposition as something worthy of note. Denying the truth of the proposition and maintaining this denial takes faith equal to the faith required to affirm the proposition.

The third group understands arguments that would lead to affirmation, as well as negation, of the proposition and thus does not make a judgment on the issue. Even if members of this group join in a community of agnostics, un-knowers, they hold this belief in an attitude of both corporate and individual faith. Thus one joins the symbolic community by assenting to a belief and then rendering a judgment on the truth value of the belief to enjoy shared knowledge; an individual maintains faith apart from these communities by assenting to the proposition of belief without making a judgment.

The end of faith comes when the tension that sustains the state of faith relative to the belief is eliminated, either with a diminution of the subjective conviction (such that faith becomes a mere opinion) or with a strengthening of its certainty, so that the belief can become a fact that one can simply hold. Converting faith into knowledge can occur relative to a community in which a shared vision and vocabulary concretizes the belief so that it no longer is in question. Although Kant would maintain the perspective that this belief remains "faith," his judgment presupposes the assumptions of a larger community that does not participate in the smaller community's symbolic matrix. Emphasizing the need for tension reveals that such "belief" acts like knowledge for believers within or relative to a community that holds the belief as certain. Smaller communities confirm our individual beliefs, allowing the tension involved in a dynamic faith to dissolve into a static knowing—at least for that time. In short, faith proper requires a lack of objective certainty in both its absolute and its relative sense, and therefore a more rigorous definition of faith manifests by weakening Kant's standard of "objective certainty."

The ultimate end of a faith that originates in a positive revelation occurs when the tension that attends faith disappears with a final unveiling. In place of the paradox that comes from being torn between two worlds, the unveiling heals brokenness by heralding the new world. This new world can take traditional religious forms, like the second coming of Christ, or wholly secular forms, such as the Marxist revolution. Entering into a community that provides the believer with symbols and a language for the revelation provides a minor form of unveiling or a pale shadow of realization, but discord can still overtake the individual who travels in the world and away from the community. A full unveilation occurs only when one's interpretation of the world serves as a universal, absolute given.

Kant and the New Possibility for Absolute Faith

Although the model of vigilant faith that I will offer is most productive in a Heideggerean philosophical framework, because both Kierkegaard and Tillich respond at least in part to Kant in their writings on faith, a brief overview of the primary ways that Kant influenced modern theology is necessary. Kant's first significant theological impact came in shifting the definition of truth: after his transcendental distinction, which differentiates the thing understood from the thing-in-itself, it no longer makes sense to define truth as a correspondence between what one thinks of a thing and how the thing "really is" in the world. Philosophers could no longer assume that humans could attain access to how a thing "really is," even through the rigors of dialectic thinking. As an alternative, Kant argues that truth is neither in the object of sensible intuition nor in the judgment produced by the understanding; instead, it is rooted in the agreement between the two. Put otherwise, Kant reconfigures the nature of the correspondence: instead of having one's subjective, sensible intuition correspond with an external or objective reality in a moment of truth, truth occurs when intuition and judgment align. Because both intuition and judgment are internal, this diminishes the importance of the external or objective world as a measure of truth, setting the stage for the rise of romanticism and, later, existentialism.

The second theological implication of Kant's work comes with his announcement that the ontological and cosmological proofs of God function only when one commits the transcendental error, falsely assuming that something necessary to think necessarily exists. Thus, although theologians such as Aquinas argued that God was understood to be necessary because God's essence is to exist, Kant points out that because "by an absolutely necessary being is meant one whose existence cannot be denied without contradiction, it follows that no being can be judged necessary in that sense,"[8] for denying the existence of this being leaves nothing to be contradicted and thus no contradiction. By revealing the gap between thinking and being, Kant opened a possibility for a new ground in theology.

Although one cannot rationalize God into necessary existence, Kant finds that needing to *think* God remains important to human experience. Rather than considering this a "proof" of God (or way to have knowledge of God's existence), Kant instead terms this "faith," through which one has a subjective conviction of God's existence in spite of the lack of objective certainty. God is in this way moved beyond the realm of the knowable, and faith emerges in a context dominated primarily by the understanding. In other words, we have faith because of what we know we cannot know, not because of a mythic image or narrative that inspires us at our deepest levels. After Kant, reason—and not only revelation—became a potential origin of faith.

Third, Kant's work shifted the content of "God" into the realm of what we cannot know. In other words, if we cannot know the ontological "God" that anchors rational understanding, despite its being necessary, the contingent God of revelation that anchors trusting is displaced just as far— perhaps even farther—from the set of things that we can know objectively. The absolute unknowability of the Kantian God in this way marginalizes the contingent God offered through revelation; while one does not invalidate the other, it puts the question of God at odds with the understanding. Theologically, presupposing the transcendental distinction required an increased emphasis on the role of the understanding as a supplement to trusting, which is why Kant (as opposed to Descartes, perhaps) is decisive in opening new ground for a theological conception of faith.

Together, these three theological implications of Kant's philosophy decisively opened up new ground for faith. Instead of being rooted in a God who, as the Good, embodies truth revealed to those who trust, the emphasis on the understanding compels modern theology (after Kant) to think truth without revelation. We still know God only through faith, but faith has become that which lies outside of reason and is no longer the understanding that follows from the initial gift of trust. Although it manifests differently, this is the basis for both Tillich's and Kierkegaard's theological understandings of faith.

Kierkegaard and Absolute Faith

Writing against Hegelianism and working to recover a rigorous sense of Christianity that would challenge individuals instead of justifying the complacency of their lives, Kierkegaard merged Kant's philosophy with his Lutheran background to create the context for an individual experience of faith and truth. Although his other texts explore a host of philosophical and theological issues, Kierkegaard takes up questions of faith largely in his pseudonymous texts, which provide different authorial points of view on the question of faith. These range from those attributed to Johannes de Silentio (who can describe the motion of faith but not perform it himself) to those of Johannes Climacus (whose brilliant dialectical abilities allow him to approach the problem of faith philosophically) and of Anti-Climacus (who brings a theological understanding to the question of faith). Although no one persona's perspective provides a complete analysis of faith, Kierkegaard's multiple layers provide enough information to construct a model of faith based on his work.

Kierkegaard establishes the *ground* of faith on the failure of reason generated by the recurring idea of paradox and reinforces the mutual exclusivity of the understanding and paradox throughout the pseudonymous literature. Paradoxes are central because they exist only through refusing the work of the understanding to explain them: anything a human can explain ceases to be paradoxical. Describing the understanding as an "organ," Kierkegaard (as Johannes Climacus) describes the necessity of the understanding "stepping aside" in order to make room for faith.

The marriage of paradox and faith evolves with (and within) each of the pseudonymous books. With each new persona's view, Kierkegaard shifts from considering the paradox in abstraction to considering it in speculation and then to focusing on human existence and, finally, on divine existence. In each text, Kierkegaard clearly argues that faith and paradox each arise in the absence of an objective certainty that contrasts with one's inward or subjective position. As Johannes de Silentio in *Fear and Trembling*, Kierkegaard begins the search for faith by arguing that it begins "precisely where thought stops" (53), expanding the paradoxicality of faith by discussing it as the retention of the infinite within the finite through an absolute relation to the absolute (37–38). The concept of paradox becomes central with *Philosophical Fragments:* Johannes Climacus defines faith as the passion that arises after the understanding steps aside when confronted with a paradox. At this stage, the importance of the paradox comes as an event, or efficient cause, which forces away the understanding to allow a space for faith.[9] The context for the event that requires faith is the irruption of the eternal into the temporal, found in the Christian narrative with its absurd and offensive claims about the person of Jesus Christ that cannot be accepted rationally.[10]

Kierkegaard's logical development of the idea reaches its nadir in Climacus's *Concluding Unscientific Postscript,* which does the exhaustive (and exhausting) work of demonstrating that a human being is capable of nothing at all.[11] This personalizes the effect of confronting a paradox and thus intensifies the despair that a paradox elicits. The absurdity of faith—relating to the content of the paradox—repulses individuals and thus makes more difficult the already daunting task of faith. As Anti-Climacus, Kierkegaard focuses on despair in *The Sickness unto Death* to show that humans are inherently and essentially paradoxical and that only with faith can one resolve the inner tension between one's finitude and infinitude.[12] Finally, in *Practice in Christianity*, Kierkegaard (also as Anti-Climacus) writes concerning the nature of paradoxicality in the God-Man, in which offense reaches its most intense and concretized moment.[13] For Kierkegaard, the *ground* of faith is paradox, as paradoxes require humans to relinquish the understanding.

The ostensible *object* of faith for Kierkegaard is thus the God-Man, who figures the paradoxical union of the temporal and the eternal. As an object of faith, the God-Man on the one hand springs forth from the revealed tradition as the central figure of the New Testament. Kierkegaard also shows how this figure satisfies the needs of the understanding by emphasizing the structural nature of the God-Man, whose essence is paradoxical. Additionally, *Practice in Christianity* highlights the need to develop faith through indirect communication because direct communication from God is impossible and, if possible, would lead to knowledge instead of faith (124–61). Accordingly, Kierkegaard contextualizes the God-Man as a sign; in particular, the God-Man is a sign of internal contradiction that separates the God-Man from the possibilities of conceptual understanding. The use of sign is important, as Kierkegaard is clear that it generates faith through paradox instead of requiring that faith come through participation (as a symbol would do). Overlapping the nature of the God-Man as a sign of contradiction is the additional qualification of offense. The importance of all of these is to underscore the *structural* manifestation of the God-Man: Jesus Christ is the object of faith not because he is the son of God but because he meets the structural requirements that underlie "paradox" and "sign," demanding a response of faith by denying the possibility of direct communication (and therefore passive reception).

Kierkegaard's cognate term for the *dynamic* of faith is "passionate inwardness," the subjective element that allows one to maintain a relationship of faith with the paradox that allows for it. The term "inwardness" is crucial for Kierkegaard given his emphasis on the hiddenness of faith: for him, the faithful alone are able to dwell in the finite world without remainder. The discussion of this dynamic is most clearly outlined as Religiousness A in the *Concluding Unscientific Postscript;* here, one achieves the actuality of existence only by continually hiding the eternal in a movement of self-annihilation before God. In self-annihilation, one is equated to a state of nothingness—but finds in that moment that God has already performed the work of reconstitution. This parallels Anti-Climacus's famous image of resting transparently in the hand of God provided in *The Sickness unto Death*. It is through this dynamic work that humans positively perform the nothing that Climacus says humans can do. Although we cannot achieve a balance between the poles that constitute a self on our own, we *can* annihilate the tension and passively accept their resolution. The dynamic in faith enables the passionate inwardness of self.

The *work* of faith, consistently explained throughout the texts, is the re-creation of the finite world. Kierkegaard repeatedly insists upon this theme, underscoring the importance of the finite world in the life of humans. The examples he gives of this are trivial and mundane—in *Fear and Trembling*, he discusses the Knight of Faith's desire for lamb's head and vegetables for dinner; in *Concluding Unscientific Postscript*, Kierkegaard discusses the need to enjoy oneself in the context of an amusement park. The highest work of a human being is to actually live in the world in which one finds oneself. The work involves the following elements:

1. Hiddenness. The Knight of Faith, like those with Religiousness A or B, hides the difference of faith (whether it is the movement that reclaims the finite world or the indwelling of inwardness). Kierkegaard repeats this concept in *Practice in Christianity* as the need to imitate the God-Man, who is always incognito.

2. Worship. If the imitation of the God-Man expresses the human similarity with God, enabled through the human effort to become nothing so that one transparently reveals the underlying hand of God, then worship becomes the expression of difference. Expressing absolute difference, necessary when one reflects on one's difference from God, requires a faith that clings to the paradox inflicted by the situation.

Absolute and Skeptical Faith

One of Kierkegaard's recurring themes is the need to relate relatively to relative ends and absolutely to the absolute. It is this paradoxical effort that drives the dynamic of faith to a twofold expression: relative ends and goods (found in enjoying oneself as a human in the finite world) and the absolute end, before which one is individuated (in an expression of worldless worship). *Fear and Trembling* depicts how revelation enables absolute faith, as

Kierkegaard—through Johannes de Silentio—contrasts the absolute with the universal through the juxtaposition of Abraham and Agamemnon. While both characters were required by external forces to sacrifice his child in a serious and profound breach of ethics, only Agamemnon (who acted on behalf of the universal) was able to do so ethically (i.e., relative to the universal and not to the absolute). Kierkegaard's claim is that Abraham is individuated in an absolute expression of faith. Abraham's inability to communicate directly with others is a symptom of his absolutely individuated state—which itself is a reflection of his absolute relation to the absolute (58–60). Revelation, here, provides the first way that one can come to an absolute faith.

As Johannes Climacus, Kierkegaard argues that dialectic provides a second way of apprehending the absolute. In his *Concluding Unscientific Postscript*, he characterizes dialectic as introducing individuals to the unknowing of the absolute. Because faith is a leap into the absurd, however, dialectic cannot become substituted for faith: at most, dialectic can show the individual the boundary, providing a vantage point from which an individual can leap toward the absolute. Nonetheless, Kierkegaard in this way accounts for the possibility that reason can lead one to the brink of faith (490).

Third, the "absolute" in the *Postscript* also refers to the type of dependence one has on God, repeating and emphasizing the importance of faith in the work of self-annihilation and reconstruction provided in *The Sickness unto Death*. Humans can will themselves at most to achieve nothing: after fully realizing this nothing, they are able to learn of their absolute dependence on God. Here, one still maintains God as the absolute end—but *after* becoming a self through the mediation of God, one also can pursue relative ends. Other goods are necessarily relative because the primary telos of one's activities is the absolute relationship with the power that grounds the self.

For Kierkegaard, each of these three origins of absolute faith—the revealed, the rational, and the existential—independently provides humans with the structure that leads to the brink of faith. Faith is never a certainty, however, and one must opt to keep faith—preserving the paradoxes of revelation, dialectic, or existentiality by withdrawing the understanding to allow the dynamic of faith to begin. One is never forced into an attitude or relation of faith, and choosing faith at one moment allows no guarantee that one can continue to make this choice; instead, one must constantly will oneself to remove the understanding. This repeated work drives the dynamic of hidden inwardness: the emphasis on "passion" that recurs reveals the extent to which one must desire to maintain one's faith.[14]

Kierkegaard does not directly attempt to incorporate doubt or skepticism into the structure of faith, although his emphasis on absurdity and offense pushes individuals to moments of suspicion or hesitation. Because paradoxes cannot be accepted in a direct or simple manner, because one must will oneself to push aside the organ of understanding and relate in faith to the paradox that presents itself, faith will never simply be a "given" at any point in a person's life. Structurally, this is paralleled by Anti-Climacus's description of faith in *Practice in Christianity* because the faith required in understanding the God-Man as a sign, necessitated because of indirect communication, is one that follows a moment of the withdrawal of a naïve trust.

Kierkegaard's indirect approach allows faith to be completely volitional: the problem is that an attitude of skepticism precludes naïve trust and thus prevents the question of faith from arising at all. One who dismisses the possibility of the truth of revelation offhandedly or grows up in a culture that has already "moved past" such stories (now seen as mythology) never hears the potential for offense and can never be introduced to the paradox. Kierkegaard's pseudonyms presume a familiarity with Christianity and a desire to embrace it that one can no longer assume is widespread in the secular age of the twenty-first century. Although this is perhaps no worse than the problem of a universal membership in Christendom, it creates a problem in that fewer see themselves as part of the intended audience of the indirectly communicated message. Those who doubt impulsively without first hearkening to the possibility of revelation never find the possibility for faith.

Secondly, Kierkegaard specifically states that skepticism itself cannot form the foundation of an absolute faith; instead, skepticism forms an inadequate parallel. Thus, although Kierkegaard clearly displaces faith beyond a first or given immediacy through the notion of paradox or indirect communication, a movement that structurally parallels the event of doubt or faith, this does not duplicate the movement of faith. This is shown in Climacus's relation of skepticism and faith. Arguing that Greek skeptics willed themselves to doubt the conclusions drawn from sensory input (and not sensation itself), Kierkegaard finds that the skeptic kept "himself continually *in suspensio,* and this state was what he *willed.*" Greek skepticism is unique because it "unfailingly used cognition only to preserve the cast of mind."[15] The willed suspension of doubt required to believe something parallels the willed suspension of the understanding required for faith, but because the doubt is not induced by a paradox, it does not come with the passion requisite for faith.

Kierkegaard's conception of faith is incompatible with a skeptical faith for several reasons. First, the existence of doubt or skepticism alone could not constitute adequate grounds for the existence of faith, as it does not arise from the presentation of a paradox. Second, absent the recognition of tradition, the skeptic would be bereft of an object of faith. Third, skepticism would seem to preclude the possibility for a dynamic faith: without an object (and lacking the help of God), the skeptic would not have the passionate inwardness that allows faith to grow deeper and forward in time. Finally, skeptics would not be able to participate in the work of faith given the lack of anything to hide and the impossibility of worship. Thus, although Kierkegaard's analysis of faith as it emerges from reason, revelation, and volition provides a good context and invaluable foundation for a definition of absolute faith, it nonetheless needs to be supplemented in order to function in a twenty-first century that increasingly would understand Christendom as an alien land.

Tillich's Two Models

Tillich provides an interesting test for the four-part heuristic of ground, object, dynamic, and work inasmuch as he offers two contrasting models of faith—an absolute faith and a symbolic faith—in the final chapter of his *The Courage to Be*, producing a tension that he resolves and clarifies in *Dynamics of Faith*. Even though Tillich favors the latter model of faith, it is necessary to understand the independent value of each model before suggesting an alternative capable of accounting for twenty-first-century skepticism.

Structurally, both of his models are situated in a modern theological paradigm, rooted in the post-Kantian era that self-critically accounts for the structural limitations of reason itself. Philosophically, Kant's critique radicalizes the problem of God's existence, claiming that it is a necessary thought without necessary ontological ramifications. Theologically, this allows Tillich to postulate God as the ground and abyss of Being, that which incorporates both Being and non-Being into itself without being reduced to either. The fact that reason cannot guarantee God's existence illustrates the importance of faith in the works of both Kant and Tillich.

The two models of faith present in Tillich's book are divided with respect to the question of the ground of faith. In *The Courage to Be*, the central object discussed is God—clarified as the God above the God of theism found through absolute faith. Importantly, the qualifier "absolute" results from the failure of symbols to mediate the experience of this God. Tillich is clear that both absolute faith and awareness of the God above the God of theism arise only when "traditional symbols that enable men to withstand the anxiety . . . have lost their power" (189). The parallel construction that Tillich uses to describe how one becomes aware of absolute faith and the God above the God of theism makes them seem almost interchangeable.

To emphasize the amorphous nature of the "object" in question, Tillich moves systematically through how traditional symbolic conceptions of God fail. Describing how once powerful symbols such as immortality and providence fail the test of critical reason, which interprets them as imaginary, Tillich argues that absolute faith "says Yes to being without seeing anything concrete which could conquer the nonbeing in fate and death." Contextually, this failure of the concrete would extend to all symbols, which necessarily attach to some concrete element to frame the transcendent content (189–90). The same reasoning works through the psychological reduction of a judging and forgiving God and also through the threat of meaninglessness. It is for this reason that Tillich can argue that absolute faith lacks "*special* content" when its content is the "God above God" (182). The "special" here should be understood as a symbolically framed conception of God, and the "God above God" understood as a God freed from symbols.

The dynamic of absolute faith is existential in nature—as is true of most modern theology—inasmuch as the presence of faith allows for the experience of existential unity in the face of an anxiety that otherwise would undermine it. The dynamic of faith in general calls for the integration of what is finite into that which is infinite: the existential unification achieves salvation from despair and the crippling effect of anxiety through accepting the infinite. Just as Tillich claims that nonbeing is that which in God allows for God to be dynamic and living, so also does our experience of existential unity allow us to be more than a mere in-itself type of object, which, determined, does not require a dynamic integration. Absolute faith, which Tillich describes as the "situation at the limit of man's possibilities" (189), uniquely overcomes existential threats and allows humans to persevere in spite of them.

The work of faith, in general, involves making concrete that which is infinite; here, Tillich indicates that the work of absolute faith is to undergird other, less radical instances of faith in concrete human experiences. Although less concrete than other depictions of works, it nonetheless makes sense in the context of the abstract nature of absolute faith. Absolute faith is the necessary precondition for other forms of faith, moving among the different symbols that do not exhaust it, and persisting beyond the failure of these symbols. The work of absolute faith, in other words, is to enable faith in every moment, just as the God above the God of theism exists behind and empowers all theistic symbols of God. The implication of this, of course, is that the ultimate ground (substance) of faith is faith alone—and not God at all.

For Tillich, an experience of absolute faith is fleeting, lasting only while we are forced to overcome what we know is beyond our capacity. He writes that "it is not a place where one can live, it is without the safety of words and concepts" (189). Absolute faith remains without words because, crucially, the experience of absolute faith is not symbolically mediated. Because it originates in an attack of nonbeing, absolute faith cannot be a state that we will or desire. We remain passive, gripped by the crush of meaninglessness and the challenge of existential doubt, clutched by the shame of guilt and conviction, made impotent by the threats of death and fate. We passively accept the support of the God above the God of theism and in this way are denied intentionality in our absolute faith.

Absolute faith, as Tillich describes it, is circumscribed by three inherent limitations that evidently cause him to prefer—or at least emphasize—the model of symbolic faith in his later works, relegating absolute faith to its background function. First, as just mentioned, his absolute faith leaves the experience of faith outside of human control and experience; although Tillich avoids making the voluntaristic error, arguing we cannot make ourselves believe, he wants us to be responsible for our faith. Second, although Tillich incorporated extreme existential doubt into the structure of faith, the extreme nature of it forces it to be too fleeting: Tillich prefers a model of faith with more prolonged human ramifications. Finally, the nonsymbolic nature of absolute faith and the God above gods deprives faith of its traditional nature, leaving humans bereft of the language and community that tradition offers.

Building on the same *ground* of faith as absolute faith, the model of symbolic faith is structured for human comfort over a prolonged period of time. As did Kierkegaard, Tillich uses Jesus as the primary *object* of faith. Unlike Kierkegaard, however, Tillich emphasizes the importance of the cross as a self-negating type of symbol (which participates in that to which it points), contrasting with Kierkegaard's emphasis on the God-Man as disconnected sign. Also parallel to Kierkegaard and identical to Tillich's own concept of absolute faith, the *dynamic* of faith in the symbolic framework is existential in nature, moving individuals who struggle with finitude toward a realization of the self as an integrated whole. Although the inclusion of the symbol causes the faith one experiences to exist relative to that framework instead of absolutely, this allows one's existential wholeness to be generated within a concrete human community that assembles around the symbol (which points to the God above the God of theism). The symbolic framework accounts for one's everyday existential needs, eliminating feelings of brokenness and still allowing absolute faith to arise when necessary. Tillich argues that the best source of the symbolic framework is the "church which raises itself in its message and its devotion to the God above the God of theism without sacrificing its concrete symbols" and therefore "can mediate a courage which takes doubt and meaninglessness into itself." The ability to face doubt and meaninglessness provides "a courage to be in which one cannot lose one's self and in which one receives one's world" (188).

Tillich ties the *work* of symbolic faith to works of love, claiming that love and faith correlate positively. Although different primary symbols encourage individuals to prioritize different kinds of actions and activities, specific manifestations of faith are less important than a focus on improving the lives of others. A second type of work occurs on the communal level, with the maintenance of ritual and ethical codes that are designed to concretize the infinite nature of the truth in symbolic expressions that reinforce the bond of the individual as a part of overlapping larger wholes.

A symbolic faith, which frames, mediates, and relativizes one's experience with the God above the God of theism, possesses limitations that do not allow it to function as a universal model. Tillich acknowledges the first limitation, relative to the nature of the individual, in *The Courage to Be*. This occurs when the symbol ceases to speak to the individual because of his or her essence or nature. Because the symbol requires an initial openness from the individual in order to mediate the individual's relation to the absolute, habitually skeptical individuals cannot encounter God or interact with the community.

The fuller explanation of symbol provided by Tillich in *Dynamics of Faith* frames a second limitation. Tillich argues that a symbol of God, which mediates any and every ultimate concern, has an element of ultimacy and an element of concreteness. The additional emphasis on concreteness seems intended to complete, or possibly correct, Tillich's original conception of God and faith. One sees this because the element of ultimacy, defined as "a matter of immediate experience and not symbolic in itself," is a distilled conception of the relation of God and faith in *Courage*. Instead of assisting in an idea of the God above God, however, the element of concretion, which "is taken from our ordinary experience and symbolically applied to God," becomes a distraction to the argument about both God and faith.[16]

The trouble with using symbols as mediators manifests at the level of language, occurring when Tillich discusses the truth of faith. In *Dynamics of Faith*, Tillich writes, "Faith has truth in so far as it adequately expresses an ultimate concern," and that it "implies an element of self-negation" (97). The notion of absolute faith presented in *The Courage to Be* clearly has no problem meeting these standards, as the struggle with nonbeing is the essence of an ultimate concern, and the absence of content means that each moment of being grasped by this faith *is* self-negating. Tillich implicitly acknowledges the fact that these criterion really serve to address the concrete element of symbols. He writes, "That symbol is most adequate which expresses not only the ultimate but also its own lack of ultimacy" (97). Although one could argue that by inserting this, Tillich reemphasizes the *objective uncertainty* that partially constitutes faith, one must also realize that this puts the responsibility for uncertainty on the concrete element framing the symbol. The emphasis on the objective continues when Tillich presents his test of the "subjective" truth of faith, which is determined by measuring whether the symbol creates reply, action, and communication (96). Here again, despite Tillich's explicit desire to make faith an act of the personality, he places the symbol in the center of faith instead of the human being.

A more obvious example of how the mediating function of symbols becomes problematic manifests in Tillich's analysis of the Cross; when he writes, "Christianity expresses itself in such a symbol in contrast to all other religions, namely, in the Cross of the Christ," he roots the truth of faith in its concrete vehicle instead of the way that the believer relates to it. Ultimately, Tillich claims that the criterion determining the truth of faith becomes "identical with the Protestant principle," which, in turn, "has become reality in the Cross of Christ" (98). This clearly shows the extent to which the objective element has overtaken and dominated the subjective. Although emphasizing a particular symbol allows Tillich to base his interpretation of faith within the context of a recognized faith tradition, crucial to Tillich's understanding of faith, the relativizing of the God above God makes the God in *Dynamics* less "above."

Thus, Tillich's sense of symbolic faith trips over the concrete element of the symbol in two ways. First, the symbol as an objective element overtakes the subjective activity, limiting the possibility of individual agency and thus absolving the individual of his or her responsibility for faith. Second, as Tillich mentions, symbols are not necessarily as open now as they once were—and having closed down absolute faith as a livable option, individuals who lack the initial belief to undertake a mediated relationship with the nontheistic God have even fewer options. Although the model does seem to function for the types of faith that Tillich lists and survives a radical existential encounter with meaninglessness, it explicitly cannot accommodate a deep-seated skeptical nature.

Finally, the importance of symbols in Tillich's late permutations of this structure of faith means that it has only negative or corrective value for a model of skeptical faith. This is because symbols require an initial movement of belief that allows them to disclose their depths and unlock the corresponding depths of the observer: those who are native skeptics do not have this minimal ability to hearken closely to symbols and thus cannot find a place within the current Tillichian system beyond occasional moments of absolute faith. In addition to expanding the possibilities of faith to account for a presymbolic faith, a more robust version of absolute faith becomes important to revisit in a theological landscape increasingly marked by atheist theologies.

Describing an absolute faith applicable to an age of skepticism requires articulating a model of faith that incorporates skepticism into its structure, following the pattern introduced by Tillich's incorporation of doubt. A skeptical faith necessarily moves beyond Tillich's model, because Tillich excluded skeptical doubt as a type of doubt his model of faith would encompass. Describing skeptical doubt as "an attitude of actually rejecting any certainty," Tillich claims that this attitude "necessarily leads either to despair or cynicism" and warns that despite its liberating function it "also can prevent the development of a centered personality."[17] Tillich's points about skepticism are valid: in order to create a skeptical faith, the model must avoid the twin woes of despair and cynicism and, as faith, must ensure that it is possible for an individual to see the self as a whole.

Because skepticism is innately unfriendly to a conception of symbolic faith, I will need to describe and test an alternative mediating structure. Crucially, however, any and all alternatives still must meet Tillich's criterion for a faith mediated by symbols. This means, first, the alternative must comprise an openness that says "Yes" to all potential objects of faith, as anything might manifest God. Second, in order to avoid the worship of idols, the alternative must also say "No" to that which is less than ultimate—and thus maintain faith as faith, preserving its dynamic function. The "yes" is necessary to prevent a skeptical faith from sliding into despair, while the "no" is crucial to prevent a skeptical faith from solidifying into knowledge.

Meeting both of these conditions is necessary in order to identify one's experience as part of the domain of faith; however, in order to define an absolute faith that incorporates an element of skepticism into its structure, additional qualifications are necessary. Therefore, third, an alternative must also have the ability to thrust the individual into a state of meaninglessness that approximates, if not re-creates, the conditions of nonbeing that engulf a symbol to thereby enable a nonsymbolically mediated encounter with the God above the God of theism. This alternative must be able to be induced subjectively to avoid making the symbol responsible for the truth of our faith. Although an absolute faith will ultimately destroy divisions between a "subject" and an "object" through the immersion of the finite in the infinite, an absolute faith must incorporate a volitional human dimension able to embrace meaninglessness without falling prey to despair.

The final two conditions of faith manifest because of the nature of skepticism. Because skepticism jumps over the first naïveté that allows a faith to be born of trusting, one can only recover trusting as a result of a second naïveté. This alters the ground of faith, which, consistent with the attitude of skepticism, cannot be located outside of the human: this becomes a fourth condition. Finally, because a consistently skeptical attitude undermines its own ground, the fifth condition for a model of absolute faith capable of including skepticism in its structure is that it demands the erasure of its own ground, reestablishing itself moment by moment. These additional criteria thus measure the extent to which a model is within the domain of faith, whether it has the quality of absoluteness, and whether it can account for skepticism.

The Model of Absolute Faith

The introduction began by sketching out the possibility of a domain of pre-belief, featuring a pretheistic faith required of individuals before a particular symbol of God is chosen as an ultimate concern. There are several types of faith that fit within this domain. In general, they have in common a status of absolute faith because any individual's faith exists without regard to a symbol. The simplest form of absolute faith is a naïve skeptical faith, the faith that upholds the naïve skeptic who simply rejects what manifests without thinking. More rare than this is the faith of the truly rigorous skeptic, who consciously creates equipollent arguments to maintain a state of uncertainty relative to what gives itself to be known.

To conclude this chapter, I will articulate a model of absolute faith that incorporates skepticism into its framework, moving through the four parts of the structure in line with possibilities already explicated by Kierkegaard and Tillich. Although the purpose of the remainder of the book is to examine each of these in detail, a small overview here offers a vision of the whole as divided into its requisite parts.

1. This model of faith finds its *ground* in skeptical consciousness. This ground expands the traditional notion of theological ground because it manifests by merging the failure of trusting with the failure of the understanding. Only in this space of overlapping determinate negations can an absolute faith become possible for a prolonged period of time.

2. The *object* of faith will be faith itself. Because any given object apprehended by a skeptical faith will be rejected, in faith, all that remains is the faith that something new will manifest over time. Because a skeptical faith sacrifices the sacrality of one central symbol and the possibility of a community that comes with it, individuals in a state of absolute faith are enabled to receive back the world as a whole. This will be shown through the proliferation of anonymous hierophanies, revealed when one intuits that all things in the world are possible manifestations of the divine, as signs, as paradoxes. Ultimately, the emphasis of "object" will transition from one focused on a thing to one focused on a goal. The object of faith is the perpetuation of faith found in watching over the world and hearkening to what might be God in it.

3. The *dynamic* of a skeptical faith will be tested against the earlier models. This requires showing how an absolute faith is able to sublate the longevity of Kierkegaard's definition of absolute faith and the structured experiences offered by Tillich. Additionally, a new model of absolute faith needs to let humans remain knowingly in faith while replicating the annihilating effects of meaninglessness required for existential unity and integration. Finally, the dynamic of absolute faith that incorporates skepticism demands a faith that can sustain faith absolutely into the future, tempted neither by mediation nor by knowledge.

4. The *work* of a skeptical faith will follow the recent writings of David Klemm and William Schweiker and will continue to expand the zone

of influence beyond human communities to include a concern for the integrity of all life—not just human communities.[18] Here, much of the work involves watching the entirety of the things in the world (consistent with an expanded sense of "object" of faith) and actively attempting to re-create the world as directed by faith.

THE NEW MODEL of faith necessitates understanding the value of vigilance for humans and faith. Vigilance will provide a function analogous to what courage provided for Tillich's model, because skepticism demands vigilance in a way similar to how doubt requires courage. The following chapters, in helping to expand on the model of faith, will therefore also explore the utility and ramifications of vigilance.

2 Skepticism as a Ground of Faith

In some remote corner of the universe, poured out and glittering
in innumerable solar systems, there once was a star on which
clever animals invented knowledge. That was the highest and most
mendacious minute of "world history"—yet only a minute. After nature
had drawn a few breaths the star grew cold, and the clever animals had
to die.

—FRIEDRICH NIETZSCHE, *On Truth and Lie in an Extra-Moral Sense*

In the twenty-first century, those for whom skepticism has become
a primal impulse no longer need to be shocked away from the openness of
their first naïveté; instead, they refuse the possibility that a new moment
may provide something of value. Without conscious or malicious intention,
these skeptics reject the world of hyperbolic description where no sale can
be missed and each election defines history. Native, naïve skeptics shrug off
such appearances, disregarding the consequences. Relative to the world of
marketing and advertisement, this strategy allows them to thrive without
accumulating goods that fail to live up to what was promised.

On a deeper level, this nonchalance problematically constructs a world in
which symbols are broken. Native skeptics, accustomed to ignoring presen-
tations of things, lack the initial faith required to unlock a symbol's hidden
depths. The world appears mute and godless, an endless series of surfaces
that lack depth or necessary meaning. The absence of depth reinforces and
exaggerates the importance of surfaces—and far too many of these are jus-

tifiably maligned. As rare instances of trusting superficial appearance inevitably lead to regret, skepticism grows more important.

Within this context, definitions of faith predicated on trusting are not useful because naïve skeptics have hardened themselves against the world to protect against the shame of being duped. Naïve skeptics see anything that requires faith as a mere confidence game, and pride requires protection from gullibility. Although this type of skepticism is a weaker and less rigorous form than the skepticism that Tillich and Kierkegaard saw as antithetical to faith, it nonetheless sufficiently precludes the possibility of a faith based on a trusting openness. The model of faith suited to the presymbolic domain therefore must achieve openness indirectly, incorporating automatic distrust. Accordingly, relative to this domain of faith the question of the presence or absence of God remains bracketed: faith's existence must be absolute, without appealing to any given symbol or sign of the divine.

Traditional models of faith begin with a revelation from God—the ground of faith thus rests in the goodness of God. Because skepticism precludes the possibility of finding depth through trusting, it is necessary to reconstitute the ground of faith in wholly human terms predicated on disbelief. Rather than understanding faith as enabled by God, a skeptical faith requires nothing outside of a human's innate capacity for suspending knowledge. Building exclusively from this human basis, a skeptical faith allows three forms of faith—one that denies knowledge received through trusting, one that denies knowledge received through understanding, and one that denies knowledge by holding trusting and understanding in tension.

In light of the challenge that skepticism posed to the theological models of absolute faith and the desirability of showing the relevance of faith to a presymbolic domain of thinking, this chapter outlines the faith that springs from the ground of skepticism. To contextualize the question of the ground of faith, I begin by analyzing how Heidegger expanded the Kantian definition of truth, thus opening a new viable domain for faith. I then examine skepticism, beginning by establishing the viability of skepticism as a human practice before determining the overlap connecting faith and skepticism that allows a conception of skeptical faith. Doing so will justify moving past Tillich by incorporating skepticism, not merely doubt, into the structure of faith. To conclude the chapter, I examine the human ground for faith that skeptical faith demands, outlining the passionate, rational, and volitional roots of vigilant faith.

The Ground of Absolute Faith

In chapter 1, I show how Kierkegaard and Tillich each offer a viable way of entering into an absolute and unmediated relationship with the absolute. Since the time of their writing, we have moved from a philosophical domain dominated by Kant to one dominated by Heidegger (at least continental philosophers have done so). I therefore will overview how Heidegger opens a new ground for faith before discussing how to find faith within a skeptical consciousness.

Conventional wisdom correlates the prevalence of "naïve skepticism" with advances in physics in the early twentieth century. Variously attributing the cause to Einstein or Heisenberg, this perspective holds that the disclosure of the power of relativism bloomed into a vaguely held mind-set that automatically accepts the limitations of one's own viewpoint: this reactionary rejection of appearances, the principle of naïve skepticism, functions adequately as protection from what appears to be good but in truth is not. Martin Heidegger, whose philosophical career was launched in the same era as relativistic physics, provides a more structured account defining how revealing and concealing come together in an event of truth. I hold that Heidegger's philosophy accounts for the cultural change that has led to the advent of a native skepticism and that this view of truth opens the ground for a more powerful definition of faith.

Heidegger contributed to changing the ground of faith from a Kantian framework through his explanation of truth as a process or event and his realization that truth involves a dynamic of revealing and concealing—the latter derived from his translation of the Greek term for truth, *aletheia*, as unforgetting. Inasmuch as the notion of truth as representation (of a metaphysical "Good" in which it participated) reflects the premodern (Greek) conception of truth, and the notion of truth as proposition (a judgment that connects a concept and intuition) reflects the Kantian conception of truth, then Heidegger's claim that all truth is grounded in the dynamic of unconcealedness suggests that his own model reflects a new and better understanding of truth.[1] Theoretical projects beginning with Derrida and Foucault in the 1970s, which transitioned into work on race, gender, sexuality, and postcolonialism in the current academic culture, remain oriented by Heidegger's definition of truth—even when this debt remains unacknowledged—as these projects presuppose that researching into what has been concealed provides a truth upon revelation.

Heidegger's essay "Origin of the Work of Art" explores the question of how art is true, or how truth serves as the origin of the art's work. Heidegger thereby reveals an anomaly that neither the "common-sense" understanding of truth nor the Kantian model adequately resolves. Art is problematic because, as it does not claim to participate in a truth, one cannot measure it in these terms. Also, art offers no proposition or judgment that one can assess rationally. Although one could evaluate art by gauging how accurately it participates in the ideal image or by how accurately it joins a concept with an intuition (perhaps form and content), such approaches miss the truth of art. The context of Heidegger's argument thus shows not only that his understanding of *aletheia* accounts for what worked best in the previous models but also that it more adequately defines the truth of a work of art—which the other models cannot fully appreciate.[2]

The first significant change that allows Heidegger's model to incorporate a work of art is his understanding of truth in a dynamic sense: as an event, happening, or occurrence. When describing the work of art, or the workly character of an "art work," Heidegger states that "in the work, the happening of truth is at work. But what is thus at work, is so *in* the work. This means that the actual work is here already presupposed as the bearer of this happening" (58). The happening of the truth requires artwork in which to work but is not limited to it.

The best explanation of the dynamic of truth in its relation to art comes when Heidegger discusses displacement. The first dynamic element occurs within the artwork as object. Consistent with his definitions of work as a conflict, or "rift," between "world" and "earth," Heidegger writes that "the more solitary the work . . . the more essentially is the extraordinary thrust to the surface and the long-familiar thrust down." The second dynamic moment occurs externally: in addition to enabling one to see the thing in a new light, the work also *displaces* the observer. Heidegger writes that "to submit to this displacement means: to transform our accustomed ties to world and to earth and henceforth to restrain all usual doing and prizing, knowing and looking, in order to stay within the truth that is happening in the work" (66). In this case, the truth works on seizing the observer and effecting a transformation as the individual receives the work. The work works through beings—through artworks, creators, and preservers (the latter "keeps the law" of the revealed truth)—in order to manifest openness to the truth of Being.

The terms "revealing" and "concealing" offer another way to describe this process. Just as revealing the "extraordinary" requires concealing or "thrusting down" the long familiar, so also does revealing the "new" require concealing what came before. By understanding truth as a tension that installs itself within being, Heidegger provides a model of truth able to describe the process, or event, of truth disclosing itself to the human being.

Focusing on the nature or essence of truth instead of that which is "true" (in the way that a fact is true) allows Heidegger to formulate an expansive model of truth whose importance has persisted through the twenty-first century—contemporary work has applied and expanded Heidegger's definition without opening a completely new or different sense of truth. The movement of revealing and concealing explains the earlier models of truth themselves, describing the relation between revelation and reason in Kant's notion of judgments. In a judgment, the "being" into which truth was brought—the "is" of a proposition—reveals a similarity while concealing a difference. Conceiving truth as work informs the postmodern theology written in the late twentieth and early twenty-first centuries. Heidegger's description of truth as a dynamic happening allows a definition of faith as a state of displacement, where one hearkens to a truth that the things in this world simultaneously conceal and reveal. Further, this definition of truth connects faith (in this understanding) and skepticism, which employs equipollent arguments as a way to account for both concealing and revealing in awaiting an absolute revelation of truth.

Skeptical Consciousness

Thus far, I have referred to skeptical consciousness using broad categories—notably the "native" or "naïve" skeptic and the "rigorous" skeptic as a point of contrast. The unthinking reaction that grounds a native, naïve skepticism is too impoverished to provide an adequate ground for faith. Because skeptical faith requires a more rigorous form of skepticism to show the potential that faith has in the pretheistic domain, I turn to Pyrrhonian skepticism as the most suitable alternative. One of the most extreme skeptical positions, the Pyrrhonians entered into skepticism through the painstaking labor of generating equipollent arguments that provided a viable alternative to knowledge. The strategy was to contrast an apparent truth with a rival argument that was equally viable in order to leave the skeptic in a continual—but active and volitional—state of unknowing.

I thus use Pyrrhonian skepticism, which rejects as ungrounded dogmatism even the claim that we can know nothing, as the exemplar of skeptical consciousness. The approach denies the certainty of knowledge that attends both the passive/receptive element of human consciousness (sense perception, trusting) and the active/grasping component (reason, the understanding). Pyrrhonian skeptics traced human error and fallibility to mistakes in judgment and therefore attempted to suspend judgments (*epoche*) in order to maintain a satisfied neutrality (*ataraxia*). The awareness that truth must be found between rival appearances has a strong compatibility with Heidegger's understanding of truth as an event, and such skepticism is key in expanding awareness of truth.

Bredo C. Johnsen's defense of Pyrrhonian skepticism articulates its viability and advantages. In his essay "On the Coherence of Pyrrhonian Skepticism," Johnsen illustrates the basic assumptions, methods, and motivations for this skeptical school, based on Sextus Empiricus's *Outlines of Pyrrhonism*. This school of skepticism is well known for its antipathy toward belief; however, its structure is homologous with a stronger, absolute faith. A skeptical faith emerges only when this deep continuity is grasped.

The goal of skepticism is *ataraxia,* used by many Greek schools to denote a state of peace or mental tranquility; the Pyrrhonian skeptics understood this to occur when individuals voluntarily deferred making judgments and therefore were able to maintain a state of continued inquiry. The first type of judgment concerned sense impressions; understanding that such impressions yield only (at best) a relative truth, the skeptic could maximally claim that something "appeared" or "seemed" to be a certain way. The second type of judgment related to dogmatic beliefs or precepts; the skeptics rejected these, also, under the same principle that what seems true to one person at one time may not seem true to another person or at another time. The suppression of dogmatic judgments reflexively applied also to skeptical principles, such that the goal was to live *adoxastos,* without belief. In terms of the model of faith presented in chapter 1, the Pyrrhonian skeptics in this way consciously and reflexively negate the ability to ascertain truth either positively, through trusting (i.e., through sense impressions, that which is given or received), or negatively through understanding (rationally derived claims).

The method undertaken by the skeptics was *epoche,* or bracketing, a term that has retained its philosophical luster in light of the twentieth-century advent of phenomenology. Johnsen explains that the *epoche* was an intentional state that the skeptics entered into because of a failure to resolve noumena and phenomena. *Ataraxia* (the peaceful state of mind) followed the work of bracketing, although the skeptics made no causal link between the two, so as to avoid its forming into a belief. As opposed to performing the *epoche* based on an overriding belief or on some grounds, Johnsen contends that the early skeptics did so out of pure frustration.[3] Further, the suspension of judgment was one that solely involved the moment at which it arose: to have suspended one's judgment on a question in the past did not mean that one had arrived at a universal truth. Instead, it was necessary to revisit the question; put otherwise, the skeptics were skeptical about their own skepticism in a reflexive awareness of the importance of time to human beings.

To perform *epoche* successfully, the skeptics constructed equipollent arguments, each of which appeared to be sound but neither of which reduced to the positivity of a belief. The equipollent argument—whether based on the relativity of perspective or time—allowed skeptics to suspend belief and adhere to appearances alone. Johnsen persuasively argues that a skeptical acceptance of the appearance of balanced arguments differs from accepting a dogmatic argument, noting, in particular, that the key to the strategy is the acceptance of appearance. Accepting the appearance of balance allowed skeptics to suspend making a decision.

At this point, an initial coherence of the logic of skepticism and the logic of an absolute faith seems clear. In faith, defined in Kantian terms as being torn between one's subjective conviction and an absence of objective certainty, an individual who desires to resist knowledge and stay in an attitude of faith maintains a state of not knowing relative to both modes of thinking—trusting and understanding. This way of describing faith thus allows it to be understood as a variation of Pyrrhonian skepticism: in faith, one could create an equipollent argument to counter the knowledge that would result from thinking *only* through trusting or *only* through understanding.

The relationship of skepticism to the question of "belief" remains complicated, however, especially as the precondition for the possibility of *ataraxia* is abandoning belief through suspending judgments. Johnsen argues for a second precondition on behalf of Sextus, however, claiming that it was necessary for skeptics to maintain an openness to finding the truth in the future. This openness served to balance out a belief that the truth, not yet discovered, would not be found in the future (543–44). Rather than contradicting each other, these positions are mutually supportive: the possibility that one can find truth in the future allows one to discard what appears to be truth in the present as potentially contradictory.

Put otherwise, to state that skeptics posit that the possibility of *ataraxia* arises in bracketing the truth value of belief is a slightly distorted characterization. Although skeptics desire to avoid making erroneous judgments, they would recognize the appearance of what might be a belief. Johnsen distinguishes between believing and the disposition to believe in order to argue that the skeptic can consistently admit to the latter while still resisting the former (550). The point here is a simple one, namely, that skeptics do not have to deny the phenomenon of belief as it appears to occur in their lives; instead, skeptics are able to recognize the appearance of various inclinations to believe and to develop a series of arguments that mitigate this inclination. It is not necessary that an equipollent argument "disproves" an inclination, only that it contextualize the inclination with a contrary possibility.

Against Johnsen, I propose that *faith* necessarily underlies this skeptical system in a second way, in spite of the absence of any and all given beliefs. Put more clearly, in Johnsen's description of Sextus's system, two moments appear akin to the notion of an absolute faith described in chapter 1. The first moment of faith occurs where Johnsen argues that Sextus contrasts with predecessors in suspending belief out of principle as opposed to frustration or anxiety. This principle appears to be one that Sextus holds with a subjective conviction (that he should act in this manner consistently) but with objective uncertainty (the *epoche* diminishes the possibility that he has truth now, and he does not know the future) (546). Thus the "principle" described by Johnsen can be interpreted as a principle of absolute faith, one that pushes a human to a state of faith that is relative to what is relative and absolute toward what is absolute.

The final element of Pyrrhonian skepticism relates to Sextus's practice. The caricature, of course, is for a skeptic to leave the room through a window when asked a question; problematically, this denies the practice of equipollence, as the window receives preference over the door out of mere contrariness. Johnsen counters this with Sextus's description of how skepticism ought to be lived. Although skeptics live holding to appearances and without beliefs, they also live according to a four-part "ordinary regimen of life," including nature's guidance (sensation and thought), compulsion of the *pathe* (eating and drinking), customs and laws, and art and crafts (550). Although Johnsen examines this fourfold regimen in detail, for the present purpose it suffices to show that the "ordinary regimen," relative to relative goods of life, society, and culture, appears worth maintaining even as one grants its status as mere appearance. One acts in spite of one's uncertainty and trusts what is most ordinary as a guide in these matters.

Although other forms of skepticism—including naïve skepticism—have surfaced in the centuries since Sextus, Pyrrhonian skepticism remains the most rigorous form of skepticism and the one most firmly rooted in a reflexive and self-aware consciousness. Because it is the form of skepticism that one engages in absolutely and intentionally, it reveals the compatibility of skepticism and faith.

Skepticism and Faith

Johnsen's description of skepticism introduces why generating equipollent arguments is imperative for skeptics and reveals how a skeptical consciousness maintains itself. First, a skeptic must be aware of his or her own beliefs as they arise. Bracketing belief requires that a skeptic also have a second type of consciousness, which looks for a viable counterargument equally as strong (equipollent) as the initial judgment that gave itself to be believed. Finally, a skeptic must maintain a consciousness open to the event of *ataraxia*, the goal of skepticism. I now build on the analysis of skeptical consciousness by reintroducing the concept of faith into the discussion.

Although there are structural similarities, and skepticism seems to require the implementation of faith as its guiding principle, faith and skepticism are not identical. As both Kierkegaard and Tillich point out, skepticism, indeed, leads individuals to despair. My point is that one can preserve the faith hidden in skeptical consciousness as the core for a new model of faith capable of taking skepticism into itself without faltering. In order to develop this model, I will specify how faith sublates elements from skepticism to create a model of faith consistent with rigorous skepticism. My use of the term "skeptic" refers to this ideal form of skepticism.

The model of faith provided in chapter 1, which describes faith as the intentional preservation of a not-knowing characterized by a failure of either trusting or understanding (the dominant modes of human thinking that convert fluidly into knowledge), has much in common with skepticism. First, faith and skepticism share the goal of not-knowing, a volitional state characterized by a subjective conviction and an objective uncertainty. The subjective conviction in skepticism—the principle that requires an openness to truth in the future—parallels the conviction in faith (which also looks to a future unveilation of truth that is not in conflict with the world). Although some might contend that the subjective conviction is different in kind, the conviction a skeptic shows when employing the principle of skepticism is analogous to the absolute faith that opposes the brokenness experienced when one is gripped by nonbeing. Because skepticism is never definitive, it forces skeptics to requestion matters that they had already considered in a never-ending task that undoes its own foundations, making skeptics vulnerable to the anxiety of meaninglessness. The ability to persist in a skeptical project thus requires a subjective conviction powerful enough to motivate its future perpetuation, a conviction analogous to the situation of faith.

Second, both absolute faith and skepticism are dynamic rather than static states; this means that individuals cannot merely rest but instead must work diligently and continually. Every moment requires reassessment, struggle, and change. The emphasis on appearance for the skeptic demands this, especially because appearances are fluid and prone to continual change: the most that one can affirm is what appears to be the case in a particular moment (including the appearance that one has balanced one's judgment about appearance with an adequately competing claim). Faith emphasizes the temporality of human existence in an equally rigorous fashion: Tillich's description of the fleeting agony that requires absolute faith and Kierkegaard's emphasis on faith as a continual work of accepting paradox without understanding individually underscore the inability to assume that one is in the desired mode of being. To this extent, skepticism and faith are equally demanding practices that require similar qualities of fortitude and dedication, qualities that employ and require one's subjective conviction.

Third, absolute faith and skepticism exist because of a series of intentionally contradictory thought processes that create a simultaneous negation of the self and suspension of the world. Theologians consistently postulate the preconditions for an absolute faith in terms of self-negation. Tillich created the terms of this negation through the intervention of nonbeing, which vacated the content of the symbol and caused the annihilation of the self. Kierkegaard used despair to show the absolute nothingness of a human being as a requirement for faith, while his use of "sign" as an offensive paradox requires a constant effort of not-understanding from the individual. Likewise, the work of skepticism intentionally negates our native inclinations toward both trusting and understanding. The effect of this overlapping negation of forms of thinking neutralizes human inclinations toward knowing and creates a view of the world filtered through overlapping possible perspectives, as though one lived inside a Picasso painting.

Although faith and skepticism share core structural affinities from the perspective of the individual, they ought not to be equated simplistically. The domains overlap, but are not coextensive. As Tillich and Kierkegaard have shown, it is possible to defend a working model of faith that excludes the rigors of skepticism. Skepticism also has an explicitly hostile relationship with belief; although there is a crucial difference between believing (the activity of faith) and a belief (a codified past judgment), any creedal statement or symbolic truth past the moment of its being presented to the skeptic as an appearance would be subject to bracketing. Skepticism holds that the traditional truths that serve as the foundation for symbolic faiths are merely possible perspectives that have no absolute claim on truth. However, the same qualities that violate a relative or symbolic faith—one held in conjunction with community and nourished by tradition—enable an absolute faith. Absolute faith, of course, also violates symbolic faiths.

The crucial difference separating a trusting faith and skepticism hinges on the question of what constitutes objective uncertainty. Traditional religious faith moves into a realm of objective uncertainty, as the world that manifests in the divine revelation is at odds with the series of connections that constitute a human world. The meaning of the objects one sees is rendered uncertain, as they seem to gather rival types of meanings—one constituted by the larger human community and another denoted by the special or particular received revelation. For example, when two religious worldviews come into geographic proximity, one is unable to comprehend why the other holds a place as sacred, as it seems no more special than a similar hill nearby. A relic or talisman functions similarly: its special value is objectively uncertain, grounded on an initial moment of trusting. Skepticism, not adhering to the truth of one world or another, undercuts types of faith experiences that depend on trusting. Such beliefs are what skepticism works vigilantly to overcome.

Although it cannot condone the postsymbolic faith that trustingly allows one to experience the objective uncertainty arising from a moment of belief (understood as a past act of trusting that one now takes as knowledge), skepticism *can* account for the uncanny experience of existing between two different worlds. For the trusting believer, the arduous nature of faith comes with dwelling in two overlapping worlds—to be simultaneously in the world of meanings that preexisted the religious transformation with the assumptions and values that had gone with it, and also to be in a more restricted world of meanings that recontextualizes these same values. For example, one who trusts in the revelation that the end is coming may not feel as motivated to pay for a new car (which had been the envy of those around)—the need for the car and for the envy alter in the face of the revelation; at the same time, because the revelation of the end is not shared, those around continue to covet the vehicle and the believer in question can perceive the appearance of envy as what it is.

The skeptic desires this very tension, this conflict between two perspectives, which still renders the object in question (either talisman or car) as objectively uncertain in two different ways. At the level of sensory perception, understanding how proximity and angle changes the nature of how the object reveals itself, the skeptic hesitates before claiming knowledge of how the thing looks. This allows the skeptic to hold to the truth that the appearance of the thing is fluid and changes as a result of contextualizing factors (the amount of light, distance from the thing, etc.).

On the level of judgments, the skeptic desires to understand the conflict of meanings that one could possibly ascribe to the object in order to render the thing objectively uncertain. To this extent, the skeptic benefits from two appearances: trusting shows the talisman as holy, an object that discloses God, while the understanding shows the object is a mere rock carved by human hands. From the skeptic's perspective, to attend *only* to that which appears through trusting (the holiness of the object) is as problematic as attending *only* through the understanding (to reduce the talisman to rock) because both reduce to a type of objective certainty. One gains certainty through the prevailing assumptions of the contextualizing community in question: the relic *is* a rock relative to a larger human community and *is* a talisman relative to the trusting community. Relative to the larger community, the believer recognizes the objective uncertainty of the talisman, but within the restricted community of believers, this object loses its uncertain status and becomes knowable. The skeptic uniquely maintains a relation of "faith," clinging to objective uncertainty while maintaining a subjective conviction that truth will manifest as knowledge—eventually.

To this extent, the skeptic is unique in the active and explicit practice of openness that leads to an access of a Heideggerean form of truth. Those who dwell in the large, general community that determines objects in wholly material terms seize on what the surface reveals: the inner riches promised by its symbolic mediation remain concealed. Those who revere the talisman's properties accept the revelation of divine depths, but this movement of trust conceals its material properties. By engaging mindfully in the practice of positing opposed but equal possible appearances, the skeptic allows for the event of truth to occur in the movement between revealing and concealing. In other words, skeptics have access to what is revealed, what is concealed, the truth that dwells in both appearances, and, most important, access to the appearance of truth as a dynamic tension that is lost to those who cling to knowledge.

It is now possible to clearly relate absolute faith and skepticism. The two share a structural affinity, equally characterized by a state of prolonged not-

knowing that relates to what is objectively uncertain and by remaining subjectively convinced of the possibility of true knowledge. This requirement
surfaces in the context of faith because of a deferred state of unveilation,
when the revelation of a world (given in trusting) is born out in objective reality. Both absolute faith and skepticism additionally serve to maximize the
potential of Heidegger's understanding of truth as a dynamic event, as each
looks through appearance in order to glean what different perspectives reveal and conceal. Skeptics accomplish this through equipollent arguments,
which allow different types of appearances to unfold different conceptions
of truth; in absolute faith, one finds the God above the God of theism in the
success and failure of a symbol.

By employing equipollent arguments that expand the number of relative perspectives, a skeptic opens the domain of the unknowable through
intentional acts of bracketing. We doubt sensory experience inasmuch as
we know some phenomena appear different from different perspectives:
because of this, I cannot claim to have objective knowledge of how the thing
is but can at most make claims of how the thing appears. Skeptics render
dogmatic arguments or other judgments uncertain through the proposition
of a contrary perspective or viewpoint—occasionally from multiple perspectives. Because skepticism expands the domain of the unknowable, previous
models of faith have been unable to accommodate it. A model of skeptical
faith must include an ability to bracket the world and persist in faith in
spite of this.

Levels of Skeptical Faith

Because faith already is situated between two rival perspectives—one of
trusting and one of understanding—humans are capable of the movement
of bracketing through the construction of equipollent arguments. In faith,
the goal is to suspend judgments, not to convince the self that both one
and the other perspective carry an absolute truth. Therefore, trusting and
understanding serve as a minimal test of skeptical faith. The many ways
in which one can use trusting and understanding as irreducible terms capable of constructing rival, equipollent arguments differentiate three levels
of skeptical faith.

Tillich's work shows how doubt is a prerequisite for faith and that true
faith is what remains after having been purged by doubt; I contend that
skepticism performs a similar function more rigorously. In discussing the
possibility of grounding faith in skeptical consciousness, I also desire to

show its advisability. The model of skeptical faith is a model or ideal version of faith for this reason: it is better able to satisfy Tillich's criterion for faith than Tillich's own version does. Minimally, a skeptical faith maintains a distance from idols, adhering to the "Protestant principle" as it makes an equipollent argument for why what appears as a manifestation of God may in fact be caused by something else. Similarly, an increased awareness of the possibility that God might appear in nontraditional places results as one skeptically refuses to ignore what the understanding would overlook. A skeptical consciousness instantly looks to relate relatively to what is relative and thus frees the individual to relate absolutely to the absolute. Ultimately, a skeptical faith allows an individual to stay in the space of absolute faith even when he or she is not gripped by the terrors of nonbeing and in this way entails a more robust faith than Tillich's system—which excluded skepticism—was able to do.

THE FIRST LEVEL of faith that skepticism opens is that of simple trusting: to trust is to not-know. Although this kind of faith is open in a strictly religious sense, in a skeptical faith it has the limited value of providing a starting point for equipollent arguments. In other words, if someone argues that he or she inclines toward one decision instead of the other, the skeptic's goal is to always already show how this desired belief is relative to at least one other possible perspective. The understanding generates counterperspectives that enable the suspension of one's belief relative to the judgment in question. To use the understanding to counter an impulse to trust creates the appearance of objective uncertainty—at least enough of an appearance to allow one to suspend one's judgment regarding the truth of the appearance. Thus, while trusting at a naïve level opens one to revelation, trusting through a skeptical lens provides an opportunity to engage in a suspended judgment.

I discussed how the failure of the understanding reveals the state of not-knowing in my analysis of Kierkegaard. The failure of the understanding that emerges as one pushes the understanding beyond its limits can be caused by encountering a paradox; alternatively, one can also reach this point through skepticism. Skepticism allows one to challenge the understanding without relying on a naïve trusting relative to a particular revelation. The critical reflection that exposes the limits of what the understanding can know, as was demonstrated by Kant, comes about only when one thinks to reflect on the thinking process itself. In addition to thinking about how one thinks, a skeptical faith also uses the understanding to develop alternate explanations or construct viable possible alternative interpretations relative to how or why things appear as they do, negating the absolute possibility of a relative revelation. This comprises a second level of skeptical faith.

Skepticism opens up a third level of faith by contrasting the determinate remainder of the negated trust with the determinate remainder of the negated understanding. This differs from the first level as it removes the skeptic's ability to rely overmuch on the understanding, which could happen at either the first or the second level. On the third level, the overlapping failures force the skeptic into an absolute relation with the absolute. Whereas the first level of skeptical faith retains the form (although not the content) of the vision one received in trust, the third level creates a new level of tension and distance from the vision. In other words, one no longer relates directly to the vision but to how the negated vision might relate with the negation of the understanding. Motivated by faith, the skeptic oscillates between the negated trust and the negated understanding and is bereft of anything knowable in either domain. The skeptic perseveres through the barren emptiness of double negation with the faith that it is possible to know the truth—in time.

This appearance of a skeptical faith, understood as the foundation of a knowable revelation, cannot be reduced to either trusting or the understanding. First, its lack of definite source (in trusting or the understanding) manifests from its origins as an equipollent argument, unlike the seeming lack of absolute truth that manifests through relativism. The principle that holds that truth will be fully unveiled, knowable, is not one revealed in a vision that would be cause for trusting; more than this, it does not in itself disclose a future world. There is no object or source of this principle, nor is there a message that the skeptic *can* trust; there is simple persistence through time. Additionally, one cannot hold the understanding responsible for this principle, as there is no objective or logical reason to believe that the truth will be knowable in the future if it is not at present. Far from deriving or receiving the proposition, at most skeptics find the principle retrospectively as an element that must have been present in order to explain their actions. In the moment of the present, stepping toward the future, one may not know that the truth will come with the certainty it seems one had in retrospect.

Being mindful about the relationship of skepticism and faith also helps to expand and regulate the nature of skepticism. In particular, one who desires a skeptical faith—as opposed to merely a skeptical status—will have two distinct levels of equipollent arguments to utilize at any time. The first emphasizes the dimension of trusting and interprets what appears as a manifestation of God in the world. The second emphasizes the dimension of the understanding and affirms a mundane judgment about the being of the thing in question. The skeptic in this way fulfills Tillich's test of faith—one always says "yes" to the possibility of God and also says "no," precluding the possibility of worshipping an idol. Neither the "yes" nor the "no" has ultimate say—at this point. One constructs both arguments equipollently and in this way moves forth in the faith of skepticism, the persistence through time with a subjective conviction that the truth will manifest eventually in spite of the objective uncertainty that continually manifests in the form of fragmented appearances.

A skeptical faith provides an adequate, suitable model to explain the domain of prebelief and account for those who move through life experiencing brokenness, bereft of the belief needed to enjoy the gifts of symbol. Although skeptical faith, as outlined above, requires more rigor than the naïve skepticism employed by many, it shows that skepticism and faith are not mutually exclusive. Even those who engage in simple and mindless acts of rejecting appearance end up in a space constituted by the highest form of skeptical faith, in which one lacks a conviction in the value of both trusting and understanding yet, in spite of this, persists in moving forward in life. This persistence is an unacknowledged work of faith and is identical in content to skeptical faith; put differently, the difference between prebelief and skeptical faith is that the latter requires the conscious volition and work of the individual, while the former is an uninspired reaction to particular cultural conditions.

The Human Ground of Faith

Although the philosophical tradition has no issue with assuming that faith is a wholly human capacity, the traditional religious formulation of faith has focused on faith's status as a gift from God. Consistently, theologians from Augustine to Tillich depict faith as elicited from humans after they collide with a truth incompatible with the mundane nature of their worlds. This view of faith puts humans in a passive position, reasonably maintaining that one cannot force faith or make belief. A manufactured faith lacks the passion necessary to sustain the tension between conviction and uncertainty—at root, one knows oneself to be unconvinced despite even a strong desire that God can help one's unbelief. In order to function as a model serviceable within the domain of prebelief, however, the model of skeptical faith needs to function without reference to trusting, revelation, or a symbol of God. Instead of a passive reaction, the domain of prebelief requires a model of faith that humans control, a faith that prioritizes the human desire to search for God over the event of God's self-revelation.

I have already defined two ways the understanding generates faith: hypothesizing alternative possibilities in order to create equipollent arguments and self-critically discovering where reason reaches its own boundaries. Building on this, I will argue how a faith rooted in the component of human thinking can originate in the domain of prebelief, growing on the exclusively human ground constituted by dwelling in a world with self and others.

Kierkegaard's *The Sickness unto Death* clearly outlines the paradoxical nature of the human being and the necessity of allowing the self to rest in a movement resembling the skeptic's faith. The tensions that preoccupied Kierkegaard—the logical categories of infinitude and finitude, necessity and possibility, and the eternal and temporal—all manifest uncomfortably within a human self. Unhappily, this self finds it impossible to be the self that it is independently. Part of why we need to relate with things constituted by a similar paradoxical tension—art, symbols, other humans—is that we require mediation to forestall the threats of brokenness.

The beginning of the work of faith comes with the construction of the self. In a symbolic universe, the symbol of God provides this mediating function—even Kierkegaard uses traditional language to describe that power which supports the human in being a self. This leap to the theistic, however, is not necessary. In *The Sickness unto Death,* Kierkegaard develops the argument he began in the *Concluding Unscientific Postscript,* showing how the human capacity to do nothing is most importantly true concerning the question of the self. Anti-Climacus systematically moves through everything humans *can* do—willing to be a self, not willing to be a self, not knowing one has a self—and shows how everything ends in despair. Despair is a self-negating state, making humans psychologically become the nothing of which they are capable. One encounters the power that establishes the self only at the point of complete human self-negation.

Skepticism allows for a structurally similar movement of faith rooted in the understanding. Tillich especially notes the connection between skepticism and despair, finding that the continual negation of knowledge leads to an undoing of a central human capacity. What humans can conceive establishes the boundaries of possibilities: what we cannot think, we can neither do nor be. Through the continual creation of equipollent arguments and by voluntarily strangling one's human potential, one can re-create the problem of the self and experience despair in a way that strongly resembles what Kierkegaard describes. The faith of the skeptic—that which undergirds the ability to continually undergo the process of skepticism with the unsupportable belief that a knowable truth will be revealed—functions in the same invisible way as the hand of God. In other words, the structural parallel sufficiently accounts for the same result despite the difference in the content that becomes negated. Presymbolically, then, a skeptical faith appears to be a viable alternative to those for whom symbols are unable to function (although this kind of faith is available only to those who engage in a skeptical faith, not to the naïve skeptics who also inhabit the pretheistic domain).

Theologians have long accorded to faith a second function: it serves as the necessary precondition of the possibility of interacting with other humans. In other words, faith provides the ability to trust others. Although this meaning of faith may seem out of place, Robert Scharlemann has argued that the theological depth of this type of basic trusting occurs only through trusting the self-in-God.[4] Any interaction with another requires faith; one does not enter into any sort of relation without some subjective conviction in the other's worth (even if the interaction is designed to deprive the other of a perceived good), even though there is never an objective certainty that the other warrants this good. In general, we understand our faith in others to correspond to the broadest communal context, which arises from shared language systems and cultural assumptions. Smaller communities are more tightly knit around concrete symbols based in revelations, ones that divide and isolate humans and offer a more perceptible whole of which to be a part. One moves into communities through the mediation of the symbol, and this modicum of faith is what allows society to function—and occasionally flourish.

I contend that faith can function on a presymbolic level, although even rigorous skeptics use language to form equipollent arguments and naïve skeptics might not understand the need to alter symbolic customs. Faith, as the willingness to recognize the other's worth, precedes even the most rudimentary of sign language. Communication grounds the desire to understand on the basis of trust, and this trust—not language—is the crucial element in generating human relationships. Thus, although faith and symbol correlate, they are not interchangeable. Just as humans who share similar symbolic spaces (at least at the level of language) can, absent faith, disregard another's moral worth, so also can those who lack any symbolic connection still, in faith, share a moment of respect. The domain of presymbolic and pretheistic faith permits a faith available to everyone—including naïve and rigorous skeptics.

The world manifests as a series of potential paradoxes that skeptics access by questioning the nature of reality. From our limited vantage point, it is impossible to verify whether the world is primarily material or ideal, whether what appears is true or illusory, whether the event of its appearance conceals its truth. Any thing in the world gathers such questions to itself, and each thing therefore becomes a "sign" in the Kierkegaardian sense. Things are *not* symbols, however, as we cannot determine whether a greater depth exists in which things could participate. To this extent, every thing we encounter offers us opportunities to humble ourselves, making ourselves vulnerable to uncertainty. Sadly, we often succumb to the temptation to master things conceptually, using calculative thought and the understanding to control the thing. Some things, those that inspire us to feel awe or the sublime, perhaps cause an initial movement toward trusting. But prior to interpreting (knowing) these things as hierophantic manifestations of a god, or even symbolically opening a greater depth or whole, we encounter things as objectively uncertain and hearken to the truths they gather. The subjective conviction that continuing to hearken to things might lead to an unveilation of a truth is a faith that precedes theism, belief, and the symbolic domain and so also exists for those who engage in a skeptical faith.

The Human Forms of Faith

Because the question of God remains unresolved within the domain of pretheistic faith, both naïvely skeptical and rigorously skeptical faiths require an immanent, human point of origin. Theologians and philosophers have produced various arguments describing naturalistic accounts for human faith, and any of these—from Schleiermacher to Nancy—justifies this assumption. Instead of retreading or slightly modifying these positions, I argue that the structure of human consciousness sufficiently accounts for the possibility of faith. Godless, this ground of faith preserves faith from something controlled by or directed toward a deity.

The human capacity to perceive what is infinite even as we maintain our finite perspectives uniquely situates us to undergo the experience of faith. Assuming that faith is an unusual state that humans enter into with conscious intention (motivated by a subjective conviction relative to a truth),

I argue that we potentially encounter one of three main origins of faith, that humans maintain their subjective conviction in the face of objective uncertainty in one of three ways. Although faith may originate in a context determined by intrusive appearances of the infinite, absolute, or eternal into human existence, the form that it takes depends on the type of compensatory effort employed by humans to maintain their subjective conviction.

The first form of faith, and what many likely assume when speaking of faith, arises in the context of passion. The *Oxford English Dictionary* lists three main senses of passion: definitions relating to physical suffering and pain (with etymological overtones of the suffering of a martyr or messiah), definitions that deal with emotional or mental states (specific definitions include anger, lust, and love), and definitions that relate to passivity. Although we can use the three senses independently or exclusively, one sense often implies the others. In each case, passion provides the context for the most personal and intense form of faith.

One explanation of why meanings among the terms overlap is that each of the senses reflects different modes of human finitude at its most finite. Embodiment itself is representative of human finitude: humans experience necessity corporeally (in terms of the need to eat, drink, and breathe), and the body also limits human experience to one point in time and space. Pain and suffering—whether from injury, illness, or age—serve as exacerbating reminders of human frailty. The suffering body that cannot alleviate its suffering must endure reminders not only that flesh is susceptible to pain but also that we are irreducibly tied to a suffering body. The doubled experience of limitation is so utterly personal that one cannot abstract from it any universal truth or awareness, to the extent that linguistic or verbal descriptions of pain cannot communicate the reality of the situation. Because it is *felt*, passion as embodied pain transcends mere physical discomfort and introduces a wholly consuming mental and emotional state lacking any given form (i.e., an emotion not identifiable as anger or hatred or love). Instead, passion reveals the heart of emotional possibilities within human beings. At extreme points of pain, we cannot discern what we feel "emotionally" or "physically": the line between the two is blurred. Additionally, the perpetuation of passion both requires and reinforces the passivity of human existence inasmuch as one cannot act against the pain that one feels; instead, one is laid open to it and before it.

In a corresponding way, passion understood as an emotional or mental state also embodies a simultaneous resistance to, and acknowledgement of, human limitation. A passionate desire—whether informed by a love for or lust after a given object—implies a lack that constitutes the self who feels powerless in its grasp. When an emotional need grows more acute, so also does the desire to have it fulfilled, and a visceral reaction—an ache in the chest, a shortness of breath, the formation of tears—is its frequent companion. A passionate anger or hatred, felt toward that which seems to impede or eliminate one's happiness and against which one feels helpless, manifests physically as well: one's heart races, blood pounds, fists clench. When passion simply occurs, with neither form (positive or negative) nor object, it maintains the physiological characteristics that both the positive and negative passions have in common (shortness of breath, ache in the chest, increased heart rate) in an indefinable discomfort or visceral knot. One can feel such passions with either anxiety or despair (when one experiences the passion negatively) or in terms of joy or happiness (when one experiences the passion, still without object, positively). In all cases, as in the corporeal dimension, the passion holds us captive, and we are helpless against its power.

Passion forms faith when we leave the state of trusting by adhering to a belief that concerns the "truth" of the person's self or world or how the person relates them. As Kierkegaard realized, faith is most passionate when it is born from an acknowledgment of personal limitations. Because my self, my world, and how I relate them are essentially and necessarily subjective concerns about which there is no objective validity, the nature of the proposition is such that it negates the possibility of a detached or objective relationship to the proposition. It can only arise through human trusting. The belief demands that the individual either affirm or negate it with a passion that unites the elements of the individual in the moment of the present. The passionate form of faith, rooted in and wholly concerning the individual, does not require a symbol; this type of faith is able to flourish pretheistically for both naïve and rigorous skeptics.

Because passion involves the fleeting instant of the present, the temporal limitations on the duration of faith are distinctive for faith formed by passion. Unlike the other forms of faith, passion requires almost no endurance: only an instant separates revelation and unveilation. Truths revealed by passion are valid for that exact moment alone. In other words, the form of passion requires a continuous reaffirmation or renegation at every subsequent moment of time so long as the proposition remains one that elicits passion from the person in question. After all, while the first answer might entail a unique or transformative event within a person's life, it does not follow that subsequent answers are any less important or that subsequent answers will be identical to the first answer.

An example of this form of faith appears in the initial writings on the psychoanalytic method. In his early work, Freud states that the goal of psychotherapy is to free patients from hysterical symptoms. He contends that this is done when the patient "reproduc[es] the pathogenic impressions that caused [the symptom] and [gives] utterance to them with an expression of affect" and that "the therapeutic task *consists solely in inducing [the patient] to do so.*"[5] The patient's utterance comes as an echo of the therapist's guess at the secret that the patient is attempting to repress. As Freud later argues during his later work with the Wolfman, the connection between a diagnosis (in this case, an utterance concerning the "primal scene" that theoretically caused the hysterical symptoms) and actual "objective" history is unimportant.[6] The importance lies in the success of the treatment (an absence of physical symptoms), which Freud directly correlates to the choice of diagnosis (i.e., the patient's verbal "utterance").

Freud's use of affect correlates with my use of passion in three ways. First, the initial diagnosis from the therapist to the patient is an analog of a belief produced at a theistic level: it is a truth claim impossible to verify objectively, yet toward which one can feel a high degree of subjective conviction. If the individual assents to the proposition with affect, *passionately* identifying with the truth (or untruth) of the proposition, then the individual has entered into a state of faith formed by passion relative to this proposition.[7] The comparison to psychoanalysis is limited because of the unique temporal element constraining faith formed by passion. Unlike the diagnosis, which is only true of a patient's past, a proposition that requires a compensatory faith-forming passion from the individual is true only of that individual's present. That being the case, to avoid Sartrean bad faith, an individual cannot make a propositional statement about the self that is true once and for all; such statements must be continually evaluated and reevaluated so that the truth of them reflects the truth of the person at present (and not one who made the statement in the past).

Of course, not every statement of personal identity (e.g., I am a father, I enjoy biking) forces an individual to enter into the state of faith, nor will every such belief elicit the form of passion from the individual. The overarching temporal arc that demands that an individual undergo a moment-by-moment assent or denial of a proposition lasts only for as long as one still responds to the statement passionately. The instant an individual ceases to have a passionate relationship to the proposition marks the instant that the individual no longer relates to that proposition in faith. In all likelihood, the final answer to the question will serve as "true" for the individual until such a time as a passionate engagement with the issue recommences.

The form of passion is the most intimate and personal way that an individual can enter into a state of faith: the belief to which an individual relates unites and defines the entirety of the individual and challenges and tests the individual at every instant of every present moment. Because it is the most personal, the form of passion is also the least universalizable—the truth to which I adhere is true only for me and for one moment of time. Thus one weakness of the form of passion is its inability to find an objective criterion by which to measure its truth. A second weakness is that humans cannot share or discuss this truth—the form of passion isolates the individual and thus removes the individual from a potential larger whole.

REASON FORMS FAITH when individuals alter knowledge-based relationships with the understanding after having applied the method of critical scrutiny to the act of reasoning and find it necessary to formulate a belief about what they determine is logically necessary but empirically nonverifiable. Using reason as a framework around thinking allows us to achieve a distance from what we think: it is an objective stance, allowing us to regard our thoughts as objects and derive from them conceptions that are necessarily and universally true of the matter at hand. This possibility extends even to my reflective engagement with my self, where I can take the subjective existential possibilities of individuals in general as an abstract object of thought while simultaneously clinging to the awareness that what will be determined at the end of that thought contains implications for my subjective experience.

One of the more compelling arguments dramatizing the movement from an objectively certain understanding to a belief formed by reason is Johann Fichte's dramatic portrayal of the "I" in *The Vocation of Man*. Here, knowledge creates the despair of the I, when beginning with the external world (which creates a world in which the self is utterly determined), or from within the individual (which creates a speculative system in which the world itself is neither more nor less than how I see it). Fichte finds that faith is a necessary supplement to reason inasmuch as it offers the possibility of acting within a world—especially on behalf of other individuals. Fichte also finds—as Kierkegaard does, later—that a judgment made in faith but formed by reason (i.e., by choosing between two choices presented by logic) unites and presents the character of the judge.

Temporally, while the state of faith formed by reason relative to a belief that cannot be empirically validated might (and likely will) stretch out through the remainder of the individual's life, the impact that this has on the individual is negligible. Unlike the incredibly taxing form of passion, the form of reason, in its universalized and objective detachment from the individual, requires very little from the individual outside of the initial failure of understanding that transports the individual into a state of faith. In other words, the individual continually persists in a state of faith relative to the belief, but the qualitative impact of that state of faith is minimal. In this way, the form of reason is structurally the opposite of the form of passion: it is impersonal and thus the most universal type of belief capable of compelling faith. At its best, one can communicate a faith formed by reason at the level of a universal truth, and individuals connect to that truth with a subjective existential awareness. The weakness of this form of faith comes, however, precisely in its failure to motivate the subjective appropriation of the "truth" it finds. The universal aspect of this form of faith, especially as it arises out of a critical or skeptical appropriation of the world, allows it to be open to both naïve and rigorous skeptics in the domain of prebelief.

One forms faith by volition when deciding to interrelate trusting and understanding on a reflexive level. What differentiates the form of volition is the willingness—on the existential-individual level—to reflect on the strengths and weaknesses opened by both modes of human thinking and pit them against each other in mutual critique. A skeptic can do this by making a set of equipollent arguments that relate to trusting, making a set of equipollent arguments that relate to understanding, and then placing the two pairs of arguments against each other. In this way, faith formed by volition—or an intentional willingness to have faith—includes the two types of human thinking and both other forms of faith, uniting them in the way that re-creates the human as a singular entity. This faith demands volition because combining trusting and understanding is a contingent and not necessary process.

Volitional faith can take a positive or a negative valence. Positively, a volitional faith allows individuals to merge the faith formed by passion in tandem with that which the reason finds as its own limits. In order to enter into this form of faith, the individual must have already received a positive revelation of God and must also have engaged in the self-critique of the understanding to find the limits of what humans can know. Following these two moments, individuals maintain a subjective conviction that the two elements denied to reason (formed through passion and reason) overlap and describe the same entity. This results in a type of volitional faith that manifests in the writings of Anselm, which defined the God of tradition as that which is greater than can be thought, placing the God in whom one passionately believed into the context also defined by reason's failing. Although this results in a reflective faith, this type of faith is suited for neither naïve nor rigorous skeptics, as the initial revelation remains uncritiqued.

A positive version of faith can also exist relative to passionate statements of belief regarding the nature of the self or others. I am gripped by an insight divulged in an event of disclosure: accordingly, I embrace the revelation in faith—regardless of whether I affirm or negate the statement of belief. This type of faith can be merged with an acceptance of the boundaries of reason to form a faith grounded in both an acknowledgment of human limitation (i.e., one that is based in the nothing that one can do or know) and possibility, interpreting the unknown as a realm open and available for human works.

The negative type of volitional faith *does* expand to the domain of prebelief and therefore is open to rigorous skeptics. I suspend judgment on a revelation of God, skeptical about the ability of the symbol to communicate the truth of God, making an equipollent argument that also accounts for what appears to be God. This skeptical moment obliterates the content of faith in a self-imposed state parallel to Tillich's absolute faith, creating the possibility of a faith without content capable of sustaining me in the space between understanding and trusting. This faith is put in tandem with the awareness of reason's failing, creating a faith born from what I cannot trust and what I cannot understand. This negative faith is thus made up of three separate moments of faith: one that brackets the initial impulse to trust, one that brackets the impulse to understand, and one that gathers these two separate impulses close together over a negative space of overlapping critique.

Every belief formed by volition in this way creates a dissonance between an actual reality and a potential, desired reality. To *will* the latter compels action and behavior, where I stake myself in bringing about the desired reality in spite of its unreality. As a mundane example, if I hear the rhetoric of a politician who describes the hypothetical world in which he or she is elected and am moved into a state of volition by assenting to the belief that this politician would be a good leader, I will strive actively to ensure that the world described by the politician comes about. I stand between the given and the desired and resolutely work toward the actualization of the latter. In this way, any activity formed by volition always already encompasses radical subjective existential involvement inasmuch as my self depends on the actualization of the proposition at hand.

The binding of the individual to the project latent within the belief is the strength of the state of faith formed by volition. The weakness of this form of faith stems from the same, very personal root as the strength—unlike the state of faith formed by reason and akin to the state of faith formed by passion, I cannot communicate either the vision of the other world for which I am striving or the reasons I desire its actualization. The form of reason tends toward an experienced state of faith that, even when subjectively motivating, nonetheless tends toward intellectual abstraction; the form of volition, however, always pushes the individual to work for the concretization or actualization of the proposition held to be true in spite of its unreal nature.

THE FIRST CHAPTER outlined a model of faith that addressed the prebelief domain of faith, populated by naïve and rigorous skeptics. This domain is *pre*symbolic and *pre*theistic in that it shares a tendency toward a symbolic rendering of an ultimate concern—such a symbol has simply not yet manifested in the life of the individual, leading that individual to experience brokenness. This chapter has shown the similarities that connect the logic of an absolute faith allowed within the confines of a pretheistic faith and the logic of skepticism; I developed this connection systematically in order to expose a model of skeptical faith. The chapters that follow discuss the importance of vigilance in this model. Chapter 3 investigates the importance of vigilance in the working of skepticism and a skeptical faith as part of an explanation for the dynamic of this faith, while chapter 4 discusses the implications of vigilance for a skeptical faith that looks out at the appearances in the world.

Part II
The Function of Vigilance in a Skeptical Faith

3 Skeptical Consciousness and the Dynamic of Faith

I believe in a personal god who cares about me and worries and oversees everything I do. I believe in an impersonal god who set the universe in motion and went off to hang with her girlfriends and doesn't even know that I'm alive. I believe in an empty and godless universe of causal chaos, background noise, and sheer blind luck.

—NEIL GAIMAN, *American Gods*

Having disclosed how skepticism provides a viable ground of faith by revealing the faith inherent in skepticism and the equipollent tensions present in theology, I will demonstrate how to sustain this experience of faith through an analysis of human consciousness. Unlike other theological frameworks, which presume the existence of a spirit/matter dualism through an emphasis on the soul, an emphasis on consciousness is germane even to those who adhere to a framework of material reductionism. Because any analysis presupposes the ability of consciousness to experience and think, and because consciousness does not require a prior acceptance of a particular historical revelation, framing an analysis of the dynamic of faith in terms of consciousness maintains its relevance to all humans—atheists, agnostics, and believers of every type.[1]

We commonly fall prey to the temptation to consider faith as a "thing." This defines faith as something that is bestowed and protected: one "keeps" one's faith or "shares" it. The ability to share unsparingly testifies to our lingering awareness of faith's infinite properties, yet the truth proposition that one shares is surprisingly undifferent from its initial translation into language. Preserved, stored, and kept, this faith is set apart, lifeless. Nothing can steal or alter this faith, but, unchallenged, it remains detached from believers' lives. Even those who manifest faith as works occasionally fall into this: the faith that informs one's values and activities remains static, a remembered motivation. Individuals desire a static faith with good intentions, longing to protect and remain nourished by the revelation. Frequently, of course, this faith concerns something about which one remains subjectively convinced and that is framed as objectively certain relative to the confines of one's smaller, symbolic community. Static faith functions as knowledge.

Although we can believe and preserve a nonverifiable statement intellectually, true faith is a *state* that one enters into and exits out from relative to a revelation or proposition of truth. Conducive to the larger goal of expanding faith to include skepticism, I attend specifically to the domain of prebelief, included in the state of faith. Most ignore the time of prebelief because of its brevity: it only exists during the time after one has assented to the viability of a proposition and before one has rendered a judgment concerning its truth value. Respecting the zone of prebelief as an important site of faith—one open to skeptics, atheists, agnostics, and believers—requires further exploration of this temporal gap. The dynamic work of faith occurs along the horizontal axis—lingering in the state of faith from one moment into the next. Rather than focusing on not "losing" one's faith (as though it were an object), the horizontal dynamic focuses on preserving the tension between subjective certainty and objective uncertainty as its own good. The vertical axis of faith, on the other hand, focuses on the role faith plays in allowing the human to become increasingly integrated with the infinite.

In this chapter, I argue that faith occurs prior to making a judgment about the truth value of a proposition or revelation and that prebelief is the most true time of faith. Put otherwise, opting toward one judgment or another causes me to leave the domain of pure faith and enter a realm of knowledge (or at least an objective certainty solidified in the context of a particularized symbolic community). I begin with a brief analysis of one of Nathaniel Hawthorne's stories of faith in order to provide a concretized vision of what faith can mean. With Hawthorne's understanding of faith in mind, I define how a dynamic faith emerges most powerfully in the prebelief time of hesitation and uncertainty. More specifically, I articulate the valuable work that a skeptical consciousness accomplishes in extending the time of a pure prebelief and the role that vigilance plays in allowing one to maintain this skepticism.

"Tarry with Me This Night"

Nathaniel Hawthorne's 1835 short story "Young Goodman Brown," set in the aftermath of the Salem witch trials of 1692, illustrates the need for a faith able to survive apart from religion and hints at how individuals can preserve the dynamic nature of faith. The story concerns a young Puritan who, ignoring his wife's plea to "tarry with me this night" (111), leaves town to keep an appointment in the forest. He meets an old man—eventually revealed as the devil—who provides detailed information about the ignoble deeds of his "religious" forebears. Despite Brown's reservations, they keep moving into the forest, where Brown encounters several religious leaders who speak amiably with his companion. The journey ends with a Black Mass, where Brown finds his wife and the whole host of his townsfolk. He calls upon his wife to resist the devil but cannot determine whether she heeds his words. He finds himself alone the next morning near where he had begun his journey. The narrator interrupts the story to ask a question, presumably of the reader: "Had Goodman Brown fallen asleep in the forest and only dreamed a wild dream of a witch-meeting?" Hawthorne then provides an answer: "Be it so if you will; but, alas! it was a dream of evil omen for young Goodman Brown" (123). The narrator describes the transformative effect of the experience on Brown, who became "a stern, a sad, a darkly meditative, a distrustful, if not a desperate man" who "when he had lived long, and was borne to his grave a hoary corpse" had "no hopeful verse upon his tombstone," as "his dying hour was gloom" (124).

Three elements of the story are important to keep in mind in a discussion of the dynamics of faith. First, Brown's wife—named Faith[2]—is central to the mechanics of the narrative. Hawthorne puts the plot into motion as Brown ignores Faith's request to tarry with her, choosing knowledge instead. The knowledge he gains, concerning the complicity of other ancestors who share his universally generic name of "Goodman Brown" in activities such as lashing Quaker women or burning Indian villages, offers the possibility of reinterpreting his past. The devil's familiarity with leading political and religious figures drives Brown to reinterpret the nature of his present world. In other words, the desire to leave a mode of tarrying with (or in) Faith causes Brown to enter a dynamic of suspicion that he is ill equipped to handle. The uncertainty concerning whether his wife resists the devil—and Hawthorne clearly shows that Brown believes she did not[3]— mirrors the reader's uncertainty, and Brown's doubt about his wife pushes him into an acceptance of evil instead of a victorious expectation in faith.

Second, the defining moment in the text is when Brown, who has literally left his Faith behind, determines it/her to be gone utterly: Brown exclaims, "My Faith is gone!" and "There is no good on earth; and sin is but a name. Come, devil; for to thee is this world given" (118). Brown understands a world in which good and sin are mere signifiers and not rooted in a participation with the divine to be a world dominated and controlled by the devil, an evil power of chaos that destroys hierarchies and obliterates differences in a work similar to that attributed to faith (i.e., remaking the finite world such that it conforms to an infinite vision). What makes this problematic for Brown—and seemingly other than a work of faith—is the "source" of the act, the devil. In this repetition of leaving the openness of faith for an assertion of knowledge—understood at a figurative and not literal level—Brown seals his fate as one doomed to a despair of his own making. Unable now to trust in a world where God reigns over a holy people in the same naïve fashion as before, the revelation of the Black Mass leaves Brown unworlded and thus in a state of despair. Relative to this revelation, Brown is tormented into a silence, as he knows that those around him would not acknowledge any confirmation of his chosen reality. He has lost his faith in the literal community of people surrounding him.

Third, by producing a proposition concerning the truth of how the world relates to religion, Hawthorne forces the reader into a position of faith relative to this proposition. The direct question to the reader—if Brown had "only dreamed a wild dream"—in truth asks the reader to determine whether or not evil rules the world. The reader's intervention is demanded by Hawthorne's addition of "Be it so if you will" (123), which puts the truth of the situation relative to the reader's volition. Although nothing will change for the fictional Brown, the story exposes a possibility of faith able to accommodate suspicion concerning both the historical tradition of religion and the nature of its practice in any present-day situation. Hawthorne challenges the reader to tarry with faith—and not assume with Brown the wickedness of the world—despite acknowledging the tragedy that evil persists in those who seem benevolent. Hawthorne invites the reader to respond to a skeptical foundation in faith.

Hawthorne's story offers four insights that ground a discussion of the dynamics of faith, accounting for skepticism and maintaining a distance capable of preventing a collapse into knowledge. A viable faith must keep individuals from being grasped by despair by incorporating fallibility, brokenness, and evil. Without this dimension, a confrontation with evil may push the ill-prepared individual into making a faith-based negation of faith in despair instead of tarrying with faith awhile longer. Second, Hawthorne points to the quality of faith as that which tarries, or hesitates: had Brown been able to tarry before deciding whether or not good and evil were more than names, he may have avoided his life of gloom and despair. Third, Hawthorne reinforces literarily the correlation between faith and corporate wholeness (including wholeness on individual, familial, and communal levels): once Brown loses his faith, he is not himself and is unable to find any comfort in the presence of his family or fellow townsfolk. Finally, Hawthorne indicates the importance of revelation and the construction of world. The revelation of the existence of a deep and abiding evil displaces Brown from a world participating in God's goodness. Choosing to reject this new world, Brown finds himself neither in a world ruled by God nor one peopled by a demonic community. In other words, Brown unconsciously assents to a proposition that he has consciously negated, and this lack of vigilant self-awareness leads to despair.

Three Versions of Faith's Dynamic Structure

On the vertical axis, faith's dynamic structure incorporates the human hunger for the infinite and the finite. This pair forms the backdrop of both the human being (according to Kierkegaard) and the symbol (according to Tillich). As I will show, theologians have conceived of the dynamic of faith as transporting humans toward the infinite and away from the finite. Individually, humans move from self-negation toward the infinite. Structurally, subsequent models of faith have become increasingly intimate, moving toward the core of human beings.

Theologically, new philosophical modes of understanding have deepened the reach of faith's dynamic, producing three distinct domains. The first model of faith—predicated on the primacy of trusting over understanding—involves a dynamic within the human being, emphasizing the need for humans to recognize sinfulness in order to receive God. The second, existential model of faith—which places understanding above trusting—sublates the internal dynamic but replicates it as an inner-human tension, eliminating the need for an external god in favor of the self's ability to become a self. The third, post-Heideggerean model of faith (to the extent that one can be generalized) understands truth as the movement between revealing and concealing; this accounts for a dynamic presence in faith that no longer requires an infinite or a finite but merely an alternating series of forces. A new model of faith would need to account for each of these domains, as well as the horizontal mode by which we maintain faith as faith. A skeptical faith maintains the advantage gained by locating the hinge of a dynamic faith in the movement of revealing and concealing but locates this faith fully within the confines of human consciousness. In other words, instead of depending on the event of disclosure as generated from the human interaction with the world where one is displaced relative to a truth, I argue that faith can be generated individually, absolutely, and without relation to the world.

WHILE THE ULTIMATE goal of this chapter is to outline the dynamic of a skeptical faith enabled by vigilance predicated on the ground of faith opened by a Heideggerean definition of truth, I begin by tracing the ways in which this differs from the faiths centered on Platonic or Kantian models. This contextualizes the advantages of defining truth as revelation and justifies this foundation's account of faith anchored in earlier definitions of truth.

The decision to equate God with Good, which marks the turn toward a theological blend of faith that takes seriously the rigors of philosophy beyond asserting the primacy of trusting, sublates trusting and understanding by showing how each participates in faith.[4] The revelation of the truth of God surpasses rational comprehension, and thus faith becomes necessary. Aquinas offers the clearest definition of this form of logic, defining faith as an act of the intellect determinate to one object of the will's command.[5] Because revelations exceed the human capacity for rational understanding, the will necessarily supplies the subjective conviction even though the object remains objectively uncertain. Unlike science and understanding, which relate to apparent objects, faith for Aquinas is differentiated by its focus on that which "appears not." Of course, many things fall into the category of that which "appears not," forcing Aquinas to differentiate common faith from the virtue of faith that maintains a relation to "the beatitude we hope for." The beatific vision allows Aquinas to hold that actions have a twofold goal: achieving their own perfection and realizing the end—to be like God. The ultimate unveiling of the beatific vision comes with a literalization of the infinitizing of the human, when one receives an incorruptible body in line with the perfection of the soul in an ultimate reconciliation with God.[6]

Aquinas offers a representative understanding of the horizontal dynamic of faith: the otherworldly nature of the beatific vision allows a faith that will not diminish into knowledge or opinion—it is different, beyond the ken of normal modes of being. Because one must continue trusting until a full unveiling of the end, there is never a time—in time—that a lack of faith is appropriate. One remains subjectively convinced about the object of faith, which, unknowable, falls beyond the realm of objective certainty. Relative to this mode of Christianity, the end of faith is only appropriate with an unveilation of the full beatific vision.

In the vertical dynamic, one integrates with the infinite through a process of an ongoing reconciliation of the soul with God. As Augustine, interpreting Paul, explains in his "On the Spirit and the Letter," the vertical deepening of faith over time incorporates multiple levels of trusting. First, one apprehends the truth of the Law that is revealed, an awareness that manifests in the experience of guilt.[7] Unable to adhere to the Law but subjectively convinced that it is the path to goodness, I unavoidably confront my own fallibility. Achieving oneness with an infinitely good God requires the work of self-negation, allowing God's spirit to manifest instead of my own.[8] This work of self-negation, the ongoing work of faith supplemented by God's spirit, leads to the annihilation of self.

The second ground of faith opens with Kant's division of thinking and being, which makes God more difficult to know in revealing how our need to think God does not mean that God (especially as revealed to a particular group on earth) actually exists. Shifting from a perspective that valorized the ideal over the material allowed a more widespread understanding of the "finite" than the limits of human fallibility. Situated primarily as an understanding (instead of trusting) faith, the second dynamic of faith moves forward horizontally through time by requiring that humans continually set aside the understanding as a way to remain in the state of faith. This particular repetition of negative willing is described by Kierkegaard as "resting" and by Tillich as "being grasped"; what both have in common is a faith that has little to do with an intellectual proposition of belief. Vertically, the sublation of the finite with the infinite is accomplished as contrasting elements within the self are harmonized. The struggle is moved within the human instead of pitting a finite human against an infinite God. Structurally, the guilt induced by Law (that requires that one trust before seeking to understand) is replaced with a despairing confrontation with nonbeing. Becoming conscious of my despair kindles a faith that accepts "Everything is possible for God."[9]

Internalizing the dynamic of faith transforms faith into a process involving the constitution of the self (instead of a dynamic between God and human). The internalization accounts for the experience of the reconciliation with the finite and the infinite that the first domain interprets literally. Additionally, internalization allows the movement of faith to exist nontheistically: the reconciliation of the self occurs moment by moment and without recourse to a symbolically determined mediator. Finally, internalizing the dynamic of faith focuses even more precisely on the temporal importance of each moment of faith and thereby prevents faith from congealing into a static mass.

The third domain of faith, grounded on Heidegger's definition of truth as an event of revealing, manifests in postmodern theologies. Postsecular theologies, in particular, build on Derrida's later writings to provide a concept of faith that is very much at odds with knowing.[10] Instead of a Being to trust or a concept to think, "God" exists as that which is both revealed and concealed in the religions that seek to contextualize or concretize specific rituals or revelations. The dynamic of faith moves forward horizontally in terms of an effort to continually stave off knowledge and preserve faith as faith. This dynamic faith depends on the understanding (to determine what knowledge is and so avoid it) as well as trusting in an unknowable or unattainable reality beyond appearance (like Derrida's sense of Justice).[11]

The emphasis on unknowability that arises out of Derrida's work on deconstruction and *différance* expands the existentialist version of dynamic faith. First, the mind-set introduced by deconstruction destabilizes the possibility of certainty in general, beyond the specific question of the self. Although Nietzsche also was aware that our worlds could be reduced to the level of interpretation, the method of deconstruction—combined with a growing realization that our "reality" is a text that has been constructed—undermines the possibility of any objective certainty. Additionally, postmodern theologies relocate faith from an alteration within myself to my interactions with the world. Assuming a world of shifting signifiers, the postmodern understanding of truth describes reality as a constant flux of meaning that prohibits absolute knowledge. Faith is reintroduced as central to human existence, as a stance of epistemological humility instead of an embrace of revealed truth.

On the vertical axis, postmodern theologies open a third mode of positively incorporating the human ability to do nothing. Whereas trusting requires accepting one's limitations to negate the self and become filled by God's spirit, and understanding views doing nothing as coming-to-rest, postmodernism appropriates nothing as the highest form of human thinking. Put otherwise, if the first domain powers its dynamic force through trusting, the second powers it in the paradoxical tension of trusting and understanding, and the third moves forward at the point of mutual failure: neither trusting nor understanding becomes a positive work.

Consciousness and the Proposition of Skeptical Faith

A trusting or passionate faith quickly departs from the home of the skeptic, the domain of prebelief. A skeptical faith abides in the understanding (an awareness of the limits of reason) or volition (willing oneself to maintain an indifference to knowledge). In chapter 2, I defined two elements of faith in skepticism. First, skeptics have faith that a truth will manifest in some unforeseeable eventuality. Second, the principle that allows skeptics to continuously suspend knowledge without being objectively certain that doing so is beneficial generates an absolute faith. Moving from skepticism to a skeptical faith—a faith reflexively skeptical about its own status as faith—takes this principle as a belief about believing. This belief arises out of the understanding and is maintained volitionally.

Based on the two elements of faith within skepticism, skeptical faith requires both the subjective undergoing based on a belief's explication or linguistic formulation and that which dutifully maintains or preserves the experience mediated by the belief in question. This chapter validates the following as a belief about faith, formed by reason and capable of both providing an individual's subjective undergoing the state of faith and the maintenance of that state: *faith is the state of being subjectively convinced of the uncertainty of objective certainty.* Because this occurs on the reflexive level, the formulation relative to the other path of reflection is also valid: *faith is the state of being subjectively convinced of the uncertainty of subjective conviction.* Based on Kant's initial definition of faith, this serves as a principle that frames a skeptical outlook, convincing me that nothing is certain. While skeptical, this belief is not nihilistic: I hold to the positivity of its truth.

Usefully, this statement of belief accommodates the definition of faith in the other three domains. Relative to trusting, holding this belief pushes one to maintain the "confidence in things unseen" advocated by Hebrews. Basing this statement of belief on Kant's formulation includes it within the domain of understanding. Finally, as the belief pushes me to refuse certainty, I view my experiences in terms of what is revealed and concealed in a comportment of openness. More important than accounting for the faith in other domains, this statement of belief adequately generates a skeptical faith. To show this, I will review Kant's parameters before describing the experience of faith based on the distinctions outlined by Robert Scharlemann.

In his *Critique of Pure Reason*, Kant distinguishes between three gradations of truth, based on differences in certainty (the degree to which a thing is determined *objectively* to be true) and conviction (the degree to which a thing is determined *subjectively* to be true). Opinions occur when one has inadequate conviction and little certainty about a proposition, while having sufficient conviction and enough certainty grants knowledge. Kant spends most of his time discussing *Glaube* (both faith and belief), manifesting with sufficient evidence for conviction but insufficient evidence to provide certainty. A tension, lacking in knowledge and opinion, thus exists in faith. While knowledge is conviction (subjectively) about what is certain (objectively), and opinion has a lack of conviction (subjectively) of what is uncertain (objectively), faith is a type of conviction (subjective) that exists *in spite of* that which is uncertain (objectively).

Kant offers four occasions when it is necessary to be convinced of what is not certain. The first type of faith (Kant calls this *pragmatic*) is necessary insofar as it compels action toward a necessary or good end. A second type of faith (*doctrinal*) persists despite not being useful—some truths are impossible to determine objectively and neither compel nor deter action. This faith becomes necessary because one is unable, for some reason, not to believe. The third type of faith (*moral*) is necessary for avoiding ends that one would find unpleasant—such as guilt. Finally, Kant argues that *negative* faith is caused by an inability to disprove the possibility of an object of faith: it is valuable in curbing evil sentiment, although it alone may be insufficient to warrant moral action.[12]

Robert Scharlemann's *The Being of God* provides a vocabulary for expressing how different experiences of truth arise. Building on this foundation, I argue that knowledge and faith are different and mutually exclusive ways of experiencing truth, that doubt is necessary to the experience of faith, and, finally, that faith is a valuable form of experience. In his book, Scharlemann outlines four ways that consciousness experiences truth, which share an experience of subjective conviction. The first type of experience corresponds to intentional consciousness and relates to physical objects or literal words (e.g., the mundane awareness of a bus existing to be caught). The second type is self-relatedness, where the object of consciousness is put in relation with the subject perceiving it (I see a bus). At the third level, reflection, one renders a judgment about the truth of a statement (e.g., "It is true that I see a bus"); at this level, the direct object disappears in order to make room for a reflective object. The fourth level, reflexivity, enables the experience of reflection (e.g., "It is true that I see a bus is true"); its utility is better seen with reflexive objects such as truth, being, or faith.

Using Scharlemann's distinctions to speak about faith requires changes at the linguistic level. Expressing my status as objectively *uncertain* requires altering the type of judgment I render. Instead of emphasizing the *truth* of my experience, verbs expressing a more hesitant affirmation ("believe" or "think") are necessary. Two types of experiences demand this type of hesitation. The first arises when I have difficulty confirming what my senses suggest. When I hear my name, I look around. If I cannot determine the source of the voice after investigation, I experience an uncanny sensation: I retain my subjective conviction although I cannot become certain this experience occurred. On a prereflective level, I register "name called." At the level of self-relatedness, I think: "I hear my name." After failing to validate the experience, I remain subjectively certain of the *possibility* that my name was spoken. Thus, at the reflective level I can state, "It is possible that I heard my name," a sentiment echoed when I reflect, "I believe I heard my name," or reflexively ascertain that "I believe that I think I heard someone call my name."

Revelations constitute the second type of experience that demands an uncertain expression. A revelation pushes me into the state of faith relative to it: unable to verify its truth in the present, I cannot passively accept the truth of the revelation on a prelinguistic level. A mundane revelation—that my friend dislikes spicy foods—forces me to suspended judgment on the level of reflection: "I believe that my friend likes (or dislikes) spicy food" equally assents to the revelation. Here, the reflexive level—"I think that I believe my friend likes spicy food"—allows for the truth and untruth of the statement to be held together, although the value of this is negligible. The historical revelations concerning Young Goodman Brown's family technically belong to this sphere of mundane revelations: Brown has trouble accepting the import of the revelation—not its factuality.

The reflexive level of faith becomes most important for revelations that disclose a new world. Because the insight is new and unexpected, it displaces the individual from the realm of immediate givenness, as would occur were one to see a ghost. Rather than thinking "Ghost is" or "I see a ghost," such encounters would move us to the reflective level, where we are able to question the subject-object encounter and ask: "Do I see a ghost?" The subject (am I really someone who sees ghosts?) and object (is that really a ghost I see?) can be interrogated separately or as a whole. Propositions can inspire this experience as well (inasmuch as words can be "objects" in a way equivalent to things): confronting truths that reveal new worlds—or new ways of understanding the world—immediately force individuals into the reflexive level. Because "God" in any paradigm cannot be given wholly over to consciousness, the proposition that "God loves me" or "I love God" cannot simply be accepted in a subject-object relational way and must be put relative to a faith judgment on a reflective level (I believe God loves me) or a reflexive level (I believe that I think I love God). Again, the reflexive level positions the object of thinking (I think I love God) in terms of a belief.

The difference between the two conceptions is easier to see and more important when placed in the present tense. A statement of knowledge, "It is not true that I see a ghost," emphasizes the objective certainty of the event (in the phrasing "It *is*") while the fact of utterance implies subjective conviction. A statement of belief, "I believe that I see a ghost," conveys the combination of subjective conviction and objective uncertainty, as the term "believe" attests to conviction without knowledge. I communicate subjective conviction by emphasizing my "I" (instead of "It is"), which also localizes the experience to an objectively uncertain standpoint. Additionally, using "believe" avoids making a statement of fact ("is"). The statement "I do not believe that I see a ghost" is also a statement of belief, holding in tension subjective conviction (of what I do not believe) and objective certainty (the event of seeing a ghost) even though it is posited negatively. Again, one assents to propositions of truth when affirming *or* when negating the content of said proposition.

Altering the language differentiates statements of faith from statements of knowledge, both of which express an experience of truth on the reflexive level. Expressing the experience of truth as knowledge, I would state, "It is true that I believed that I saw a ghost." Expressing the experience of truth as faith, I would state, "I believe that I think that I saw a ghost." This reflexive statement of faith manifests subjective conviction at each level (excepting "saw," the way that I perceived the "ghost") in the emphasis of the subject (the "I") and subjective affirmation and emphasizes the uncertainty of the object (which, at the reflective level, is the event "I saw a ghost" and, at the reflexive level, is the event of "think that I saw a ghost"). As was true at the reflective level, a reflexive statement such as "I do not believe that I thought I saw a ghost" is still a statement of belief (and not knowledge) for reasons outlined above.

Faith, then, occurs when one is subjectively convinced and objectively uncertain about an object or experience. In Kant's view, these experiences are valuable even when unnecessary. This is true about the faith that occurs relative to doubt—either a belief that exists instead of doubt (bad faith) or a belief that exists because of doubt (skepticism). Faith occurs when one cannot answer a question with objective certainty (e.g., Did I see my friend Roger?). Expressions of faith blend subjective conviction with objective uncertainty: "I believe" and "I do not believe" express the conviction as personal while emphasizing the doubt that clings to the object (which keeps it from the realm of knowledge, characterized by certainty).

Scharlemann's framework clarifies how one can experience the Kantian tension between conviction and uncertainty as faith throughout different levels of consciousness: the process of faith is revealed as the question of faith moves into increasingly abstract levels of consciousness. On a self-relational level, I am subjectively convinced of something that is objectively uncertain; the belief that arises from both bad faith and skepticism dwell on this level. On a reflective level, I am subjectively convinced that I have experienced the tension between subjective conviction and objective uncertainty. On a reflexive level, my experience of faith remains subjectively convinced of the uncertainty of subjective conviction and convinced about the uncertainty of objective certainty. Each of these experiences is a manifestation of faith. Accepting this twinned definition of faith as a "law" or "principle" that primarily governs human interaction allows us to attain a comportment of faith relative to all experiences. Because this faith is born through the intentional negation of the understanding, it is primarily formed by the understanding (although maintaining it depends on volition).

This definition of faith succeeds negatively against the situation of Young Goodman Brown. Were Brown to have filtered his experiences through a subjective conviction concerning the uncertainty of subjective conviction, the force of the experience of the revelation would have diminished: instead of concluding that the world is of the devil, he may have been more capable of disbelieving that the experience occurred at all. More important, this stance on faith would have allowed him to experience his fellow Puritans with the same degree of faithful mistrust: Brown would have viewed their external expressions of piety with an understanding that his subjective conviction regarding their righteousness may be misplaced. Put otherwise, a relation of faith would have provided him with a more accurate (and therefore less destabilizing) sense of what occurred. Rather than stating, "My faith is gone! . . . There is no good on earth," which expresses an unwarranted objective certainty that appears (inaccurately) as a truth, Brown had grounds only to claim: "I think that I believe my faith is gone" or "I believe that I think that there is no good on earth." The postulation, put at a reflexive level, would have allowed Brown time to examine whether this is *truly* what he believed or thought. Tarrying uncertainly about either of these statements would have saved Brown from a life of despair.

Faith and the Hesitation of The Fantastic

Skeptics acknowledge the importance of lingering in uncertainty, refusing knowledge and embracing the relativity of appearances in order to adhere to a deeper and more accurate sense of truth. Assuming faith as a human good, an end in itself, requires a parallel (if not identical) desire to linger in uncertainty. Even Hawthorne points out the importance of hesitation relative to faith; more than believing, in other words, faith is a matter of tarrying. Young Goodman Brown's choice to cease uncertainty and pursue knowledge—to no longer tarry with faith (or Faith)—leads him to assert with illegitimate objective certainty that his faith was gone. A living faith, spawned (in some cases) by adhering to the principle described above, requires us to intentionally prolong unknowing lest we stumble into false certainty.

Tzvetan Todorov's *The Fantastic,* which defines a specific literary subgenre, offers another example of how tarrying requires a sustained suspension of certainty. Todorov defines the birth of the fantastic with the event of "an uncanny phenomenon which we can explain in two fashions, by types of natural causes and supernatural causes. The possibility of a hesitation between the two creates the fantastic effect" (26). The effect is a transitory one. As Todorov explains:

> The fantastic . . . lasts only as long as a certain hesitation: a hesitation common to reader and character, who must decide whether or not what they perceive derives from "reality" as it exists in the common opinion. At the story's end, the reader makes a decision even if the character does not; he opts for one solution or the other, and thereby emerges from the fantastic. If he decides that the laws of reality remain intact and permit an explanation of the phenomena described, we say that the work belongs to another genre: the uncanny. If, on the contrary, he decides that new laws of nature must be entertained to account for the phenomena, we enter the genre of the marvelous. (41)

Thus the fantastic is born with the inability to determine the nature of a phenomenon and dies once one makes a decision about the uncanny phenomenon.

Hawthorne's story meets Todorov's criterion, as natural causes (the fact that it was a dream) and supernatural causes (the existence of devils, witches, and sorcerers) each sufficiently explains Brown's experience. The overt gesture from the author to the reader solidifies the story's place within the framework of the fantastic: by saying to the reader, "Be it so if you will," Hawthorne allows the reader to leave the fantastic by asserting that the story is either uncanny or marvelous. Emily Brontë's *Wuthering Heights* provides another example, as the reader is unsettled when the narrator raises the possibility of a ghost without satisfactorily settling it. Textual evidence suggests the workings of ghosts, yet the existence of ghosts falls short of being a requirement: the characters could be delusional. I can read the text as uncanny, understanding the ghosts to be merely appearances and refusing to adjust my secular sense of reality that excludes supernatural beings. On the other hand, my reading may find that the secular sense of reality is inadequate: the text becomes *marvelous* as I redefine reality with the new understanding opened by the text.

The experience of the fantastic—in which an event or object resists an ordinary understanding, demanding clarification and provoking investigation— exceeds narratives in its importance. The situation of indecision into which certain narratives thrust readers (and/or protagonists) is more fundamental than Todorov's emphasis on natural and supernatural events. The *situation* requires an ambiguous phenomenon that I can explain in one of two competing paradigms, and it lasts as long as my uncertainty about whether or not the phenomenon demands that I change my conception of the world. If I can reconcile the phenomenon to previously held notions, then it was a merely uncanny phenomenon (following Todorov's use of the term). If the challenge to what I had previously accepted cannot be met, then the phenomenon invites me to reconceptualize the world.

An example of this in a domain outside of literature is the discovery of quantum particles (which functioned as a new kind of thing). These particles demanded hesitation, as nobody knew whether Newtonian physics could explain them or they required a new paradigm to explain their operations. In this historical situation, the new phenomenon required the creation of a new model of understanding, moving science into a domain analogous to what Todorov described as "the marvelous."

Situations that push me between two competing explanatory paradigms demand the language of faith. I encounter an unsettling event or object that, like Brown's Black Mass, I cannot easily assimilate. I am gripped, troubled, dismayed. I hesitate, uncertain as to whether or not my senses are deceived, unable to know whether they are attempting to reveal a truth requiring unprecedented levels of openness. Uncomfortable, I rub my eyes and admit I was mistaken. Comforted, I continue with my day. Alternately, I can summon others as witnesses, verifying what has been found, and we all can expand the borders of possibility.

The phenomenon itself allows for an experience of knowledge: discomfort with the objective uncertainty of the phenomenon compels me to decide whether it conforms to old laws or requires new ones. In other words, the revelation of the phenomenon causes me to assent to a proposition regarding the truth of the experience of its existence: within the domain controlled by this phenomenon, I can either affirm or negate it. Deciding to accept my previous notions (and believe that the senses were mistaken) parallels the decision to reject my previous notions and redefine reality: both allow me to understand the experience with the phenomenon using the language of knowledge. Thus, after reflection, I can say, "It is true that I saw something new" (rendering the subjective conviction as objectively certain) or "It is not true that I saw something new" (where I am subjectively convinced that the experience was objectively disproven).

The language of belief best characterizes the time of hesitation—Hawthorne's *tarrying*—between the initial moment, when I assent to uncertainty, and the final moment, when I render an objectively certain decision. The initial hesitation requires me to skip past the self-relational level (where I put myself in relation to an object) and instead ask, "Am I really seeing this?" After reflecting on the experience, I maintain this uncertainty in a statement of faith: "I believe that I saw this" or "I doubt that this is what I saw." On the reflexive level, I continue to hesitate, subjectively certain of the uncertainty of subjective experience: "I believe that I think I saw this." Each subsequent reflection sublates the element of doubt taken from the initial skepticism present in the initial question.

Understanding how faith relates to the fantastic conflicts with Todorov, in part because it applies beyond narratives. Todorov explains the relation of faith to his schema by replicating traditional structures that see faith and doubt as mutually exclusive. He writes, "Either total faith or total incredulity would lead us beyond the fantastic: it is hesitation which sustains its life" (31), where "faith" places me in the realm of the marvelous and "incredulity" moves me into the realm of the uncanny. In the realm of human experience, it seems more accurate to define the true place of faith as the realm of the fantastic itself, in the space and time of hesitation. This interprets shifts from the fantastic to either the marvelous or the uncanny as an exactly parallel act toward knowledge (away from faith), moving either toward traditional certainties (the old paradigm) or toward new knowledge able to account for foreign phenomena (a new paradigm). Because the uncanny and the marvelous are equal possibilities within the domain of the fantastic, and because the fantastic perpetuates possibilities, only those able to maintain positions of openness demanded by the fantastic have a Kierkegaardian faith that *anything* is possible.

The ambiguous phenomenon of the fantastic resembles Kant's negative faith. The Kantian formulation (the inability to disprove the possibility of an object of faith) focused on the existence of an object (i.e., the inability to disprove that God exists). The situation of the fantastic expands the need for negative faith. I can bracket questions concerning the *existence* of the phenomenon, for its existence is given to consciousness. It is more important to maintain my inability to disprove one of multiple (at least two) possibilities for *understanding* of the phenomenon. Because these possibilities are mutually exclusive (I cannot understand the anomaly in terms of two opposing paradigms in the same way at the same time), I cannot simultaneously *know* both. Instead, I neither affirm nor deny the ability of either paradigm to explain the phenomenon: I assent, then hesitate.

The process of hesitation and suspicion exists on a moment-by-moment basis. When I am subjectively convinced of a proposition's objective certainty, I hold it as fact. It can become an experience or an object that I possess in certainty. Because the lived experience of hesitation resists the tendencies toward classification and possession, faith is purely experiential: I cannot *have* faith but can only *experience* it. The experience of faith in this way exercises the human possibility for having nothing, which, in turn, makes everything possible.

Intending a reflexive faith by adhering to the principle that I will remain subjectively convinced of the uncertainty of subjective certainty rewrites all experience as moments when I undergo an absolute uncertainty. All subjective experience, every object I encounter, each moment of revelation, becomes like the ambiguous phenomenon encountered in the fantastic. Remaining convinced of the uncertainty of objective certainty, a person with a skeptical faith understands that even seemingly mundane or trivial things may contain hidden value. A discarded cup becomes as difficult to classify as a ghost and demands the same kind of hesitation. So long as I remain willing to undergo and not have my experiences, I can experience faith instead of having knowledge. This continual experience keeps me in faith, holding trusting and understanding in tension, and thereby avoids knowing. Convinced only about the uncertainty of subjective conviction, *nothing* (and only nothing) can be held or taken for granted.

Reflexive faith and the fantastic both engender an uncertainty in which I can neither affirm nor negate a proposition to which I have assented concerning objects or events responsible for a revelation. A skeptic can neither "say yes" to including the proposition in a preexisting paradigm of thought nor "say no," that it cannot be so included. The paradoxical stance of saying "yes and no," affirming some aspects while negating others, also violates a skeptical orientation. All three decisions equally move me away from the fantastic, making certain the "subjective experience" about which a reflexive faith remains convinced only of its uncertainty. Reflexive faith, like the pure fantastic, never makes certain that to which it relates.

Don Cupitt's model of antirealist faith in *Is Nothing Sacred?* provides a helpful point of contrast with this definition of faith. According to Cupitt, realists find that religious language describes a world beyond our own, while nonrealists define reality as a shifting scheme of fluctuating interpretations. Claiming that everyone today is a nonrealist (in a move anticipating Taylor's claims in *A Secular Age*), Cupitt refuses to make his claims absolute, positing them as interpretations of how things seem.[13] The implications for religion are straightforward, as Cupitt argues: "For the realist, what makes the Truth obviously true is its preservation unchanged; for the nonrealist, what keeps truth true is the vividness with which it is re-imagined and re-expressed" (52). Cupitt identifies as a nonrealist "a person who does not accept the old two-worlds doctrine, and therefore does not need dogmatic belief" who believes "there is only one world, the world that we have built up around ourselves, the world produced by our language" (54).

Problematically, despite Cupitt's emphasis that he provides only a new interpretation, the one-world doctrine seems just as dogmatic as a two-world doctrine. Understanding antirealism as another interpretation and not a doctrine in a consistent fashion requires an attitude of belief: one must *hesitate* before accepting the validity of it as an interpretation. Faith should interpret both realism and antirealism as possibilities, each of which might be true. The two persist in equipollent tension, disrupting a single explanation for my experiences. Adhering to the principle of hesitation, I tarry skeptically for the ultimate unveilation of *a* truth that removes all tension and all doubt. The goal of an ultimate unveilation separates my faith from the adoption of the deconstructionist sense of *différance* that it otherwise resembles.

The fantastic provides an understanding of reflexive faith on two levels. First, it reveals that hesitation and the withholding of assent and denial are ontological possibilities that manifest as ontic instantiations when I read a certain type of literature. The experience of reflexive faith, when I am subjectively convinced of the uncertainty of subjective experience, is the ontological foundation for the experience of the fantastic: humans are beings able to hesitate and withhold judgment. This capability, however, runs contrary to human nature: even though we can tarry, we do not prefer it. Although reason primarily forms this approach to faith, it still requires some amount of passion (to affirm it in each moment in the present) and volition (to ensure that one continues to will this faith into the future).[14]

Finally, it seems important to investigate the temporal nature of the hesitation described above, insofar as time—especially duration—is important to both reflexive faith and the fantastic. To survive, both must be endured. Todorov warns that the fantastic is fleeting, existing only while I hesitate. This hesitation, unsettling and uncomfortable, is difficult to desire to maintain: instead of hovering above options, undecided, it seems more *natural* to settle on one option. In the realm of literature, the consequences of such settling are not dire; however, the possibility of experiencing a reflexive faith requires a method for perpetuating this hesitation. The way to prolong this hesitation is through an act of consciousness—maintaining a type of self-consciousness during which I keep watch over how I am self-conscious, ensuring that an object characterized by uncertainty to which I have assented is neither affirmed nor negated.

Neither defining ambiguous phenomena nor actualizing possible understandings of events is an irrational activity. Knowledge is useful, and the maintenance of openness is uncomfortable. Rather than refusing knowledge, the hesitation produced by the fantastic arises in the humble realization that I do not yet possess enough information to make a decision, that I require more information. Faith looks to possibilities excluded by knowledge and holds that the possibility of possibilities is a sufficient reason to hesitate between a "yes" and a "no" or even a "yes and no." This is a transient attitude: faith desires to extend the experience of hesitation indefinitely. If things provide the ground for faith to concretize itself eventually, then hesitation is the dynamic that pushes faith into the future. This is accomplished through a consciousness characterized by *vigilance* as it keeps watch over itself.

Hesitation, understood through the mediation of the fantastic, thus fulfills the second notion of faith understood through Hawthorne, that of tarrying. Although the initial relationship between faith and tarrying presented by Hawthorne seems trivial or accidental—a plot device intended to add tension to Young Goodman Brown's desire to leave—it can be seen as a crucial ingredient to a reflexive mode of faith, which tarries between two conflicting explanations for an object or event—one that conforms to the familiar world, and one that betokens the existence of an as-yet unknown world. Tarrying prolongs the time of uncertainty that begins after I assent to a possible truth. Subjectively, tarrying would not only have allowed Young Goodman Brown to avoid the experience in the forest but would also have allowed him—in faith—to not simply accept the domination of evil over the world.

In addition to expanding the horizontal dynamic of faith by prolonging the time in prebelief, hesitation also exerts a force on the vertical axis. Vertically, faith moves us toward unification, the sublation of the finite into the infinite. Given this dynamic thrust toward integration, the tarrying enabled by defining faith as the subjective conviction concerning the uncertainty of subjective conviction allows individuals to unite with two truths held in tension with each other at a point of origin; this is the essence of truth in the Heideggerean sense. The implication of tarrying allows one interested in undergoing a skeptical faith to move from understanding faith as rooted in the negation of the understanding (which occurs at every moment that one hesitates) to a theological vision of faith. In concrete terms, I am always able to hesitate before knowing the world through understanding or trusting, choosing between a natural and a supernatural option. The experience of tarrying in light of these situations thus becomes the comportment through which one achieves a unity with the truth that springs from a proposition based on a revelation from things in the world. The human relates finitely with this infinite essence of truth, which contains its own dynamic direction within itself. The relationship is necessarily one of faith, as the finite relation with the infinite cannot be one of knowledge.

This definition of faith, which entails the task of hesitating or tarrying, enables humans to manifest the capacity for doing nothing in an active sense. Thus, rather than resigning myself to the fact that "human beings are capable of nothing" in despair, this definition of faith approaches nothing as a type of good, an important human quality. Remaining subjectively convinced about the uncertainty of subjective conviction continually reminds me of my finitude, emphasizing the limitations of sensory intuition and the fallibility of interpretation. Tarrying is the task associated with this mode of remaining, one that continually reaffirms that human beings are capable of nothing and one that enables humans to understand this affirmation as meaningful.

The task of skepticism, and therefore also of a skeptical faith, requires a complex effort from the one who intentionally accepts the principle that affirms the value of not-knowing. In addition to observing the world with a critical lens, withdrawing from appearances, I must keep watch over my habits of perception to ensure I have maintained a skeptical orientation, an activity made possible through vigilance.

Vigilance and Consciousness

Vigilance is a specific mode of seeing. To search vigilantly requires more than merely looking; it requires attending to the way that I look at things, seeing (in consciousness) how I am seeing. Scharlemann's distinctions between experiences of truth in different levels of consciousness show why skepticism requires vigilance. The experience of the first level, the presentation of an object to consciousness, precedes my awareness of seeing. Experiencing my being aware of the object, relating my subjectivity to the object, lets me state: I see a bus. Reflecting on this experience takes the experience of the second level as the object of consciousness and relates the self to this experience. Reflexive consciousness attends to the experience of reflection.

We commonly fall from a reflexive mode of faith, failing to maintain the subjective conviction concerning the uncertainty of subjective conviction, embracing knowledge, and clinging to subjective experience as certain. I pass from faith into knowledge, seeing past and present as fixed and objectively certain. This is to choose to *have* instead of *undergo*. Because consciousness defaults into seeing its experiences as certain, skeptics must maintain vigilance over their understandings of past experiences, after they are filtered through consciousness, to ensure that appearances were not, in fact, taken as certain. Vigilance, watching how I watch, monitors how I was aware. Vigilant skeptics avoid objective certainty that they were vigilantly skeptical, as this would violate the principle of skepticism.

A necessary component of the work of skepticism, vigilance plays a critical role in driving the dynamic of a skeptical faith. The dynamic of faith pushes the finite to integrate with the infinite, healing feelings of brokenness. A skeptical faith vigilantly searches for more possibilities capable of fueling equipollent arguments. My task is a heightened awareness, a drive toward possibilities that I maintain as possibilities and a faith that yet another overlooked possibility awaits discovery. Most important, a skeptical faith requires a vigilant mode of consciousness to extend the duration of hesitation: subjective experience remains uncertain only so long as I remain open to the possibility of an additional possibility. Vigilance allows the skeptic to live within this openness.

Vigilance is sympathetic to the stance of faith discussed at the beginning of this chapter: like faith, vigilance refuses what is given to consciousness and prompts interrogations at the self-relational level: Am I certain I see a bus? At the level of reflection, one who has chosen vigilance can only claim, "I believe I saw a bus." Consciousness is limited, attending to one thing at a time. Because of this, a reflective or reflexive experience requires speaking of the self-relational experience in the past tense. I can only reflect on experiences that have already passed and cannot reflect on what I experience in the present. Vigilance provokes reflection, or a reflexive state of consciousness. Thus, in asking, "Was I being vigilant yesterday?" I reflect on how I reflected on my relationship with the bus. I may answer "no," admitting that, at the time, my reflection on the bus was characterized by a less-than-vigilant sight. I might answer "yes," understanding that while reflecting on the relationship with the bus, I was simultaneously attempting to understand whether I critically understood how I understood my experience with the bus. Of course, this "yes" would prompt further questions about whether or not I was properly vigilant relative to the question of my own vigilance.

Because vigilance involves a reflexive experience and the question of vigilance can only be answered about the past, vigilance, as a mode of being in the present, can neither confirm nor deny the truth of any experience. Vigilance is a way of seeing that takes how I saw as its object, meaning that the answer to the self-reflexive question "Am I vigilant?" can only be answered—in the now—with neither a yes nor a no. I can render a verdict on my vigilance, reflecting on my past reflection, only after time—perhaps only a moment—has passed. Even then, remaining vigilant, I cannot *know* that this experience of the certainty of vigilance is itself altogether certain. Vigilance continually demands that I test the certainty of the test of the certainty of the test of subjective conviction: only in so doing can I claim to remain subjectively convinced of the uncertainty of subjective conviction.

Consciousness is always consciousness *of* something. Consciousness can take as its object either a thing or event outside of itself (which manifests as an experience of the literal level of consciousness), or it can take itself as its object (which results in either the self-relational, reflective, or reflexive level of consciousness). Vigilance is a willed project that has the goal of maintaining openness to possibility. The stance of skeptical openness relative to further possibilities is a matter of self-consciousness, and vigilance, in addition to being a function of will, is also a form of self-consciousness that takes consciousness as its object. Instead of merely becoming conscious of what consciousness is conscious of, vigilance makes an inquiry of the *mode* of consciousness, seeking to be conscious of *the way in which* consciousness was conscious of itself. The project of vigilance is sufficient to grant it the status of being a form of self-consciousness and not mere self-consciousness.

As Friedrich Schleiermacher argued, forms of self-consciousness have specific subject matters that filter what consciousness attends to when it takes an object. This allowed him to identify aesthetic, social, and religious forms of self-consciousness.[15] As forms of self-consciousness, they maintain their form without regard to the specific content attained by the intentional or direct level of consciousness. Thus, when in a mode of *religious* consciousness, I understand the religious implications of an aesthetic object without seeing its artistry. Alternately, if I will myself to be in the mode of aesthetic consciousness, I appreciate the artistry of a religious artifact without attending to—or even noticing—its religious importance.

Lacking specific subject matter, vigilance differs from the other forms of self-consciousness, remaining open to possibilities that they exclude or assume in becoming knowledge. The content of vigilance thus depends on whatever another form of consciousness has repressed. Vigilance resists any certain (whether through affirmation or through negation) relationship with predetermined content. The positive work of vigilance is its bringing to self-consciousness how other forms of self-consciousness function. For example, skeptics use vigilance to reveal how the truth of the religious self-consciousness's experiences with (for example) an aesthetic object is achieved only at the *expense* of vigilance (which also would have attended to what was concealed). While other forms of self-consciousness result in knowledge, the vigilant form of self-consciousness alone preserves the possibility of faith.

The dynamic of faith sustains believers through the time between events of revelation and unveilation. From the perspective of the "absolute future" or the "eternal," the revelation is given completely, re-presented in all things and at all times: from this perspective, there is no need for faith, and there is no dynamic movement. From the human perspective, driven into relative futures and ontologically prevented from attending to the absolute future directly, the revelation cannot be *understood* but only *trusted*. Vigilance is required as part of the dynamic of faith that connects the absolute and the relative future: it simultaneously maintains an indirect orientation toward the absolute future that generates the revelation and also keeps watch over things to preserve their openness to the oncoming truth. In vigilance, one expects the full unveilation to arrive in the next moment of relative time—and one's expectation is always victorious, as all things re-present and gather this truth (from the eternal) into each moment of relative time. Using Christian metaphors, one could say that the Kingdom of God is imminent as well as immanent, at hand—temporally as well as physically—for those who have eyes to see.

Because, in relative time, we allow the present world to conceal the coming world and permit finite things to hide the absolute, vigilance comes alongside the work of tarrying. While tarrying expresses human finitude and limitation, manifesting the nothing of which humans are capable, vigilance searches for the impossible possibility that prevents possibilities from eroding into certainties. The vigilant regard for possibilities attends to the existential dynamic of faith, repeating the movement from the human capacity for nothing to the fact that with God, all things are possible. In vigilance, one is able to view *with God*, providentially. After all, Young Goodman Brown lost God only after losing sight of possibility as possibility.

Theological Implications of Vigilant Faith

In his "Postmodernity and Faith," Alan Olson claims that thinking more productively about consciousness "is, *a fortiori,* to think more productively about the process of faith."[16] A truly skeptical faith, a reflexive faith that uses a vigilant form of consciousness responsible both for looking at the possibility of other possible ways of understanding an experience and for attending to the way in which consciousness is conscious of itself and its experiences in order to maintain a subjective certainty in the uncertainty of subjective experience, adds three important elements to an understanding of the process of faith. First, a skeptical faith resists idolatry, the greatest threat to a nonvigilant faith. Second, a skeptical faith remains open to the possibility of *anonymous hierophanies*, sites where God potentially manifests in the mundane. Third, and possibly most important, a skeptical faith enables a relationship with a nonobjectifiable source or depth of faith, accounting for the potential of God as process.

A skeptical faith requires vigilance, and a vigilant faith requires skepticism. Before determining that a skeptical faith is a form of faith that has theological significance (the weak version of my argument) or that the domain of prebelief is the most pure or essential time of faith (the strong version), it is necessary to show that a skeptical faith accounts for the dynamic of faith opened by other domains of faith. I therefore conclude by testing the capacity for a skeptical faith to allow a nonsymbolically mediated way of accessing the divine.

LIKE TILLICH, Scharlemann argues that symbols have a reflexive structure in line with Heidegger's theory of truth, insofar as they are simultaneously true and not true. A symbol is simultaneously what it is and what it is not—the way that a flag is both what it is (cloth) and what it is not (the country it symbolizes). Thus, "the 'infallible truth' is the truth that no one possesses the truth, and this is not imposed on faith but is in the symbol of faith."[17] Again following Tillich, Scharlemann argues that the Cross is a second-order symbol whose structure symbolizes the relativity of all symbols. He writes, "The symbol of the cross is to other symbols of truth what reflexivity is to reflection. Reflexivity can see that reflection is capable of seeing both the true and the false (it can see the duality of reflection); the symbol of the cross symbolizes the depth that comprises both the true and the false" (179).[18] The Cross manifests the depth because the truth to which it points is both true and false at the level of reflection and symbolizes this truth of all symbols.

Tillich's own writings on the nature of symbols and the Cross, one of the best articulations of the relation of faith and symbols, point to the potential problem with giving symbolic objects the responsibility of the truth of faith. As Tillich writes,

> In the same way, Biblical research in Protestantism has shown the many levels of Biblical literature and the impossibility of considering the Bible as containing the infallible truth of faith. The same criterion is valid with respect to the whole history of religion and culture. The criterion contains a Yes—it does not reject any truth of faith in whatever form it may appear in the history of faith— and it contains a No—it does not accept any truth of faith as ultimate except the one that no man possesses it. The *fact that this criterion is identical with the Protestant principle and has become reality in the Cross of Christ constitutes the superiority of Protestant Christianity.*[19]

Although Tillich's terms are tantalizingly general, they nonetheless carry the particularity of the context. Modern readers confronted with a pluralistic religious landscape may desire for Tillich's "yes" to apply to any or all religions, but this desire is thwarted by Tillich's method of grounding the universal within a concrete particular, yielding a conclusion that appears as the return of Christian triumphalism (the ability for Protestantism to trump the truth of all other religions). Although the criterion of yes and no approaches the status of reflexivity, Tillich's conclusion about the truth of this criterion—put into particularistic Protestant terms—is merely true on the level of reflection. After all, the functionality of the Cross as a meaningful reflexive experience is limited to a relatively small community: those who are able to see the Cross as a symbol of an ultimate concern who are *also* able to see the truth of the symbol and *also* able to see the symbol as being false and *also* adhere to a transcendental and not immanent religious worldview.

Tillich's statement also reveals the problem with paradoxically affirming "yes" and "no" instead of skeptically withholding affirmation and negation (neither saying yes nor saying no). The paradoxical stance reveals the universal in the particular—yet, as shown in Tillich's reduction of a universal criterion to something that "became reality in the Cross of Christ," it also fails to tarry and plunges into certainty. The fact that God "became real" in this symbol does not exclude the possibility that other writers could see the principle as "becoming real" in their own symbols.[20] That Tillich saw this as constituting the "superiority of Protestant Christianity" does not exclude Muslims from seeing the Koran as constituting the superiority of Islam, yet it is more clear and accurate to resist saying "yes" and "no" in a response to a question of ultimacy. Hesitating before saying "no" allows me to consider the possibility that a given symbol of faith *does* manifest the ultimate. Hesitating before saying "yes" rejects exclusivity, remembering that all concrete symbols bear, in their concretion, the possibility of idolatry.

When we step back from language and are mindful of the value of grounding a definition of faith in things (a perspective I will consider in the next chapter), definitions of faith that depend on symbols have major problems. First, symbols have no power over how they are used. At best, a symbol that points away from itself (as Scharlemann claims of the Cross) merely makes possible the truth of faith: symbols risk becoming idolatrous because they depend on the "good faith" of the believer. One can see the Cross as pointing to what is true and *not* to a depth that combines truth and falsehood; too many approach every symbol saying yes, forgetting to say no.

Second, the truth of a symbol partially depends on one's subjective experience of that symbol. This is the danger of idolatry, of the desire to say yes to something that, in one's experience, represents the ultimate. That relating improperly to *true* symbols is idolatrous reinforces the danger of depending on external symbols for the truth of faith. The epidemic of violent fundamentalist groups of all persuasions testifies to this danger.

Finally, depending on subjective conviction also renders a symbolic faith that testifies to the certainty of ultimacy, itself unable to be *known* certainly. Those who mediate their relationship with the divine through symbols can state "I have faith in _____," revealing the tendency for what starts as faith to become knowledge. Beliefs that become possessions cease to mediate a true experience of faith. In knowledge, one no longer is *close* or *near* to a hierophantic object: it loses its proximity when held only in a consciousness that overwhelms it. Symbols are always limited to a context or a community able to understand them as symbols. No symbol is truly universal, especially in a culture shattered by brokenness.

The first advantage of a skeptical faith is as a guarantee against idolatry. Skeptical faith is a reflexive structure in a skeptical consciousness, which, when utilized consciously, provides the subjective counterpart to the reflexive objectivity of symbols. Vigilance, as a mode of being, is open to everyone in a way that symbols and objects are not. A skeptical faith resists the comforting temptation of knowledge and embraces the insecurity of doubt. Additionally, a skeptical faith allows for a proper relationship between the self and a concrete thing that potentially reveals the divine. For Tillich, faith's truth requires it to adequately express an ultimate concern.[21] In vigilance, one expresses concern for the ultimacy of one's faith. Vigilance is a heightened concern about one's own being concerned, a desire to know the truth of one's concern. Only if I am vigilant can I inquire skeptically about the truth of my concern or the truth of the ultimacy of my faith. Vigilance is therefore the necessary means for knowing whether my faith adequately expresses an ultimate concern.

The second criterion Tillich offers for the truth of a symbol of faith is that it expresses an ultimate that is truly ultimate—that the faith is not idolatrous.[22] Instead of placing responsibility for ultimacy on the symbol, my concern about the truth of the ultimacy of the belief keeps me responsible. Being vigilant prevents me from having faith in a symbol that fails to express the ultimate: thus, a skeptical vigilance is the necessary precondition even for those who wholeheartedly subscribe to Tillich's definition of faith. Whatever the symbol, a vigilant faith is the only sufficient guarantee of its ultimacy. Refusing to accept or reject a symbol by constantly testing both symbols and my vigilant relationship to them, I understand the inadequacy of the mediating thing or word. In this way, minimally, a skeptical faith supplements all of my interactions with symbols or things. When it merges with the form of religious self-consciousness, vigilant self-consciousness resists the comfort of accepting the subjective experience of ultimacy. This keeps me from giving myself to an idol—a symbol that is less than ultimate yet nonetheless demands everything. Put in terms of consciousness, vigilance maintains the state of faith as a *dynamic tension* instead of allowing it to reach stasis in knowledge: the point at which faith calcifies or is "had," is the point where one has erected an idol.

The second advantage vigilant faith offers the practice of religion involves its openness to *anonymous hierophanies*. When the form of vigilant self-consciousness merges with the form of religious self-consciousness, it opens the awareness of the self to multiple possible hierophantic sites that unaided religious self-consciousness, desiring certainty and unaware of the uncertainty of subjective conviction, would ignore. These possible hierophantic sites exist in art (sculpture, literature, painting, film, music), nature (mountains, trees, rivers, oceans, heavenly bodies), civilization (buildings and cities), and refuse (used coffee cups, plastic bags). In this way, vigilant faith attends to all possible manifestations or revelations of a "God," even as it goes about in the world of the everyday. These new modes of encountering "God," of course, remain tempered by the first function of a skeptical faith: I test my subjective experiences of revelation, appreciating them as possibilities but hesitating before saying "yes" or "no" to a proposition that this thing mediates the divine.

Third, vigilant faith transcends the requirement that symbols mediate the divine. Vigilance is a self-conscious effort to resist knowledge, supplementing a faith grounded in a concrete thing. By refusing to put myself in a knowledge-based relationship to a given concrete manifestation of God, by vigilantly maintaining a distance from such knowledge-tainted manifestations, by remaining on the path of the fantastic, neither refusing nor accepting concrete manifestations of the holy in the fantastic, I stay open to the possibility of the positive relationship with the absolute that cannot be symbolically mediated—Tillich's God above the God of theism. This is neither a faith in nothing nor a faith in absence. Instead, it is a way, in faith, of vigilantly keeping myself in a skeptical relation to what I, in faith, hope to see in spite of the impossibility of such a relationship. The radical openness of a vigilant faith, manifest in suspending judgment and neither saying yes nor no, allows unique access to a nonsymbolically mediated relationship with that than which none greater can be conceived.

The tension between the infinite truth and its confinement in finitude creates a dynamic of faith that attempts to unify the infinite with, or in, the finite. The *experience* of the dynamic of faith moves from an experienced awareness of finitude (which, at its limits, confronts humans as the potentially terrifying prospect that nothing is possible) to a contrary awareness of infinitude (the impossible surplus of possibilities offered through a god for whom everything is possible, or "humanly" by vigilantly attending to the possibility of other possibilities).

Throughout the accounts of the dynamics of faith—from Augustine's struggle between Law and Spirit to Kierkegaard's movement from despair to faith—the emphasis has been on the relationship of *consciousness* to the situation. In relation to the dynamics of faith, consciousness is responsible for faith's preservation. Therefore, in addition to the faith one possesses relative to the truth revealed in the interaction with a hierophany (which constitutes the depth or verticality of a faith, formed by passion on a moment-by-moment basis), the dynamic of faith also makes necessary and possible a horizontal understanding of faith capable of endurance. This sense of faith, formed by reason, is the *subjective conviction in the uncertainty of subjective conviction* and depends on vigilance to ensure that I remain in the state of faith instead of sliding into knowledge. Although it may be grounded in a thing that supplies its depth, the *object* of this type of faith is faith itself: it is a supportive element that keeps the dynamic of faith alive. The faith in the domain of prebelief differs from nihilism as it is predicated on hesitation, not rejection: tarrying is required only for as long as it takes the truth to be unveiled. The power of faith enables me to always believe that my expectation that the unveilation has been fully manifest in the moment has been realized; the cost of this belief is both a suspicion that it has not, in fact, been realized and that the next moment in time needs to be attended to as well.

With this, it is possible to return to Hawthorne's four criteria for faith. I have shown how a skeptical faith prevents despair from grasping believers, insofar as the believer remains open to further possibilities and maintains a relationship with the nonsymbolically mediated absolute. Second, a vigilant faith is the necessary precondition for the possibility of tarrying in faith—without it, the human drive toward certainty would remain difficult to resist. Third, a skeptical faith keeps me vigilant to the possibilities of interacting with others: in Christian terms, it allows me to see in the least of these the God that I await. Finally, a skeptical faith vigilantly protects against a sudden, violent, re-creation of the world, as it tempers the truth of a revelation with the possibility that something may have thereby been concealed.

4 Anonymous Hierophanies and the Mundane Possibilities of God

> But if you really learn how to pay attention, then you will know there are other options. It will actually be within your power to experience a crowded, hot, slow, consumer-hell type situation as not only meaningful, but sacred, on fire with the same force that made the stars: love, fellowship, the mystical oneness of all things deep down.
>
> —DAVID FOSTER WALLACE, 2005 commencement address at Kenyon College

The Secularization of the Sacred

When we listen, the world sometimes whispers secrets that we cannot understand. Things reveal themselves with unrelenting meaningfulness in ways that violate the language-based and controlling dictates of reason. Reason cannot contemplate the fleeting pleasures and riches of the sensory world. The comfort provided by feeling a hard ground beneath one's feet or a soft pillow behind one's head are not rationally accountable. Our intuitions regarding the reverence appropriate to particular sites, the awe inspired by the sight of a lonely tree's profound struggle to touch the sun or a weed's tenacity in making a home between slabs of concrete are not false simply because they do not make sense.

Individuals in other times perhaps felt more comfortable associating the feeling of being gripped by a sacred revelation of a nonlinguistic truth. Gods could manifest in objects or locations that literalized and concretized the feeling of trust inspired when summoned to behold the flash of the infinite within the finite. German romantics knew this truth about nature, as did the American transcendentalists: their art and writings testify to a desire to reencounter and preserve the unintended magic of a clear and starry night or clouds gathering on a shoreline. For this reason, perhaps, reading Mircea Eliade's work on "primitive" religion—the sacred depth of bodies of water and stone, of plants and planets—evokes a chord of nostalgia that echoes beyond our own personal history. We mourn when realizing that we cannot experience nature as they did: often, the call of wild places is answered by a national park, where guides invoke a staged feeling of wonder and everyone leaves with a souvenir. Our regimented lives are scheduled and planned around avoiding the troubling disruption that other truths might cause. As secularisms wash away the magic of life, we forget how to treat such moments. Our discomfort grows as we re-create the world in strip malls and suburbs, where every house and city becomes a tasteful echo of hollow anonymity.

Optimistically, I would like to argue that this impressionable dimension of our humanity persists but has only been numbed by an increasingly urban life promoted, regulated, and enframed by technological efficiency. Reducing what is good to what is knowable (quantifiable, determinable, controllable), finding value in terms of money and the things that money provides, we remain blind to other possibilities that vie silently for our attention. This type of calculative thinking, a subset of the understanding that does not respectfully step aside when it senses paradox, cannot account for the value of the fragile and fleeting mysteries that manifest when we encounter what once was called the sacred. Although it may be true that gods have died and have no place in the modern world, it is also true that we fail to seek out the traces of divine presence that might manifest even in unlikely places.

Put otherwise, reducing faith to a variety of diseased knowledge has left us unequipped to fully appreciate wild beauties. Bereft of a true sense of faith, moments that speak to the space between trusting and understanding unsettle us. Too commonly, we attempt to obliterate all such moments and reminders, building cities that glorify anonymity and repetition, stilling uncontrolled rumors of awe. The alternative solution is to attend to a definition of faith that invites the sacred in the secular world without requiring the blasphemy of defining it as God. The sense of faith formed by passion lasts for an extended moment of appreciation. Such moments, however, also need to be accounted for without violating the skepticism and the domain of prebelief.

Chapter 3 articulated the importance of vigilance to a skeptical faith, for the need to watch carefully and intuit natural and supernatural possibilities for everything encountered in the world. Formed by the understanding and powered by the will, this emphasis resulted in a dynamic faith that was empty, hovering over the possibility of being concretized through a hesitation that stops short of refusal. In discussing the object of faith, the goal of this chapter is to outline how a skeptical faith keeps to its telos object (hesitation) by testing itself against thingly objects (the things in the world that beckon as sites of revelation, signs of God's visitation). Because thing-objects communicate the revelation, the thingly object of faith co-creates a revelation of truth that allows me to enter into a state of faith relative to it; claiming I "believe in" this object is inaccurate. The term "object" contains an internal tension conducive to a skeptical faith, such that one can check the telos of faith against its thingly carrier and the thing of faith relative to the telos.

In order to examine the object of a skeptical faith, I begin with an overview of a film that forces viewers to contemplate a sign of atheist theology. This leads to an overview of theological speculations concerning how God might interact with our surrounding world in ways that do not require transcendence. I move from God to things, exploring the necessary preconditions for how objects speak to us. Attending to this leads to a theological interpretation of the testimony of things, and then to a more robust appreciation for the everyday, mundane things with which we surround ourselves. I conclude by testing the possibility that the world—despite its maddening monotony—might still disclose the truth of God against standard theological tests for an object of faith.

Finding the Entire Life behind Things

American Beauty opened in theaters on October 1, 1999, and generated a worldwide box office gross of over $350 million (making it one of the top 250 domestic and top 150 worldwide films ever). Depicting brokenness in the life of a man who finds his middle-class suburban role as husband, employee, and father to be meaningless, the film won five Academy Awards, including those for best picture, best actor, and best director, indicating that this satiric revelation of emptiness at the century's end was both important and well done. The film concludes with, in the words of the script, the vision of an "empty white PLASTIC BAG being blown about. The wind carries it in a circle around us, sometimes whipping it about violently, or, without warning, sending it soaring skyward, then letting it float gracefully down to the ground." This image is initially introduced by a character who describes it as the "most beautiful thing [he] ever filmed." As the image replays at the movie's end, the deceased protagonist is heard to say, "It's hard to be mad when there's so much beauty in the world." Although incorporating a piece of discarded refuse is a potentially vexing aesthetic problem, its theological import is more pressing: the bag becomes an object of faith for Ricky Fitts, the individual who initially experiences, films, and describes it.

The first indication that this bag is a potential object of faith concerns how it offers a revelation to the one whom it displaces. While showing the movie to a friend, Ricky narrates the initial experience, explaining, "And this bag was just . . . dancing with me. Like a little kid begging me to play with it. For fifteen minutes. That's the day I realized that there was this entire life behind things, and this incredibly benevolent force that wanted me to know there was no reason to be afraid." Several truths are revealed in the dance of the bag: a total life located "behind things," a "benevolent force," and the comfort, protection, or consolation this benevolent force desired to offer. The difficulty with this revelation—to use aesthetic terms—comes in the conjunction of a traditional content and an unusual form. The content of the revelation is an almost Augustinian depiction of a consoling, protecting, transcendent deity. The form of the revelation (its origin in a bit of trash) and its rhetoric (which avoids any mention of God, Christ, or sin) make the seemingly straightforward intent of the revelation more difficult to understand. In other words, because it lacks an appeal to any traditional revelation of God (through any accepted symbolic manifestation), a traditional theological model would interpret the plastic bag as unimportant. The content of the revelation, the consoling fatherly protection of the "incredibly benevolent force," is too affirming and transcendent for most postmodern theological interpretations. Nonetheless, that a truth is revealed to Ricky provides a first sense that the bag invites faith.

The second way the plastic bag is a potential object of faith arises in Ricky's steadfast orientation toward the object and the truth it discloses. The initial import of the plastic bag is revealed in the fifteen minutes that he stood watching the bag and realizing what it offered. The repetition of his viewing, found in his comment that "video's a poor excuse, I know. But it helps me remember . . . I need to remember," shows that the revealed truth remains important to him after the event of disclosure. Part of his task of preservation—beyond his own ritual of reviewing and remembering—manifests as evangelism, sharing the good news of this truth to others. This element unfolds as he shows the video to his friend Janie. The experience of the bag, even as a poor reproduction of the event on video, is thus lived and relived. Ricky's description of the scene as he watches it reinforces the power of the original experience for him, even as he shares it with others. Although the repetition of viewing the tape, explaining it to others, and remembering the moment can be seen as ritualistic, it is a ritual particular to the initial experience Ricky has with the bag—not one that is universalizable. Thus, although the plastic bag is difficult to ground in a particular theological paradigm, the movie nonetheless offers it as a viable object of faith, and its importance in the movie—in the context of the movie's popular and critical acclaim—indicates that its potential was taken seriously.

The choice of a plastic bag as a potential object of faith challenges traditional theological and aesthetic ways of understanding how things convey meaning. While Ricky's decision to film the bag (and the director's decision to produce the film) is an aesthetic choice, the bag itself is not a meaningful artistic statement. It lacks the ironic value that has enabled artists since Duchamp to push the boundaries of what art can mean. Part of what makes Alan Ball's script and Sam Mendes's choice of a shot so powerful arises from Ricky's ability to pause and preserve a moment with an intentionally unremarkable object. Not only is the object an intentionally odd choice, but Ricky's interpretation of it is also unusually slanted enough to draw attention. Traditionally, objects worthy of theological contemplation (inducing notions of a benevolent force) have been limited to items rooted in a given mythology (icons or relics) or nature; if there could be an antithesis, a cast-off bag might be it.

And yet the movie works in such a way that Ricky's interpretation does not unsettle the viewer; instead, the image and music, combined with Ricky's description, invite the viewer to participate in being gathered by the bag as well. The importance of describing "God" generically emerges as the juxtaposition of the bag with a more specific invocation of a deity would undoubtedly jar and distract viewers. The choice to use a discarded plastic bag to carry tidings of a bland deity makes a profound statement about the theological possibilities opened in an urban environment. Overlooked refuse appropriately reveals the anonymous God that might persist in a secular world, a type of God open, perhaps, to a vigilant faith.

Before speculating on secularized objects of faith—the end goals, the concrete vessels, or the intended presences—more work is necessary.

Grounding a theological perspective able to explain the event of the plastic bag depicted in *American Beauty* first requires presenting a structural explanation of how objects are able to testify to truth at all. Heidegger's explication of how natural things, equipmental things, and art things convey meaning will suffice. After explaining how traditional theological interpretations of nature (as hierophany) or art (as symbol) fail to grasp what is presented in *American Beauty*, I combine the late Heidegger's amended explication of equipment with Thomas Altizer's theological perspective to provide a theological model capable of explaining how the plastic bag and other common types of things might reveal God. At its heart, this chapter offers a meaningful interpretation of objects suited for our secular age, objects capable of revealing nothing and concealing nothing.

Defining Objects of Faith

Postmodern models of faith, rooted in (or working against) a Heideggerean approach to truth, are splintered into two rival factions that share a faith that *trusting* theology adequately critiques the *understanding* offered by modernity. The Radical Orthodoxy approach finds that a return to the roots of theology is the only way to critique a nihilistic and secularizing logic that arises in modernity. Deconstructionists adhere to a neo-Kierkegaardian mind-set that retrieves *trusting* through the negation of the *understanding* necessitated by the dynamic of faith rooted in Heidegger's model of truth. The unsuitability of these formulations is especially unfortunate because the Heideggerean conception of "truth," formulated as an event of disclosure occurring within a dynamic of revealing and concealing, has the potential to serve as a consistent framework for faith and theological thinking. Inasmuch as faith comes with a suspension of knowledge on an existential level, and theology holds in tension the types of knowing resulting from both *trusting* and *understanding,* a theory of truth that arises in the event of conflict and an anthropology that roots human beings firmly and concretely in a finite world seems well suited for the work of theology and a definition of faith. Thus, in addition to offering a constructive notion of the work of faith, the failure of postmodern theologies to provide a model of faith relative to Heidegger's conception of truth highlights the need for a new model of faith.

The models of truth outlined in chapter 2 develop in increasing levels of abstraction. God served as the object of faith in the Platonic model of faith: revelations *about* God were issued *by* God to the human, and the goal of faith was uniting *with* God. The switch to the Kantian model provided an increased emphasis on the subjective element of faith as well as an increased affirmation of finite reality (no longer deemed secondary or illusory). While the object of faith was the God-Man, who served as a model for faith by having paradoxically merged the infinite and the finite in a self-negating manner, the way that this God-Man was an "object" differed from the way that God had served as an object before Kant. An example of a postmodern "object" of faith is the *khora,* which simultaneously eliminates the material dimension of object and emphasizes the inability to "have" faith through "possessing" its object, understanding faith as a process symbolized by, or as, *khora.*[1] The *khora* grounds language such as "religion without religion" or "God without God," which often appears in works of postmodern theology. Although the notion of God as process sounds like a regression back to the intangible, if faith ends up building on faith and serving as its own ground, then any God that would be an "object" of faith would become identical with—or at least analogous to—the process of faith itself.

In addition to connecting faith and consciousness, Alan Olson's "Postmodernity and Faith" suggests countering postmodern ideologies by understanding faith as a process. Taking the position that we need to stop grounding faith externally, Olson argues that "the quest for faith's proper reference . . . may be viewed as being the battleground of faith in all phases of modernity." Olson's option, which I expand upon, is to understand faith as "'faith in . . .' something which grounds consciousness and legitimates belief."[2] While I ultimately argue that faith serves as its own object in the domain of prebelief, I agree with Olson that we must incorporate the concrete world at the beginning of an analysis of the object of faith. Doing so instantly incorporates the element of finitude necessary to all definitions of faith. The objective, thingly quality imparts to faith the plentitude present that consciousness lacks. Paul Ricoeur's description of a symbolic sign analogously depicts the importance of the concrete: "contrary to perfectly transparent technical signs, which say only what they want to say in positing that which they signify, symbolic signs are opaque, because the first, literal, obvious meaning itself points analogically to a second meaning which is not given otherwise than in it. . . . This opacity constitutes the depth of the symbol, which, it will be said, is inexhaustible."[3] To use one of Ricoeur's examples, depicting guilt as a stain or burden is powerful because people are familiar with the physical task of scouring stains or the labor involved with carrying a weight. In terms of faith, revelatory events that push an individual into the state of faith enter consciousness primarily through an experience with a thing, as the bag in *American Beauty* reveals. Following Olson, we must understand the "object of faith" in such a way that it maintains the notion of faith as a process while simultaneously emphasizing the importance of material objects in mediating revelations.

This chapter provides a generalized, structural description of ways that all things can serve as the foundation for a truth to which faith can cling and also describes the particular value of *anonymous hierophanies* for truths meaningful to a culture assailed by brokenness. These, in traditional Christian language, allow humans to find the Kingdom of God at hand within the things in the world that surround us. My analysis of the relation of faith and consciousness requires an adequate explanation of the "object" of faith to articulate a foundation for the possibility of a passionate origin of faith that opens to a faith formed by passion and/or volition. This concrete depth of faith emerges for the vigilant skeptic, who remembers that what appears conceals as much as it reveals.

The Testimony of Things

Faith is a state into which one moves (or is moved) after having assented to a revealed proposition. Because humans are finite beings who mediate experiences through consciousness, we cannot gain propositions ex nihilo: they must be mediated through experiences with the concrete world. Even one's choice to undertake a skeptical faith, remaining subjectively convinced of the uncertainty of subjective conviction, is shaped by external factors. The importance of concrete reality is revealed in Jesus's parables, as Jesus describes events centering on concrete and mundane things as a way of opening humans to new truths. The basic possibility for hearkening to a parable and the potential for it to be meaningful is rooted in an ability to hearken to the testimony of things. This section explores Heidegger's distinctions about things to open the possibility for a new understanding of how things speak.

The starting point for identifying the foundation of *Dasein's* relation to things within Heidegger's writings is a statement from *Being and Time* discussing the relationship between thing, truth, and *Da-sein*. In this definition, Heidegger roots the subjective attitude toward truth unequivocally in the objective revelation: "One mode of certainty is *conviction*. In conviction, Da-sein lets the testimony of the thing itself that has been discovered (the true thing itself) be the sole determinant for its being toward that thing understandingly" (237). On one level, the sentence relates to the opening of *Being and Time*, where Heidegger provides his phenomenological definition of truth, which, as discussed above, is "to let [beings that are being talked *about*] be seen as something unconcealed (*alethes*); to *discover* them." He then adds, "In the Greek sense what is 'true' . . . is *aisthesis*, the simple sense perception of something," and that "perception is always true" (29). In this basic sense, each thing offers true testimony about itself—but only in the most limited sense, as when a plastic bag discloses that it was originally white in color. Additionally, because a vigilant skeptic cannot simply cling to an ontic awareness of outward appearance, a deeper sense of how things convey truth is necessary.

A clue appears in Heidegger's word choice for discussing conviction: using the term "testimony" to refer to the action of the thing is an odd choice, as testimony seems beyond the capacity for *things* to offer. Testimony, defined by the *Oxford English Dictionary* as "personal or documentary evidence or attestation in support of a fact or statement; hence, any form of evidence or proof," is the result of a three-part process: witnessing, bearing witness, and giving witness (or testifying). Generally, this is understood in a legal or religious sense; however, Heidegger's use of the term seems peculiar, as "things" might initially seem incapable of this—lacking organs of perception, things cannot "witness," lacking consciousness they cannot "bear witness," and lacking voice they cannot give witness. Bereft of speech and perception, it is difficult to comprehend how things reveal truth.

Understanding the testimony of things requires attending to how things relate to truth beyond their mere witness to material persistence. The key is Heidegger's disdain for a detached vision of objects, seen in how he favors a definition of truth as revelation or *aletheia* instead of a correspondence model. A true thing, suitable for *Dasein* to be toward understandingly, corresponds to *Dasein*'s own structure of revealing and concealing, of dis-covering. The event of revelation occurs when *Dasein* comports itself openly toward the thing, eschewing a calculating or instrumental mind-set. Events of truth are temporally restricted to the length of their occurrence. In terms of the initial example, the truth happens because Ricky is open to the truth of the bag, and it occurs each time he remembers or reenacts it (either alone or when sharing it with a friend). Its truth does not occur when Ricky attends to other things or when Ricky fails to attend to the bag in a suitably open manner. The prebelief domain of *openness* to the testimony of things—preceding an attitude of *trusting* or *understanding*—emerges as the most basic and necessary element of faith. One cannot *trust* or *understand* things that one does not first hearken to in an openness that remains the object of a vigilant skeptic's faith.

Instead of a world filled with "subjects" and "objects" that correspond, Heidegger emphasizes the interrelatedness of things with the world in which they are found; this emphasis allows him to characterize things as signs that refer one who perceives them to the context in which the thing is located. Heidegger discusses mass-produced suits, which point first to "the random and average" and finally the world of "wearers and users." The *world* expands from the "world of the workshop" where suits are made to the larger "public world" in which suits are worn. Things like covered railroad platforms testify to the "*surrounding world of nature*" (78–83) and human desires for light and dryness. Plastic bags testify to a need to carry various objects and a social disregard for the environment. In this sense, things give witness to natural and human worlds by simply being present.

In addition to the practical testimony that things offer to the world around them, things also always bear witness to the ontological structure of referentiality. Heidegger writes, "*Signs are something ontically at hand which as this definite useful thing functions at the same time as something which indicates the ontological structure of handiness, referential totality, and worldliness*" (77). The referential totality, or world, is not a "thing" the way that a sign is—it is never ontically at hand. The *reference* is what allows the possibility of testimony but never itself gives witness; the structure is therefore unidirectional, as humans can never grasp, see, or understand the reference itself. The explanation within *Being and Time* shows how things testify to worlds beyond their ontic existence, although this explanation reveals neither the nature of a true thing nor how one can understand it.

Although all things exist as signs, the early Heidegger distinguishes three types of things—mere things, equipment, and art—on the basis of their respective testimony. The "mere thing" is dominated by its earthly or concealing component—wood or stone, for example.[4] While this mere thing has a sheltering quality, it nonetheless testifies. A tree witnesses drought or flame, bearing witness in its trunk and carrying its testimony into its future. A mountain that witnessed the passage of glaciers bears witness through the scars left on its face. Although mute, the fact that earth has the ability to witness and bear witness allows it to *give witness* to the passage of time. Witness occurs in the presence of the earthly and is borne physically, on the material of the thing. This witness moves throughout the existence of the thing, becoming part of the thing and borne with it thereby, allowing its witness or testimony to shine forth. Mere things give witness to time's passage, testifying to the power of earth's endurance.

Humans, aware of time, would not seem to require this testimony of other things in terms of its truth, as the historical occurrence of a drought or fire is true merely at the ontic level of sense perception. The gap between testimony and truth is helpful, however, because understanding the ability of the earth to testify despite its inability to reveal truth demonstrates two things. First, because all things composed of an earthly element bear witness, all mere things are constant witnesses—surrounding us in a great cloud, witnessing sleeplessly all that passes by. Second, the fact that truth requires the testimony of phenomena reveals that the ability to testify, built into the earthly, makes truth possible but falls short of guaranteeing that truth inheres within all types of earthly things. The impoverished relationship to *truth* that seems to exist with regard to this type of thing does not allow *Dasein* to maintain a relationship of *conviction* with mere things (which would require that the testimony of the thing be the sole determinant for my being toward that thing understandingly).

The second kind of thing that Heidegger distinguishes, based on the interpretation of a thing as "formed matter," is *equipment*. Our tools, characterized by usefulness and reliability, exhaust the earthly or material component by directing it toward a given use. In this way, the worldly feature of equipment swallows up the earthly aspect—a shirt, for example, testifies more readily to a factory than to a cotton field. Thus, unlike the mere things that conceal, equipment is instrumental in allowing there to be a human world and is itself made possible by the human capacity for revelation.

Partly made up of the earthly, equipment testifies with the earthly as would a mere thing, revealing the passage of time (as rust testifies to the age or ill treatment of an ax blade). In mediating human values and needs, equipment *also* gives witness to the nature of the human world (as Heidegger's example of public lighting systems or covered railroad platforms suggests). Additionally, equipment's testimony is temporal in a new way, as can be seen when we contrast arrowheads with shotgun shells. Both testify to a need for humans to utilize projectile weapons for hunting, but the arrowhead, which uses an antiquated technology, gives witness to a world long past. The shotgun shells, whose spent uniformity contrasts with the hand-chiseled arrowhead, bears witness to a world that uses a technology of mass production as well as to the physical trauma of an explosion of gunpowder. Although the earthly element of an arrowhead allows it to persist into the modern world, it is only *in* the world—it is not *of* this world. It becomes an alien good, a strange thing in a world strange to it, recognizable but not useful. When an object is removed from its world (in space or in time), Heidegger describes this as "world-withdrawal and world decay," which "can never be undone" because the "works are no longer the same. . . . Their self-subsistence has fled from them."[5]

In sum, equipment testifies to earth and its origins of production, to the nature of a world in which a thing fulfills a need and to a natural world that creates such needs. In its worldliness, equipment *bears witness* to the needs of both the world and the earth that give rise to it and *gives witness*, reflecting world on earth. It does not create this world, but reflects and reveals the world that finds its existence to be useful.

Art, Heidegger's third type of thing, is uniquely characterized as a *striving* or conflict between world and earth and the opening and concealing tendencies manifest in each. Heidegger first acknowledges in art the possibility of a true thing, as such, coming into existence. Art is set into work by preserving the conflict between world and earth, and the nature of this ongoing conflict opens the possibility of the emergence of a truth predicated on the continued tension between world and earth. Thus it is less art as "object" than art as a *work* that enables it to open up a world. Heidegger writes, "In setting up a world and setting forth the earth, the work is an instigating of this striving. This does not happen so that the work should at the same time settle and put an end to the conflict in an insipid agreement, but so that the strife may remain a strife."[6]

Heidegger discusses how strife and conflict merge by way of two examples: a van Gogh painting of shoes and a Greek temple. The temple contains an "emerging and rising in itself" as it reveals a world at odds with the given or normal world of equipmental referentiality, as, "towering up within itself, the work opens up a *world* and keeps it abidingly in force."[7] This world does not simply float as an idea: Heidegger argues that the temple, which opens a world, also "sets this world back again on earth," which "only thus emerges as native ground."[8] Although the dust and dirt are omnipresent, the work of the temple *opens* this earth as ground *for that specific world*. The temple introduces humans to their particular world, which allows Heidegger to argue that "the temple, in its standing there, first gives to things their look and to men their outlook on themselves."[9]

Art testifies to the truth, revealed through the work of *displacement*—a term Heidegger uses to refer to what happens to both humans and art in the work of truth. Heidegger correlates what the art work does and its effect on humans, arguing that the work's ability to enter a self-opened openness is echoed in its ability to move humans from the ordinary. The openness that opens itself structurally adheres to the depiction of the work of the temple cited above, and, importantly, this self-opening work is what is initially transported. Heidegger's "ordinary" refers to the situation *equipment* reveals, where the world overtakes and brings forth the earthly in a familiar and usable way. This ordinary allows an unquestioning human relationship to world: the event of displacement is the necessary precondition for humans to relinquish control and engage the world through trusting.

Unlike equipment, which bears witness only to its world, art transports its preservers or guardians to the world that it opens, an alien world unconnected to the equipment of the preserver. Art *bears witness* to the new world in its figuration, and it *gives witness* of that new world through the setting-into-work of its truth: creating and preserving, art reveals to humans the nature of an otherwise unknown world and invites one willing to preserve it as a "projected sketch into the work of the unconcealedness of what is." Within this sketch, the revelation effects a complete transformation, such that "everything ordinary and hitherto existing becomes an unbeing," which loses "the capacity to give and keep being as a measure."[10] Average experience theorizes idly about such revelations for purposes of entertainment: movies such as *The Matrix* feature a revelation of a new reality in light of which none of the protagonist's former ideals or goals retain even marginal importance. As in the movie, revelations *transform* by providing a comprehensive way of seeing all of existence from a new structured beginning instead of through a simple twist of fate where a merely unanticipated future arrives.

A second way to understand the power of the revelation that Heidegger discusses is in the form of a contrast with equipment from other cultures. Through its continued reflection of its own world, an artifact (such as the arrowhead) possesses the power to provoke an uncanny feeling in the one who contacts it: in bearing witness to its bygone era, it gives witness to the transience of all worlds. The two stone legs of Ozymandias reveal this transience to the traveler standing before them. Another world, contained within the refuse of a past time, pushes against the world of the viewer—but its strangeness occurs only in relation to the familiar and everyday world in which the person exists. Dropping the arrowhead is enough to sever one's relationship to it and allow one to return to the unthinking ordinary world.

The revelation of art is different: gripped by art, preserving the world revealed within it, the reminders of one's former existence (prior to revelation) become artifacts akin to an arrowhead—the car one desired before one entered the new world is an uncanny shadow afterward. The revelation is so completely transformative and previously unsought that "the truth that discloses itself in the work can never be proved or derived from what went before. What went before is refuted in its exclusive reality by the work. What art founds can therefore never be compensated and made up for by what is already present and available."[11] Functionally, the state of being gripped by this truth requires *trusting,* as one cannot reason from what was known—or what could be known a priori—as a way to understand the new world.

Thus, at this stage in his career, Heidegger argues that things produce three forms of revelation. The first form of revelation is through the earthly: earthly things witness the passage of time, they bear witness through a material alteration—marks on the body—and give witness to those who wish to see what occurred. The second type of testimony offered by things is as signs to the surrounding cultural world; this form of testimony is unique to equipment, and no sense of world would be possible without the ability of things to embody the projects of humans. The final type of testimony comes through art, which reveals a new world through a displacement of both the "object" that bears witness to the world and the "subject" who bears witness to this "object." World—the present one or another—comes to presence through the property of language: language initially institutes a dynamic within being (which is other than the dynamic between being and nonbeing).

Theological Interpretations of the Testimony of Things

Although the distinction of three kinds of things reveals how different things bear witness on an ontological level, Heidegger's work does not provide an adequate explanation of how an equipmental object such as a plastic bag could bear witness to the truth of another world in a way that demands the effort of preservation. Because a plastic bag would fall into the category of "equipmental" objects, in which the function (carrying things) uses the material without remainder, it would seem incapable of conveying the promise of a new world, especially a message of comfort from a benevolent deity. It remains necessary to examine specifically theological interpretations of how God might appear in the world of things. Two dominant modes of theological interpretation that flourished in the twentieth century emerge as capable of explaining the event encountered in *American Beauty.* Specifically, Eliade's description of a hierophany can be seen as both congruent with and adding to Heidegger's conception of the revelatory potency of a mere thing, while Tillich's discussion of a symbol echoes elements of Heidegger's description of equipment and art. Relative to the thing, these analyses would allow a movement from a first-order trusting to a second-order faith.

Eliade, in his foundational text *Patterns in Comparative Religion*, uses the term "hierophany" to refer to "manifestations of the sacred in the mental world of those who believed in it" and includes in this category all "rite, myth, cosmogony or god" (10). He almost instantly expands this definition, urging the reader to "get used to the idea of recognizing hierophanies absolutely everywhere, in every area of psychological, economic, spiritual and social life." This is true to the extent that anything humans have "ever handled, felt, come in contact with or loved can become a hierophany" (11). In what might be his most extreme formulation, Eliade writes: "God is free to manifest himself under any form—even that of stone or wood. Leaving out for a moment the word 'God,' this may be translated: the sacred may be seen under any sort of form, even the most alien" (29). This view presumes a fully sacralized cosmos where humans, in experiencing the world, discovered and created points of access to a sacred or divine presence within the course of their daily lives. The term "hierophany" offers the most expansive notion of how things, especially mere things, exist within a theological framework.

In his theological writings, Paul Tillich gleans much from Eliade's phenomenological understanding of how things mediate the human and divine worlds. The function of hierophanies parallels Tillich's depiction of symbols, which "[open] up levels of reality which otherwise are closed for us" and which "[unlock] dimensions and elements of our soul which correspond to the dimensions and elements of reality."[12] The difference between the thinkers arises concerning the role played by things. While Eliade emphasizes the importance of the material uniqueness of the object in serving a hierophantic function (inasmuch as a large tree or smooth stone is a more likely candidate for a hierophany than an anonymous bit of shrubbery), Tillich's notion of a symbol as self-negating seems to view the materiality of the object as masking or distorting the represented transcendent reality. Self-negation is of such importance that Tillich finds that the intentionally self-negating Cross is the only appropriate symbol for the ultimate Ground of Being. Thus the contrast between Eliade and Tillich is exemplified when one realizes Tillich's claim that faith must be articulated symbolically precludes Eliade's insight that stone and water hierophanies are sacred in and of themselves, without regard to another dimension. For Tillich, objects are not an end in themselves. The movement to a language of symbol pushed theology into a transcendent framework, where the objects are important relative to acts of material self-negation.

Ultimately, Tillich's sense of a symbol—although it is able to speak for, or from, another world—functions like equipment as the element of world (or the referent) swallows the "concealing" potential of its material foundation. On the one hand, theologically, Tillich's sense of symbol reveals the potential for an equipmental revelation to present an absolute new world. On the other hand, Tillich's theory is inadequate to explain Ricky's revelation, which depends upon the juxtaposition of the unnatural materiality of the bag and the breeze in the air. Eliade's hierophany also cannot explain Ricky's revelatory encounter with anonymous, mass-produced material because of his emphasis on unique attributes.

A theological model capable of explaining the phenomenon of the plastic bag or any anonymous hierophany must merge the theological theories above. Expanding on Eliade, it would allow God to be present anywhere— even in a generic item whose unnatural qualities are as important to that particular revelation of "God" or "world" as a gigantic "tree" would be to the hierophany of an axis mundi. Expanding on Tillich, this site would open up a level of reality in the form of a revelation of a new world, a different way of understanding all things. In order to keep it an object of *faith*—as opposed to something easily understood—the additional corrective from Heidegger (which also repeats Kierkegaard's understanding of the God-Man) is to conceive of the thing as a *sign* that points to a still-clouded and unknowable referent. The notion of symbol, as Tillich describes it, could be appropriate only after a full unveilation of the truth—but one can make even this modest statement uncertainly and in *faith* (held in the tension of the negation of *trusting* and *understanding*).

Today, those desiring a skeptical faith must explore the potential capacity of equipmental things to reveal the presence of God. In a postindustrial twenty-first-century context, we increasingly confront more of an equipmental world than a natural one. Restricting points of divine access to nature or symbols would prevent vigilant skeptics from finding gods or things to question. On the other hand, expanding the possibilities of a theological universe to include common equipmental things would immerse vigilant skeptics in a world calling out for beholders. In such a world, each plastic bag or abandoned building would hold the potential for vigilant skeptics to apprehend the divine—but hesitate to call it such.

Reevaluating Equipment (and All Things)

Heidegger provides the deep structure for a rehabilitated conception of equipment capable of disclosing the capacity of things to play the role of a hierophantic sign as discussed above. Heidegger advanced his philosophical project in the early 1950s by focusing on the equipment that he had neglected in the thirties. First, Heidegger applied his concept of "work" to seemingly mundane items (bridges, jars) and revealed the wonderful life behind things. Second, Heidegger expanded the simple conception of world to reveal how things gather a complex series of relationships: earth and sky, mortals and divinities. These two expansions lead to a third advance, a more robust description of activity in which *displacement* (an extraordinary event) is redefined as *co-responding* (granting more applications to the everyday). *Preservation* (which depends on one's recognizing a revelation "worth preserving") becomes *vigilance,* a heightened awareness active at all times. Heidegger's "The Thing," given as a lecture on June 6, 1950, and published in 1951, is a culmination of the focus on things advocated by his mentor, Edmond Husserl, whose line "To the things themselves!" became the slogan of the phenomenological method.

In this essay, an analysis of a jug framed by the problem of nearness and distance, Heidegger amends his earlier insights. Although Heidegger maintains his determination that equipmental things represent what is near, his linguistic description of use-objects emphasizes the practice of a new way of looking, which he describes as vigilance. The alteration is subtle: instead of seeing equipment as lacking the artwork's self-sufficiency, he views equipment as "something self-sustained, something that stands on its own," "self-supporting or independent."[13] The difference is caused by a new understanding of how a thing relates to its status as object. He explains, "As the self-supporting independence of something independent, the jug differs from an object. An independent, self-supporting thing may become an object if we place it before us, whether in immediate perception or by bringing it to mind in a recollected re-presentation. However, the thingly character of the thing does not consist in its being a represented object, nor can it be defined in any way in terms of the objectness, the over-againstness, of the object" (166–67). Objectifying a thing by causing it to depend on our perception or memory erases the independent element of thingliness from the thing itself and thereby negates the thing as thing. Objects, existing "inside" consciousness, lack distance from the "subject" who relates to it. In contrast, things maintain a status as nearby. The nearness of things preserves a distance that maintains the thing's independence. Independence is thus named as the first determining quality of things.

Although objects possess an abstracted, permanent, static quality, in analyzing the jug, Heidegger determines that things engage actively and dynamically with their world. In claiming that "the jug presences as a thing. The jug is the jug as a thing," Heidegger transitions to discussing things in general and correlates the jug's jugness with its status as thing (as opposed to its status as container or void). Heidegger next explores the question of presence, writing: "But how does the thing presence? The thing things. Thinging gathers. Appropriating the fourfold, it gathers the fourfold's stay, its while, into something that stays for a while: into this thing, that thing" (174). Heidegger's own discussion of the presencing of the thing is a type of thinging as he gathers verbs. A thing "things," "gathers," "appropriates." The end of this paragraph, the phrasing as "this thing, that thing," retroactively emphasizes the terms "stay" and "while." These terms relate both to the thing and to the "fourfold" of earth and sky, mortals and divinities. The thing *is* a thing as it gathers and appropriates these intertwined relationships that then "stay" as, in, and through the thing's continued thinging. This analysis allows Heidegger to think "this word by way of the gathering-appropriating staying of the fourfold," which requires an independence and distance not permitted by mere objects. Already, the compatibility of the thing with divinities makes things—which exist relative to our ability to attend to them properly—a potential site for witnessing gods.

Heidegger clarifies the notion of "gathering" in the essay "Building, Dwelling, Thinking," published one year after "The Thing." In the essay, Heidegger reveals how a bridge gathers together the fourfold. The bridge, by producing banks that "emerge as banks only as the bridge crosses the stream," as "one side is set off against the other by the bridge," "*gathers* the earth as landscape around the stream." The bridge gathers sky, as "where the bridge covers the stream, it holds its flow up to the sky by taking it for a moment . . . and then setting it free once again." Mortals are "gathered" inasmuch as the bridge "escorts the lingering and hastening ways of men to and fro, so that they may get to other banks and in the end, as mortals, to the other side." Finally, the "bridge *gathers*, as a passage that crosses, before the divinities—whether we explicitly think of, and visibly *give thanks for*, their presence . . . or whether that divine presence is obstructed or even pushed wholly aside." The bridge's gathering is done "in *its own* way."[14] The individual way that a thing gathers emphasizes the importance that the materiality of *each* thing plays in offering a unique revelation. The bridge as location is built to preserve the fourfold in a way that Heidegger formulates as a chant: "to save the earth, to receive the sky, to await the divinities, to escort mortals" (158).

Things gather the elements of the world into a space wherein each of the elements of the fourfold are spatially related to each other, brought near: the corresponding activity within the human domain is *dwelling*. Dwelling is important for vigilant skeptics, as Heidegger indicates that its comportment requires a meditative vigilance. Although dwelling involves cultivation and construction, Heidegger argues that the essence of the activity is protection, a "sparing and preserving" that occurs "when we leave something beforehand in its own nature, when we return it specifically to its being, when we 'free' it in the real sense of the word into a preserve of peace" (149). Like things, the activity of dwelling gathers the fourfold (or world) as it occurs "in the sense of the stay of mortals on the earth," which "already means 'under the sky,' both of which *also* mean 'remaining before the divinities'" in the context of "belonging to men's being with one another" (149). Humans, in other words, *dwell* within a world that is safeguarded and preserved through letting things be.

The relation of thing and world invites humans to be gathered into this relationship to which, as mortal, they belong. Determined in this relationship, humans dwell by relating to the way that *each thing things*. Relating to things in this way requires understanding our locatedness in the world, our contingency: we need to remain mindful of our own limitations and appropriate them joyfully. In "The Thing," Heidegger describes the process in these words: "If we let the thing be present in its thinging from out of the worlding world, then we are thinking of the thing as thing. Taking thought in this way, we let ourselves be concerned by the thing's worlding being. Thinking in this way, we are called by the thing as the thing. In the strict sense of the German word *bedingt,* we are the be-thinged, the conditioned ones. We have left behind us the presumption of all unconditionedness" (181). The terrifying understanding that we are conditioned, structurally forbidden the perspective of the absolute, drives me to the small solace provided by a vigilant skepticism. Becoming concerned about things, keeping things close without assuming that they are "objects" over which I can have an absolute regulation and control, reveals a new potential for being in the world. As be-thinged, a vigilant skeptic arrives self-consciously into the world as such; only with things themselves as models can humans hope to find traces of the divine.

Things are beings that reflect world, a reflecting gathering more akin to *sign* than *symbol* (in other words, better read by Kierkegaard than Tillich). The testimony of the thing provides a *reflection* of this world (as denoted by Heidegger's term "mirror play"). The explication of world into its four parts and the recognition that things possess a truth with potency sufficient to produce conviction grant the testimony of the thing new power. The thing as *thing* (not as object) gathers and, in the gathering, brings forth testimony that prompts language, discourse, and thought. Things—including equipment such as plastic bags—in this way reveal new worlds. Heidegger discloses "the testimony of the *thing* itself" capable of bespeaking humans, and "Building, Dwelling, Thinking" and "The Thing" in this way read as a performance demonstrating how one can "be toward the thing understandingly," vigilantly letting things be. This attitude provides the basis upon which one can truly hearken to things, enabling a revelation from equipmental things. This revelation provides an opening to a time of faith through trusting instead of the understanding, when a vigilant skeptic can assent to its proposition and hesitate before affirming or negating it.

"The Thing" moves in a direction opposite that of "Origin of the Work of Art": in the earlier essay, Heidegger magnified the world of things to include everything and then instantly narrowed the scope of things to mere things, equipment, and art. In "The Thing," after discussing the specific example of the jug as a thing, Heidegger expands the scope of things farther than "Origin" had been willing to go, allowing the word "thing" to include mere things, equipment, and art, as well as such classically immaterial "things" as the soul or God (whom "Origin" had hesitated to call a thing). Ultimately, Heidegger calls upon the idiomatic English use of "things"— the kind of thing referenced when one "knows one's things," or "how to handle his things." Heidegger expands the term beyond entities with an obdurate physical presence—instead of being a type of thing, as a jar is a type of thing, anything and all things are things.

The account of things given in these essays clarifies how a plastic bag reveals a new world through its capacity to reflect and gather. Both the new world and the new site of revelation are important for the vigilant skeptic, demonstrating the power of the domain of prebelief (on the ontological level) and allowing a faith appropriate to the conditions of a broken twenty-first-century world (on an ontic level). Because three of the components that the thing gathers are determined—earth, sky, and mortal— Heidegger's explication of the origin of a world suggests that a revelation of a new world comes with, or through, a new or different manifestation of the absence of the divinities for whom expectant humans are doomed to wait. Heidegger's explanation thus accounts both for how Ricky understands co-responding as "the bag . . . just . . . dancing" with him and sees revealed "this entire life behind *things*" (my emphasis). This explanation also accounts for Ricky's apology for the video: the video demands the distance that allows the revelation to come as a dance but annihilates the materiality of the bag crucial to that thing's original *thinging* of the world, a thinging that Ricky attempts to supplement with a description that cannot fully reproduce the initial moment. Ricky could dwell in the revelation that there is no reason to be afraid, he could share the event with others, and the movie ensures the viewer remembers it by replaying the bag's dance as the protagonist dies.

Theological Interpretation of the Testimony of Equipment

Although Heidegger's account of the testimony and constitution of the thing adequately accounts for the bulk of the scene in the movie—the need to wait and watch for fifteen minutes, the need to remember and reenact the event, the revelation of comfort—it provides neither resources for understanding why the plastic bag as a particular thing revealed comfort nor explanations of why the plastic bag depicted God as a blandly benevolent life force. These questions push beyond Heidegger and require a theological model capable of grounding a more universal hierophantic sign that shows the peculiar relationship between empty refuse and God. This analysis connects the activity of a vigilant skeptic described above with the virtue of faith outlined in the first two chapters and clarifies how a vigilant faith emerges from a passionate moment of trusting (in addition to the principled adherence to a skeptical understanding explored in chapter 3).

Don Cupitt in his essay "Is Anything Sacred?" offers an initial insight into a theological matrix that would justify interpreting a plastic bag as the visitation of an anonymous god. Explicitly going "beyond Eliade," Cupitt uses Heidegger's sense of truth as an event that reveals and conceals. Contextualizing his statement with reference to Pascal and Kierkegaard, Cupitt writes, "In Christ, God is incognito . . . let us extrapolate this idea to its furthest limit: if the more God reveals himself the more he hides himself, then his completest self-revelation will coincide with his final disappearance." Echoing Altizer and Vattimo, Cupitt makes a dialectical argument that "Christianity does indeed start out by positing certain sacred objects and themes—but only in order to secularize them and so make them belong to everyone."[15] The process of secularization and universal accessibility is a movement congenial to a skeptical faith, as it is open to theological forms of revelation (and thus trusting) without adhering to a particular concrete revelation.

The object of faith that remains after one accepts that God is fully revealed when fully hidden (and vice versa) becomes rather difficult to describe. Cupitt's term for this is the "Abstract Sacred." A study of van Gogh leads Cupitt to argue that "to be effectively Christian nowadays, art must leave out Christ himself. To be truly religious, it must be 'flat,' entirely of this world and quite unconsoled. The Abstract Sacred gets its religious weight from its very repudiation of the supernatural."[16] The relationship to art is hardly accidental, as Cupitt (following Heidegger) argues that art provides the language that we can use to articulate the Absolute Sacred. Cupitt's characterization and interpretation explain why Ricky finds a revelation of a "benevolent life force" instead of a god and explains why the antidote for fear that Ricky feels becomes religious precisely in its banality. The "entire life behind things" that Ricky senses is at least analogous to Cupitt's "Abstract Sacred" and provides a starting point for understanding the theological possibilities opened by fusing atheism and the mundane.

If Cupitt offers the language necessary for understanding the dance of the plastic bag, then Thomas Altizer's Death of God theology offers the structural justification that undergirds Cupitt's thoughts. Altizer continues the trajectory of theological interpretations of objects provided by Eliade and Tillich—but with a dialectical twist. The unveiling of the nihilism revealed to Nietzsche and its normalization within the world allow Altizer to argue that the self-negation that Tillich had inflicted upon materiality through his theorization of symbols is more appropriately applied to God. Put otherwise, God repudiates the supernatural by (or in) Godself, eliminating all otherworldliness. The self-negation of the *spiritual* dimension causes a resacralization of finite materiality but not in a way that would resemble pantheism or a simple return to an Eliadesque system of hierophanies. The resurrection of the Godhead within materiality and finitude results in an infinitization of anonymity, and the anonymous is reproduced, in Heideggerean language, as *equipment* found ready to hand in a mass-produced supply of interchangeable parts or things: Styrofoam cups, cell phones, plastic bags.

Altizer's theological framework enables a theological interpretation of how equipmental objects, those things that are closest to hand, offer a uniquely important access to the truth of God. Altizer writes: "Theologically, what is now most difficult is to name a totally and actually anonymous presence as the image and identity of God for us." Warning against the temptation to speak of God as having withdrawn from our barren existence, he states, "Our anonymity does name God, and it names God if only because it embodies a total presence . . . which we can see only because we can no longer see or envision what we once named as God." Because a purely anonymous vision is impossible without the loss of both an immanent and a transcendent center, and the loss of each is at the heart of anonymity, Altizer states that we know the loss is "present when we discover and embody a pure immediacy in response to a totally anonymous presence. And we know or remember that this is an immediacy which once was a response to the 'I' of God." Although the "I" of God no longer elicits a total response, the fact that anonymity *does* do this reveals "a new presence and a new identity of what we once named as God."[17]

The indirect revelation of God, mediated through a human response to what is finite instead of an idea of the holy, requires us to change our preconceptions about how material objects reveal God. Although objects in an Altizerean universe are like hierophanies in enabling an interaction with the Godhead, a direct presentation of anonymity makes a *knowledge* of the divine impossible. Arguing that things act like traditional symbols, participating in the God toward whom they point, is confusing. Because these things participate with nothingness, humans experience the symbolic dimension as broken (the symbol has been disconnected from God) or nihilistic (it participates in nothingness). In terms congruent with the later Heidegger, things gather the absence of divinities through anonymity: because absence is not a complete negation (which would not enter into a relation at all), what things can gather is reflected in terms of anonymity.

Instead of looking to hierophanies (the direct revelation of God through distinctive objects) or symbols (via the displacement that occurs in art), neither of which are able to produce an immediate and anonymous response, a God conflated with the anonymous is best experienced through equipment seen as a sign. "Sign" here should be understood as conflating Kierkegaard's theological understanding of the God-Man (which required faith precisely because it did not participate in God but served as an obstacle to the *understanding*) with Heidegger's structural understanding of things in the world (which emphasized the role equipment plays in the perpetuation of a world). Equipmental objects, ready to hand and referring to an unknowable backdrop implied by the existence of the object, do *not* "participate" in any sort of divine understanding or truth: this is precisely what allows them to function as a sign of the anonymous that may or may not be the resurrected god (which has, at this point, little to do with the Christian revelation). Equipment—anonymous, functional, ready to hand—embodies the anonymous presence that generates a response of pure immediacy. While natural things are alien—increasingly so in a mechanized and industrialized world—and artistic things increasingly generate alienating displacements, equipment allows individuals to gather the self and the world together in a moment of use. In a broken universe—where shopping malls symbolize the nature of culture—such anonymity manifests as a potent source of theological potential, a potential that only Altizer's theology can truly or clearly explicate. Finally, Ricky's description of the "entire life behind things" that took the anonymous form of an "incredibly benevolent force" can be explained. Rooted in a confrontation with that which was both empty and anonymous—what can be termed an *anonymous hierophany*—no other and no better reflection of that which once was called God can be found.

Mark C. Taylor's *Disfiguring* also describes how trash and refuse offer a privileged insight into the nature of the postmodern divine. In Taylor's reading, disfiguring "neither erases nor absolutizes figure" but allows for a Freudian type of denegation "through which the repressed, or refused, returns" in an affirmation of negation (instead of a Hegelian type of negation). Taylor explains his aesthetics through an analysis of Bataille, who contrasts a profane world of work and reason where desire is repressed with a more primal, sacred world of "'immanence' where clear differences and articulate distinctions are lacking." The sacred domain is found through sacrifice, an excessive act that is neither reasonable nor useful, a surreal world where distinctions between "rational" categories like good and evil are overcome in a fusion of opposites. This attitude materializes in the solicitation of "the refused that realism refuses," including "impurity, disorder, transgression, irrationality, and uselessness."[18]

The notion of a "flat" universe, described by both Cupitt and Altizer, requires further explanation. Because things, understood as reflecting back an anonymous presence, function as signs instead of symbols, it is impossible to know what, if anything, lies beyond them. Viewing things as signs permits vigilant skeptics to undergo a faith open to atheistic, transcendent, and immanent possibilities (that there is no God, that there is a God outside of the universe, and that God is fully within the universe). Because I remain co-responsible for the creation of the world—including any new world revealed through the eventful interaction with a thing—I necessarily embrace a close distance from the thing, unable to be united with the thing absolutely yet remaining tied to it, proximate with it, dancing. Equipment reflects a new or different world to the individual, one where anonymity is a total presence and not merely something that allows the thing to become a consumable object: incorporating equipment, especially the banal and refused, into our worldview makes its omnipresence meaningful. Retaining a watchful distance from such objects as we move through the world becomes imperative, as maintaining this distance frees things to gather earth and sky, humans and divinities, into a total presence. Because each thing is capable of manifesting a total presence, vigilant skeptics can remain fully integrated with a world that faith draws into the enlightened darkness of an absolute unknowing.

The event of faith cocreated in conjunction with an anonymous hierophany speaks clearly to a postindustrial, twenty-first-century world. The possibility of this event presupposes both a resacralized world where things serve as signs reflecting a world not yet present and the vigilance of the individual willing to search for and hearken to the testimony of things. The revelation itself is intensely personal and manifests only through the effort and cocreativity of the person. Accordingly, individuals form this type of faith *passionately,* uniting the self during each moment spent attending to the revelation. Although the revelation that emanates from an anonymous hierophany is conceived of as a future world, because world is always necessarily a cocreation from the self, that which is revealed concerns the individual personally and powerfully. The preservation of this truth over time allows the faith to perdure and accomplishes the work of actualizing the reflected world into existence; at this level, one forms the faith relative to the revelation from the anonymous hierophany by *volition.*

The Standards of an Object of Faith

Our secular age inspires a normalized nihilism that justifies the defensive posture of naïve skepticism. Increased technological prowess has led to a surplus of goods, and the development of careers in marketing has led to a consumer society dominated by the need to possess identical types of brand-name objects, to eat the same types of meals in the same chain restaurants. Plastic surgery and fashion trends allow individuals to redefine their external features, providing an increased sense of homogenization. Globalization magnifies this artificial sameness on a worldwide level, where each culture participates in the creation of the emerging global culture, in which all are producers and consumers—especially consumers. Because of this, each culture becomes increasingly anonymous: one can sip on Starbucks coffee or drink a Guinness while eating sushi, eat at Pizza Hut or McDonald's, or shop for leather jackets or khaki pants in almost any major city in the world. Additionally, the prominence of electronic communication (e-mail, text messaging, instant messaging) further depersonalizes human interactions: face-to-face contact is replaced by interactions with impersonal textual interfaces. A distanced state of chronic unbelief is prudent in such a situation.

The benefits of homogenization rely on our ability to personalize content within an impersonal format. Although iPods and laptop computers look identical, we individualize this equipment to make it an extension, an externalization, of our personality. Social networking sites such as Facebook or Twitter offer this opportunity as well. Customers at coffee shops can get "their" drinks by selecting from a set number of options. Similarly, technological advances allow individuals to "custom-design" homes or automobiles, negotiating a certain number of fixed variables in order to achieve a "unique" and "personal" object that "represents them" and nonetheless remains part of a larger structure of brand-name goods. In this way, material objects and goods—equipment, to use Heidegger's term—replace religion as a way of mediating the finite and infinite, the possible and the necessary. As equipment, these objects are not "religious"; in what has become archaic terminology, they are "profane," not "sacred." Endowed with the task of mediating the finite and the infinite, however, these objects are not merely secular. Generic, these objects would serve neither as hierophanies in Eliade's sense nor as symbols in Tillich's.

Altizer's theological vision, which locates God as the total presence of anonymity, is the most appropriate theological matrix with which to interpret this social phenomenon. The anonymous stands equally near to all things, providing an absolute sense of an Abstract Sacred. Unthingly objects reveal and conceal, serving as signs that confront consumers with the anonymous—but only indirectly, for the object itself is given in its wholly finite mundane way, and the finitude obscures the total presencing of the anonymous without denying its presentation. Similarly, the anonymous itself is a sign that potentially reveals and conceals the resurrected Godhead. The totality of the anonymous is a covering large enough to conceal the Godhead underneath it, but, like Kierkegaard's God-Man and Knight of Faith, no hint of the Godhead manifests through the anonymous. In this way, equipment testifies to that which lies beyond it as a sign; read through

Altizer, this testimony would include the world whose anonymity may include or exclude Godhead reborn.

Chapter 3 described how one could "undergo" an experience of faith relative to a revelation—the experience of which was formulated as a proposition to which one gave assent (in the forms of affirmation or negation). This is consistent with Heidegger's statement that a projected sketch (revelation) gives rise to language. One undergoes faith relative to this proposition until the truth of it is fully unveiled; until then, its status is a becoming-true. In Christian theological terms, a revealed "truth" has an infinite quality that can be experienced and put into abstract or universal terms as a "belief" but requires a certain duration in time in order to manifest as wholly finite. Because the truth cannot be determined, one can understand the "truth" in terms of faith: until the truth is wholly unveiled, one relates to the truth through faith instead of knowledge, realizing the faith through an internalized transformation that is repeated through an externalization implied in the individual's actions. *Faith* is the most appropriate term for one's interaction with the anonymous hierophany, as the infinitude presented within the revelation prohibits an *understanding* just as the self-negating anonymity limits one's *trusting*. Further, while a vigilant skeptic might well view a religious icon with a sensitivity to what it simultaneously offers and lacks, an anonymous hierophany seems a more likely site where one could, like Ricky, find a moment with the anonymous that appeared as God.

Our postmodern age is grounded on understanding that truth occurs as part of a dynamic event of disclosure and that it does not "exist" as an object to be found or located. The model that understands truth as an event accounts for fully unveiled truths that function like "objects" for consciousness to apprehend, but it also accounts for the truth of art that occurs through such a dynamic movement. The postmodern emphasis on the interpretability of truth thus takes truth itself out of the realm of knowledge, characterized by subjective conviction and objective certainty, and puts it into the realm of faith, characterized by subjective conviction and objective uncertainty. Within this model, every revelation of truth is received in faith.

Appreciating the value of equipment and refuse as objects of faith and mastering the attitude of vigilance that co-responds to this appreciation—the model of faith that understands that things reflect a resacralized universe—demonstrates how objects of faith function in other models of faith while also explaining how a plastic bag can offer a revelation of the divine. If things are signs that reflect the total anonymous presence that hovers in the places where gods once were, humans can see them as *participating* in God, as symbolic interpretations (ranging from Augustine to Tillich) would hold. The traditional approach problematically leads individuals toward *knowledge* (or a nonnegated *understanding*) instead of the uncertainty of faith, allowing a type of distanceless consumption of other objects that prohibit a possible dance with the divine (and thereby obscuring what Ricky was able to experience). The model of the object of faith presented here accounts for a self-negating component (which Tillich held to be crucial), but in shifting this self-negating to the divine, this model allows for the virtue of materiality to manifest in a uniquely important way. The Kingdom of God, in a sense, is literally at hand and embodied in those objects that are handy. The vigilant skeptic watches for these objects and, in faith, allows them to come close without annihilating them through an active affirmation or negation of the potential truth that they disclose. For a vigilant skeptic, everything becomes a possible object of faith, which allows for faith's object—its own continued regeneration into the future as an end in itself—to be maintained.

Part III
The Works of a Vigilant Faith

5 The Work of Vigilance

Of course, it is strange to inhabit the earth no longer,
to give up customs one barely had time to learn,
not to see roses and other promising Things
in terms of a human future

—RAINER MARIA RILKE, First Duino Elegy

Enlarging the domain of prebelief, the initial space of all faith, has revealed a model of faith suitable for native skeptics (who instinctively reject appearances and thus lack the initial suspension of disbelief required for unlocking symbolic worlds) and rigorous skeptics (who mindfully make equipollent arguments with an eye toward finding an eventual truth). While believers who choose a particular symbol to mediate their faith exit this domain, a skeptic with vigilant faith can intentionally dwell in this domain.

The practice of a skeptical faith requires vigilance. As the underside of consciousness, vigilance is the reflexive awareness that grants awareness of our awareness and thereby grounds both skepticism and faith. On the one hand, skeptics necessarily engage in vigilance as they question the extent to which they have consistently bracketed the world; vigilance separates rigorous from naïve skeptics. Vigilance is also a necessary precondition for the possibility of a reflexive faith. Preserving the dynamic axes of faith, vigilance prevents faith from sliding into a static condition. Vigilant skeptics maintain both a passionate subjective conviction in the possibility of a full unveilation of the truth and a critical attitude that ensures they keep searching; traces of God remain objectively uncertain.

Chapter 4 described the need for vigilance relative to possible objects of faith that one might encounter. Unable to embrace traditional symbols and therefore beset by brokenness, a vigilant skeptic (who remains open to the possibility of future revelations) investigates the world vigilantly, expanding the zone of possibilities of objects that might reveal the God above the God of theism. This outlook exposes the theological potential of human artifacts that many theologies of culture overlook, focusing on the anonymous objects most conducive to revealing the anonymous divine. Whether or not there is (or was) a god, vigilance infuses the world with a skeptic's faith and—at worst—donates the shining appearance of the sacred in a world that might otherwise grow forgetful of it.

Part 3 moves from a skeptical faith to a vigilant faith, highlighting how skeptics can work to realize unseen truths. Chapter 5 constructs an account of vigilance as an end in itself, underscoring its importance to both the vigilant human and to the surrounding world. Having established the importance of vigilance as the work that activates the dynamic of faith and generates the proliferation of objects of faith, this chapter contextualizes the particular importance of vigilance as an independent work relative to atheistic paradigms. After examining how Emily Dickinson's work exemplifies how vigilance is a work of faith differing from those grounded in trusting or understanding, I contend that vigilance works without violating skepticism, based on the existential functions of vigilance in Heidegger's philosophy (preserving, questioning, providence). Finally, I define different senses of what "godless" means, the distinct form of godlessness that vigilance promotes, and the relationship between a godless vigilance and the absolute. Ultimately, I show that humans uniquely access the absolute through a faith that shuns symbolically mediated representations of the divine. Incorporating a dimension of positive work, the vigilant faith described in part 3 differs from a skeptical faith to the extent that a skeptical faith differs from naïve skepticism.

Apprehensions Are God's Introductions

Emily Dickinson demonstrates how vigilance serves as the work of faith through her distance from theistic conceptions of God and her dedication to creating such spaces for others. Her hesitations regarding theistic devotion appeared at an early age: when seventeen at Mount Holyoke, only Dickinson consistently advertised that she was without hope of salvation, impenitent and unrepentantly so despite the efforts of her family, friends, and classmates. This antipathy toward organized religion, revealed in her refusal to attend services, did not extend to a dismissal of the divine. Her letters and poems portray the problems with traditional Christian conceptions of God, despite a respect for and familiarity with the Bible itself. Consistently, Dickinson's life and poetry show a drive away from familiar, ritually prescribed centers and toward the experiences at the boundaries of language and reason.

Instead of manufacturing passions designed to meet social expectations and quell her own misgivings about ultimate concerns, Dickinson devoted her life to unsettling certainties through a poetic work of vigilance. Her writings create a theological ground, marrying a criticism of traditional Christian values (Paradise, Eden, Christ, God, Sabbath) with a commitment to pushing language beyond the boundaries of reason. The resulting spaces deprive her reader of an object: her poems are doors to an absolute faith, bound up in a joyful appropriation of the finite world of flowers and insects that surround her. Her writings testify to a life spent in a work of vigilant faith: one that skeptically refrained from the temptations of both reason and revelation, one that scoured the world for sites of the divine without clinging to any particular moment. Beyond this, Dickinson kept watch over those around her, inviting them to perceive the world with a faith steeped in vigilance, testifying to the possibilities of a godless faith with a loving concern for those around her.

Dickinson details how a vigilant faith potentially resacralizes the mundane world. In "By my Window have I for Scenery" (Fr849), she demonstrates how envisioning the tree outside her window permits a work of faith beyond skepticism:

> By my Window have I for Scenery
> Just a Sea—with a Stem—
> If the Bird and the Farmer—deem it a "Pine"—
> The Opinion will do—for them—
>
> It has no Port, nor a "Line"—but the Jays—
> That split their route to the Sky—
> Or a Squirrel, whose giddy Peninsula
> May be easier reached—this way—
>
> For Inlands—the Earth is the under side—
> And the upper side—is the Sun—
> And it's Commerce—if Commerce it have—
> Of Spice—I infer from the Odors borne—

Of it's Voice—to affirm—when the Wind is within—
Can the Dumb—define the Divine?
The Definition of Melody—is—
That Definition is none—

It—suggests to our Faith—
They—suggest to our Sight—
When the latter—is put away
I shall meet with Conviction I somewhere met
That Immortality—

Was the Pine at my Window a "Fellow
Of the Royal" Infinity?
Apprehensions—are God's introductions—
To be hallowed—accordingly—
[Extended inscrutably]

The first stanzas gather perspectives on what the tree might mean to others, holding them at odds. Dickinson initially depicts the scene as "Just a Sea— with a Stem—" (invoking an instant connection with "See") and then lists the relative opinions of bird and farmer, gently chiding their affirmations of the obvious by emphasizing "for them." She then contemplates how the tree allows a squirrel to reach its "giddy Peninsula," and how the tree has its own "Commerce . . . / Of Spice" that she "infer[s] from the Odors borne." The first two stanzas reveal how keeping watch embraces the evidence of the senses, projects likely but uncertain possibilities for others (Bird, Farmer, Squirrel), and allows deductions based on nonvisual senses such as smell. Delighting in the unknowable, Dickinson demurely demands faith from her reader by destabilizing a central perspective of knowledge.

The third stanza moves past inferences of what is unknown but likely into an affirmation of what is unseen and unevidenced; this step uses faith to reintroduce mystery into the world. Still discussing the "Pine" as the "It" in question, Dickinson writes, "Of it's Voice—to affirm—when the Wind is within— / Can the Dumb—define the Divine?" First, her idiosyncratic punctuation (it's) indicates that the tree both is and has a voice, affirming a "Divine" in what is paradoxically intuited and gathered without words. Using a question to invoke the divine keeps its presence uncertain, although the plausible context of a tree's testifying to an invisible wind pushes readers to affirm the possibility with her. Suggesting trees serve as possible sites for divine visitation with a question, Dickinson refuses to locate the tree as either sacred or profane, either idol or icon. The tree is not sacred; Dickinson hearkens instead to the possibility that the Divine might be communicated through the mundane. The verse reveals the miraculous possibilities of nature that our drive toward certainty causes us to ignore.

The fourth stanza explicitly merges Dickinson's vigilance with the concept of faith, when a moment of openness invites a divine presence that demands a faith that surpasses theistic limitations. Dickinson locates Paul's admonition to live "by faith, not by sight" into a natural—not supernatural—setting, expanding the domain of faith to include all moments. Defining the Divine in the "Dumb" insinuates not only that we can encounter God without recourse to symbols, but also that experiences of the absence of God result from our obdurate refusal to consider that trees themselves may prophesy. The first four lines gather the terms "they," "sight," and "Conviction" with ironic coldness: opposing what "it" suggests to faith against "their" emphasis on sight, Dickinson invites her readers to reflect on the foundation for their convictions. The occurrence of the poem thereby demands the reader's self-disclosure.

The fifth line of this stanza is the sole exception to the quatrains that comprise other verses. A short line, it adds "That Immortality—," a pinch of doctrinal language that fails to speak the "Holy" summoned by the tree. The fourth line completes the thought: the supplement of this fifth line is made extraneous. Even if one could be convinced of immortality, Dickinson's dash indicates that no more can be said about it. Unlike the tree, which gave birth to a number of different interpretations, "Immortality" offers very little beyond itself. Dickinson's faith focuses on expanding what life means now, not on theorizing about the possibility of an afterlife. There is enough on earth, perhaps, that remains unseen.

The contrast of what the tree gives, as opposed to what "They—suggest to our Sight," is developed finally in the last stanza, when Dickinson wonders, "Was the Pine at my Window a 'Fellow / Of the Royal' Infinity?" The line break at "Fellow" puts Dickinson on equal terms with the pine at that moment. The final lines confirm a faith that requires and transcends vision: "Apprehensions—are God's introductions— / To be hallowed— accordingly—." Sacralizing perceptions, Dickinson shows that scenery contains as much God as one is willing to see—and that a willingness to see vigilantly, a willingness to gather the Divine dumbly, qualifies believers as fellows of the royal infinity. The truth of this possibility—scenery that both conceals and reveals the infinite—gathers within Dickinson's poem, which, like the tree's branches, gives witness to the infinite. Disregarding both immortality and "God" as objects of faith, Dickinson's vigilance produces intimations of the infinite that are drawn out of hiding and hallowed. The poem ignores "facts," things that "they" might say, to gather a truth built on an individual work of vigilance: the *how* of looking invites the appearance of the scene that we do not (Fr978), which relies on faith as its sole support.

Dickinson's poetic variants destabilize her poems by making it impossible for her manuscript readers to treat her poems as objects: one cannot know which words are included or excluded in a poem. The variant in Fr849 replaces the final line with "Extended inscrutably." Beyond hallowing what we sense in the world, in faith, Dickinson implies that "God's introductions" are meant to be "Extended inscrutably": we should remain skeptical of what is given (able to be scrutinized), anticipating the unseen beyond. The faith projected in the poem invites readers to revere the world with a holy awe, to assume that appearances are introductions to a divine who might appear through the vigilant work of faith.

The Preserving Function of Vigilance

Dickinson's defiant works of faith, resacralizing the world, illuminates the ontic potential for vigilance. Having opened this potential, I devote the remainder of this chapter to outlining the ontological work of vigilance based on Heidegger's late essays. I begin by discussing vigilance as a practiced openness toward things and the world they gather. Next, I discuss how vigilance works to provide Heidegger's philosophy with a rare moral imperative: Heidegger finds that human vigilance becomes necessary for the shepherding of beings against the twin dangers of thinking technologically and thinking poetically. Finally, the vigilance defined and demonstrated by Heidegger serves as an ontological model for a spiritually ontic discussion of vigilance; in other words, the ability to engage in vigilance as a work of faith rests on the structural possibilities of vigilance.

CONCEPTUALLY, vigilance first appears as part of the work of *preservation* in "Origin of the Work of Art." In the 1950s, Heidegger contends that vigilance is the work that enables *building* and *dwelling*, the everyday modes of preservation understood as world making and world sustaining, respectively. A vigilant comportment invites our mindful watch for the truth of things we can preserve. Becoming explicitly conscious of the crucial role vigilance plays in our everyday lives reveals the importance of vigilance relative to the banal and the mundane. A vigilant faith, in particular, uniquely allows us to suspend judgment and thereby enables the preservation of multiple worlds simultaneously.

In "Origin," Heidegger provides a useful definition of "work"—which works both on the art and on the viewer who receives the art—focused on the work of *displacement*. Submission to displacement—being determined by the truth revealed in a work of art—requires restraining the normal relations of earth and world, employed when we engage with equipment and the equipmental. This mode of restraint is parallel to the hesitation required by skeptical faith. Through restraint, the work's unique vision or configuration of world, placed back onto the earth, can occur. *Preservation* causes the observer to become *bewahrenden. Bewahrenden* means not only "guarding"—it is a particular type of maintaining or keeping that relates specifically to the truth (*wahr*)—of the thing at hand. Preserving the truth of the work by letting be the particular truth of the specific world opened by the work is accomplished only by reconfiguring modes of activity that generally are assumed and not reflected upon. Skeptical and vigilant self-examination enables the task of reflective thinking. Dickinson's displacement (hearing the divine in the dumb) transformed her habits, values, and life as she appropriated the disclosed truth. The work of preservation (writing a poem), enabled by a subjective conviction concerning a revealed truth that is not reflected in an objectively certain world, extended the duration of that revealed truth to each of her readers beyond her own lifetime.

Building describes how humans transform the world into anchors capable of gathering the truth in an objectively certain manner. This transformation preserves a particular balance of earth and sky, mortals and divinities (the fourfold, or *Geviert*) in things. We *build* creatively, *cultivating* those things that grow and *constructing* things that do not grow. Some constructions are places or locations, which create a space in which the fourfold can be installed. Other constructions are crafts, examples of *techne*—Heidegger discusses how a silversmith forges a sacrificial chalice with a sense of co-responsibility. In all of these things, humans form earth in ways that meet the mortal need of sustaining life. The need to work like this reflects the absence of divinities, and the changes that *building* occasions emerge in contrast with an unchanging sky.

In addition to the work of *building* that describes how humans make the world, Heidegger discusses the function of *dwelling*, used to signify the way humans receive their world. *Dwelling* mirrors the activity of things, which "hold" or "keep" the fourfold, and expands the notion of *preservation* from its earlier relation to the truth claim found in the work of art. Because all things stay, or hold, the fourfold, dwelling intentionally preserves all things. Thus, *dwelling* and *building* are different modes of preservation. In dwelling, one accepts that all things echo the truth of one's world; in building, one promotes the vision of that truth in the creation of new goods offered in this world's image. Put concretely, building new roads promotes a vision of a world that prioritizes efficiency and convenience in transportation over the value of nature. We dwell as we receive this world, purchasing vehicles to drive on roads and houses where these roads end.

Functionally, *dwelling* and *building* are conceptually similar to the notion of *bewahren,* the preserving guardianship to which the art-thing's work of *displacement* calls humans.[1] But whereas *dwelling* and *building* are activities that constitute world making and world preserving in its ordinary function, *bewahren* allows humans to stay determined by a displacing revelation of a new world; put otherwise, it is world preserving in its extraordinary version. The term *bewahren* as a relation to a special type of comportment transforms into the term *vigilance,* which grows in power and importance through Heidegger's later writings. Vigilance is a more attentive way of being in the world, which hearkens to things and the way things preserve the fourfold; this increased attention becomes imperative as Heidegger becomes more aware of the number and power of things. By the end of "The Thing," Heidegger explicitly states that things depend on human vigilance to allow people to hear and understand the things' way of reflecting the world of earth and sky, mortals and divinities. Although he warns that humans cannot simply "make" things, Heidegger adds that "neither do [things] appear without the vigilance of mortals" (181). Vigilance requires a movement away from explanatory representational thinking to a thinking that "responds and recalls" (in the manner of Ricky Fitts) and "takes up its residence in a co-responding which, appealed to in the world's being by the world's being, answers within itself to that appeal" (181–82).

Co-responding indicates a watchfulness through which a human, acting like a thing, mirrors—or produces—a dwelling wherein the newly revealed world can stay. The thing's ability to gather depends on a human's attentive response to the event of the thing's gathering; without humans, the gathering enacted by things does not constitute an event. When co-responding with things, humans gather and stay the mirror play of earth and sky, mortals and divinities. Our mortal finitude is brought near to that of the earthly thing without being made identical. While co-responding emulates the structure of *displacement* in "Origin," in that both the entity and the human are moved into a world, it differs because co-responding occurs with regard to whatever is near—a jug or a bridge, for example—and does not involve the singling out of the displacement event. Dickinson's poetry, which gathers and displaces, exemplifies this kind of vigilance.

In Heidegger's thinking, vigilance manifests as the highest human capacity, necessary for creating, receiving, and spreading the world gathered and localized by things. We gather the world intentionally through vigilance and thereby appreciate the truth revealed in thingly gatherings. The skeptical root of a vigilant faith, however, requires a more nuanced type of creating, constructing, and cultivating. World making and world preserving normally occur without a tension between worlds—they place, instead of displace. A vigilant faith, which maintains the gap between relative and absolute worlds or (minimally) between two relative worlds in order to perpetuate the truth of objective uncertainty, cannot engage in building or dwelling in the same fashion as Heidegger outlines. Rooted in its responsibility for preservation, the worth of vigilant faith is determined by its capacity to construct and cultivate toward a future and in light of a revelation *in spite of* its hesitations.

The Questioning Function of Vigilance

Heidegger's concept of *destining* opens a second type of work, as vigilance contrasts ways of seeing in technology (*techne*) and art (*poiesis*), the common ways we fulfill our destiny to be unconcealing. These are not equal: Heidegger contrasts the first, a "bringing forth" (or *Hervorbringen*) such as a farmer does with a small plot of land, with the second mode of "challenging forth" (or *Herausforden*), exemplified by human extraction of natural elements such as coal or oil from the ground.[2] Art and technology provide different contexts through which we engineer objective certainty. Vigilance preserves the human capacity for openness (*Gelassenheit*), found in questioning and resisting the answers art and technology provide.[3]

Humans engage in revealing and concealing as they interact with the world in trusting and understanding. Although this process is a powerful way of being, Heidegger dispossesses humans of instigating the process; instead, he finds, "That which has already claimed man . . . has done so, so decisively that he can only be man at any given time as the one so claimed."[4] Without revealing the nature of the "That" at this time, he presents two different responses to being claimed. One, *Herausforden*, occurs as humans treat nature as an object of research that conceals energy sources that humans can demand from the earth. The common alternative, *Hervorbringen,* occurs when humans give themselves over to "meditating and striving, shaping and working, entreating and thanking" that allows them to find themselves "everywhere already brought into the unconcealed."[5] In general, the human capacity for revelation occurs through either of these modes. *Herausforden* and *Hervorbringen,* as ways of revealing, correlate positively with the earlier sense of displacement: although humans are involved in the process of challenging forth and bringing forth, they do not control it.

Heidegger describes why we engage in revelations using the term destining *(Geshick),* a term related to a "sending-that-gathers" *(versammelde Schicken),* similar to the projective saying that sublates the emphasis on *gathering* undertaken by almost all of his discussion of revelation. Heidegger argues that Enframing (the claim on humans preceding *Herausforden)* is an "ordaining of destining,"[6] and *Hervorbringen* (explicitly related to *poiesis)* originates in destiny. Heidegger connects *aletheia* to freedom on the basis of our being destined, writing: "Always the destining of revealing holds complete sway over man. But that destining is never a fate that compels. For man becomes truly free only insofar as he belongs to the realm of destining and so becomes one who listens and hears [*Hörender*], and not one who is simply constrained to obey [*Höriger*]."[7] The word for "free" that Heidegger uses is *das Freie,* which echoes his terminology in "Building, Dwelling, Thinking." There, the nature of the free came about through a sparing or preservation that "left something beforehand in its own nature," or returned it "specifically to its being" (149). Freedom requires a destining that allows for a return. Structured as disclosing and discovering, humans are destined to be revealing; Enframing and *Hervorbringen, poiesis* and a certain element within *techne,* vie as two possible modes of fulfilling this destiny. Vigilance is the third and most free way of revealing, grounded in skeptical questioning rather than enframed by knowledge.

Heidegger's greatest concern in his late work is with *Herausforden*-related concepts, a challenging forth that Heidegger identifies as the dominant mode of revealing within modern technology and the most dangerous way that humans fulfill their destiny. *Herausforden* is a utilitarian and pragmatic way of relating with the world that demands from nature the revelation of energy that can be extracted and stored as such. *Herausforden* frames the world as potential energy: plains are wind farms, hills are coal mines, rivers are dams. Driven toward maximum yield at minimum expense, *Herausforden* involves the two actions of regulating and securing. What *Herausforden* reveals falls into the category of "standing reserve"; such items lose their autonomy and sense of nearness, no longer a joint partner in cocreation.

Enframing, *Herausforden,* and *techne* are dangerous because they are closed to questioning, blinding us to the full possibility of our own freedom. The danger increases with Enframing's successes, as we embrace "correct" answers at the expense of possible truths. Annihilating possibilities, Enframing destroys wonder: Heidegger warns that even God would lose the mystery of distance, sinking to the level of a cause.[8] Even more worrisome to Heidegger is the point when humans will take themselves as standing reserve, as objects of control, regulation, and manipulation. Heidegger warns that Enframing conceals its origins as a spoken project, making it unlikely we apprehend Enframing as a claim. Heidegger thus argues that Enframing is more dangerous than the destining of *poiesis,* which remains mindful of its origin in language; thus Enframing is the "greatest danger" that threatens humanity.

Yet, although Heidegger originally contrasts *poiesis* and *techne,* the revealing enabled by *poiesis* and *Hervorbringen* cannot counter the threat of Enframing. The final sentence of "The Question Concerning Technology"— "For questioning is the piety of thought" (35)—indicates the importance of generating questions in thinking by allowing a conflict between modes of revelation or bringing forth. Warning against "sheer aesthetic-mindedness," in which "we no longer guard and preserve the coming to presence of art," Heidegger indicates that a pure *poiesis* presents problems structurally similar to the blind concealing of Enframing. The saving power lies exclusively in an attitude of vigilance (being mindful, not minded) that balances questioning and safekeeping in watching over, and in the maintenance of conflict between the revealing "world" and concealing "earth." The saving power occurs in the intentional holding-in-conflict that accompanies the work of a skeptical faith.

Art shares with Enframing a tendency to collapse tension, converting things into "unbeings." Enframing eliminates this tension by reducing "objects" to the objectlessness of a standing reserve, while Heidegger argues that art-based revelations overpower the potential resistance of things: "By virtue of the projected sketch set into the work of the unconcealedness of what is, what casts itself toward us, everything ordinary and hitherto existing becomes an unbeing. This unbeing has lost the capacity to give and keep being as measure."[9] The revelations of Enframing and art consistently push humans to reducing experiences into knowledge. The "object" that has been regulated and secured as standing reserve is an "unbeing" lacking "the capacity to give and keep being as a measure. "Enframing," as well as art, is described as a "projected sketch," "sending," "destining," or "grounding." Art and poetry are neither "bad" nor "wrong," however: unworlding occurs through the work of revelation itself. As revelation, and without regard to whether the conflict is held within a figure (art) or between two destinies, *unworlding is a constant and ever-present danger that attends all revelations and all truths.*

Thus, Heidegger calls vigilance the "saving power" that appears at the moment of the "greatest danger," represented by Enframing. Heidegger writes: "For the saving power lets man *see* and enter into the highest dignity of his essence. This dignity lies in *keeping watch* over the unconcealment—and with it, from the first, the concealment—of all coming to presence on this earth. . . . Everything, then, depends on this: that we ponder this arising and that, recollecting, we watch over it."[10] The "destining of revealing," occurring as a "granting" or "sending," is the originary work: a bestowing, a founding, a new world that was once projected forth and unconcealed as a way of understanding the relationship between earth and world. Vigilance, which keeps watch over truth, locates the origin of Enframing's concealing at the heart of its original bestowing. The "arising of the saving power" thus appears in the form of *Wahrnis,* safeguarding, preserving, vigilance. The safeguarding prevents unworlding and making things unbeings—but requires that the vigilant one refuse to embrace what is revealed as an absolute truth. This is why Dickinson's poetry is more vigilant than other, closed poetic worlds: her poems are riddled with moments that deny human desires for objective certainty by juxtaposing multiple visions of a world. The perspective of the bird and farmer, who see the tree as pine, balances her own view of the tree as prophetic voice: her vigilant balance preserves the being of the tree within multiple possible worlds.

Heidegger uncovers key elements of the work of vigilance that inform a vigilant faith. First, vigilance performs a work of gathering and revelation that parallels what *Hervorbringen* and *Herausforden* enable. Second, vigilance carefully watches over the unconcealment as it happens and reflects on the event of revelation, protecting things from the unworlding that follows other forms of revelation. Finally, vigilance keeps watch reflexively over its own activity, ensuring that the one watching watches over the way that one watches. These functions of vigilance make it central to the work of vigilant faith: mindful engagements with the world, self-scrutiny over one's comportment, and bracketing judgments about the ultimate truth of revelations.

Vigilance therefore also always already contains an active dimension through which it enters into the world as a co-responsible mode of gathering. Heidegger explicitly indicates that revelations motivated solely through preoccupations with technology or aesthetic-mindedness induce an unworlding dangerous to humans. The conflicting understanding of revelation offered through Heidegger's example of the silversmith[11] allows a vision of dwelling co-responsibly, in a vigilant freedom that gives being to things and humans. Like Dickinson's pine, each thing gives witness to multiple truths simultaneously and thereby enables our freedom to question. In a questioning vigilance, we interpret our destiny as preserving this tension in being determined by the truth of things.

The Providential Role of Vigilance

Vigilance is also *providential:* Heidegger argues that we are called to serve as guardians, preserving the beings abandoned in the default of the gods. Vigilantly dwelling between two worlds allows us to preserve things from unbeing and the unworlding that revelations cause. A vigilant guardianship requires a skeptical faith, as remaining subjectively convinced of the uncertainty of objective certainty allows me to gather two possible worlds around the things I encounter without opting for one or the other. For example, my iPod is simultaneously an anonymous technological device that plays music and a sign of an anonymity that could only be God.

The true power of vigilance manifests when related to the portion of the fourfold Heidegger allots to *die Göttlichen,* "the divinities," a term that Lawrence Hemming translates as "that aspect of beings in their being which God might '*sich ereignen,*'" bring God forth in eventuation and reveal God's self.[12] On the one hand, our work of building and dwelling preserves *die Göttlichen* in things as part of the fourfold. On the other, the relation to divinities is unique as one *awaits the divinities.* As Heidegger writes in "The Thing": "The default of God and the divinities is absence. But absence is not nothing; rather it is precisely the presence, which must first be appropriated, of the hidden fullness and wealth of what has been and what, thus gathered, is presencing, of the divine in the world of the Greeks, in prophetic Judaism, in the preaching of Jesus. This no-longer is in itself a not-yet of the veiled arrival of its inexhaustible nature" (184). Vigilance uniquely enables us to gather what is not manifest and *appropriate* it within the self. Heidegger's examples of divine presence demonstrate this: for the Greeks, gods enriched the world as they walked through and on it. In prophetic Judaism, the hidden fullness and wealth was made a function of time made relative to the truth of the coming Messiah. In the preaching of Jesus, the Kingdom of God is neither in the world, as was true for the Greeks, nor of it in a futural sense, as was true in Judaism; instead, the Kingdom of God remains *at hand,* an overflowing hidden fullness waiting to be gathered and made present (or freed) through human vigilance.

The remainder of the passage confirms the unique importance of vigilance (as opposed to *dwelling* or *building*) in receiving and gathering *die Göttlichen:*

> Since Being is never the merely precisely actual, to guard Being can never be equated with the task of a guard who protects from burglars a treasure stored in a building. Guardianship of Being is not fixated upon something existent. The existent thing, taken for itself, never contains an appeal of Being. Guardianship is vigilance, watchfulness for the has-been and coming destiny of Being, a vigilance that issues from a long and ever-renewed thoughtful deliberateness, which heeds the directive that lies in the manner in which Being makes its appeal. (184)

While dwelling and building concern themselves with existing things, vigilance spans times and persists through realms of the no-longer, the not-yet, the has-been, and the coming. If the nature of the divine is a "hidden fullness and wealth," vigilance enables a true guardianship that preserves more than what merely manifests. The task of vigilance is endless, as *die Göttlichen* are "inexhaustible." As Dickinson's pine tree illustrates, no thing in a world that awaits our vigilant regard should be overlooked.

Problematically, the appropriation of the hidden fullness of *die Göttlichen,* a fullness that has been and is coming but is *not now,* creates a new and different type of displacement. As with displacement, I am determined by a truth unique to a specific revelation and am forced to "transform . . . accustomed ties to world and to earth and henceforth to restrain all usual doing and prizing, knowing and looking."[13] This transformation is necessary in displacement, as the "ordinary things" become unbeings that do not share in the cocreation of the new world that has been revealed. Unlike displacement, the appropriation of the hidden fullness intimated here comes with all beings, universalizing our need for vigilance. The fact that vigilance requires an "ever-renewed thoughtful deliberateness" is not accidental because guardians, individually determined relative to the revelation of the hidden, are trapped between an old world filled with unbeings, which has vanished, and a new world yet to come into existence outside of the guardian's own appropriation of it.

Our vigil enables a revelation powerful enough to cause an unworlding transformation but also serves as the necessary precondition for keeping the old and the new world extant before a final unveilation. Unlike modes of building or dwelling, the ordinary modes of being in the world (which manifest in the activity of "worlding"), unlike the *techne* and *poiesis* that stand beyond them in generating unconcealings (which manifest in the activity of "unworlding"), vigilance is an open mode of comportment that hearkens to things and attends to their gatherings. In the context of a godless world where *die Göttlichen* have absconded and the theistic God is lost, humans as vigilant watchers-over-being occupy the place of Providence.

Vigilance is a word that, in English, stands between the related German verbs *wahren* (to look after, protect, safeguard) and *währen* (to last, endure), both of which relate to *bewahren* (to preserve or protect), and all of which, of course, relate to *Wahrheit,* truth, and *wahrnis,* safekeeping. Vigilance, defined by the *Oxford English Dictionary* as "The quality or character of being vigilant; watchfulness against danger or any action on the part of others; alertness or closeness of observation," uses the same connotations embedded in the particular German family of terms that Heidegger emphasizes. Vigilance emerges in the ability to watch closely: instead of merely preserving what is found, humans look out for things so that the truth offered by things—and the things themselves—arrives. Further, vigilance is a necessary element within *dwelling,* as we let things be only through watchful safeguarding. By dwelling in vigilance, humans are able to free things—and themselves—to and for each's own most possibilities.

Holding Vigil in a Godless World as a Work of Faith

Heidegger outlines the necessary function of vigilance during the default of the gods. "Godlessness" takes different forms, however, and faith works differently relative to each. Chapter 1 defined the work of faith as converting the infinite truth into finite expressions or manifestations, complementing the dynamic of faith in which the finite self merged into an infinite whole. While traditional understandings of the dynamic of faith emphasize how the infinite transforms humans into passive vessels, discussions of the work of faith have embraced human capability and creativity in installing divine truth into finite locations through the things of this world. This work differs from labor in the world, as it cannot be equated with money, possessions, or earnings: it is essentially meditative, impossible to regulate, unquantifiable.

Holding vigil, its own work of faith, inevitably involves labor whose subjective urgency is at odds with any objective results. No profit results from keeping watch over a friend whose illness has rendered her unresponsive or standing over the corpse of a dead relative. Frequently, holding vigil requires sacrificing potential objective benefits: I cannot go to work or may have to stay up late at the expense of productivity the following day.

Because this-worldly consequences are often harsh, I hold vigil only when confronted with existential crises that preclude activities beyond watching in silence. While shopping, I notice a man weeping uncontrollably, clutching a phone. The motivation to keep watch differs markedly from voyeuristic curiosity or the shocked paralysis resulting from the introduction of unabashed reality within a public space. The man's grief is overwhelming: his needs are beyond the capacity of language—especially a platitude that I might offer an acquaintance. Holding vigil requires remaining present, even though my watch provides no comfort. Sensing a need beyond reason, I keep watch.

Volition emerges as the core motivation of vigilance as the work of faith. Certain that I can say or do nothing reveals that the understanding does not prompt me—it would speak against my mute, helpless presence. Knowing neither the person nor the situation, my passion does not spur me to stand vigilantly over the one who mourns: doing so is awkward and uncomfortable. Rather than be mistaken as a gawker, my instinct is to leave. My volition battles against these impulses: I will myself to stay and watch, overcoming the protests of passion and reason. Eventually, the man dries his eyes, steels himself, and leaves. My watch, unnoticed, comes to an end: I depart. The vigil—not a work of faith here—has ended. Watching over a stranger's grief is not necessarily a work of faith, although the watchfulness that a vigilant faith demands might manifest in similar moments.

Vigilance reduces to neither faith nor skepticism, and neither faith nor skepticism is vigilance: although faith and skepticism each requires vigilance, vigilance is not exhausted in these tasks. The work of vigilance is critical to the function of a skeptical faith, for it is only with vigilance that one can continually undergo the state of faith, remaining subjectively convinced of the uncertainty of both objective certainty and subjective conviction. Vigilance enables skeptics to tarry, preserving an openness to possibilities others overlook. A skeptical faith requires vigilance, but deciding to pursue a vigilant faith requires additional willpower: vigilant faith repeats the movement of skeptical faith one step further. While reason perpetuates a skeptical faith and the objects of skeptical faith provide a passionate anchor, a vigilant faith emerges through the volition that pits the one against the other.

The problem of how vigilance provides the work of faith in a broken, godless world cannot be resolved with an encounter on a street. Unlike works of faith motivated through interactions with a symbolic truth, a vigilant faith hesitates before embracing any one truth of any revelation. One with vigilant faith both recognizes the absence of the full expression of God in the world and takes seriously ancient edicts that warn against worshipping idols. I continuously will reason to oppose my passion and vigilantly hesitate before affirming a truth. Unlike earlier models of faith, however, a vigilant faith willfully deprives itself of an infinite truth capable of concretization—the basic standard of the work of faith.

Not everyone experiences the godlessness of the world. Communities that cling to traditional symbols find their passionate desire for God met in sacred texts, natural landscapes, quiet hearts: integrated, their knowledge conceals the truth of absolute godlessness. The world offers hints and suggestions of the divine that connect believers with a God—but native skeptics who hunger for God experience the contrary truth of godlessness. When one understands God's absence as a broken connection, the revelation that reality is nothing more than what appears at its most mundane moments differs from finding a Tillichian revelation of God as abyss. The importance of holding vigil vigilantly and the need for a vigilant faith requires distinguishing different modes of potential godlessness. Doing so will disclose the unique contribution of the domain of prebelief, the pretheistic ground for faith, and vigilant faith.

The first experience of godlessness appears in common and popular discourses, a simple negation or disavowal of the Christian God. This mode of acknowledging the absence of God is as superficial as the parallel mode of knowledge arising from those who "know" God exists. The knowledge in both cases arises from the abstract level of "proofs" and argumentation. Reducing the question of God to a truth that can be answered or known implies that the god who does not exist is a mere being like other beings. The absence of this god attains the level of a historical curiosity, such as the absence of dinosaurs or dodo birds. This type of atheism, at its best, expresses godlessness as a celebration, an affirmation of human capability and freedom. At worst, such atheisms are militant and unable to see the value of faith or religion. Ultimately, although this kind of atheism is easy to trumpet, the question of this god's absence is not robust enough to merit discussion.

A second experience of godlessness arises in the situation of naïve skeptics, who lack the belief required for forging a symbolic connection with the divine. Traditional resources prove wanting, and they cannot make belief occur despite the apparent fervor that others feel. At best, naïve skeptics remain blissfully unaware of the potential of religion and untouched by the infinite passions that burn within others. At worst, naïve skeptics experience godlessness as despair, a crippling sense of inadequacy gnawing at their sense of worth. This experience of a passionate unbelief, akin to the passionate involvement one might have with a symbol, is equally impossible to communicate.

The atheism of a vigilant skeptic is not limited to "knowing" there is no God (usually a specific monotheistic entity); instead, it involves the more profound work enabled by hesitation relative to one or more revelations of God. Prolonged hesitation allows the vigilant skeptic to anticipate God's location in any given thing or event without affirming that God was revealed. The situation is analogous to the pools of nothingness that Sartre argues spring into existence when one expects to meet a friend in a café who is not present.[14] An unexpected absence differs from the friend's simply not being in places foreign to that friend. Vigilant faith projects possibilities of God into every thing I find and just as vigilantly hesitates to affirm its actuality. Choosing to constantly project the possibility of God into the world in a certain way is an expression of freedom and creativity, the most profound work of human capability. A skeptical faith opens the possibility that each place is uniquely blessed with a particular gathering of God without affirming what is revealed as God. A vigilant faith preserves the openness of these found sites—and also creates new things capable of installing the truth of God's possibilities (presence and absence) within new witnesses. The incorporation of absence distinguishes this reenchantment of a secular age from nostalgic attempts to revive traditional transcendent anchors. As Dickinson's poem demonstrates, works of vigilant faith require faith instead of knowledge: simultaneously affirming and negating appearances of God, these works preserve beings through a providential act of remaining open to the question of God in faith.

Works of vigilant faith manifest as pools of possible godness that resist simple affirmation and require volition beyond the operation of a skeptical faith. Grafting skeptical faith onto the structure of vigilance projects the skeptic's latent "faith" that truth will eventually emerge, simultaneously remaking and preserving that truth in every thing around. Continuous efforts of vigilant faith expand the spaces of possible-God, inviting the unique absence of God that calls for renewed vigil, a reminder that God remains at hand. The anonymous grief of a stranger may be a sign that discloses the God I refuse to see. Attending to that possibility, I gather the opportunity for God to manifest during my vigil—but I ensure that this possibility dwindles into the space for a godless faith by negating its objective certainty.

Vigil and the Absolute

Contextualizing a vigilant faith in terms of godless spaces does not lead to the ultimate triumph of atheism; instead, doing so reorganizes both the *arche* and telos of faith. A vigilant faith begins beyond one's relative understanding or trusting: preserved through an effort of volition in the domain of a presymbolic mediated encounter with the divine, it enables a human faith available to everyone. The universality of this faith allows all to engage in the work of preserving, questioning, and providence. The end of faith comes in the possibility of opening and preserving an indirect relationship with the absolute. In line with the "absolute faith" described by Tillich, a vigilant faith both intentionally creates constant conditions for such moments (instead of finding it through a dizzying encounter with nonbeing) and preserves and projects such moments as valuable.

Kierkegaard defined faith in terms of remaining in absolute relation with the absolute and in relative relation to what was relative. Those with skeptical faith meet this definition inasmuch as they gather those things that appear as locations of the human world and simultaneously reject a passionate relationship with any truth that might be revealed lest they maintain an absolute relationship with a merely relative good. The absolute, therefore, cannot manifest during times of revelation; at most, possibly, the absolute appears after the truth has been fully unveiled and made manifest without conflict or remainder.

Those with skeptical faith attain an indirect awareness of the God above the God of theism, which appears indirectly—a manifestation of a possible future unveilation that unfolds only with each passing moment of hesitation. Although revelations are gathered, located, and presented within each thing that those with vigilant skepticism encounter, the concrete thing simultaneously preserves and alters the nature of the absolute truth, disguising and obscuring it. A vigilant faith emerges as a repetition of a skeptical faith through the incorporation of a new axis: a vigilant faith prepares for the arrival of the absolute God. Vigilant skepticism through the constant recognition of and denial of God in things is necessary to this task, but a vigilant faith pushes past this movement of hesitation to summon and encourage manifestations of the absolute.

The absolute, like God, does not manifest in or through our direct experience; as Kant pointed out, humans lack the capacity to do more than conceive the absolute. Even Tillich's "absolute faith" is relative to the individual experience of the person, arising in contrast to the relative faiths opened by traditional symbolically mediated theisms. The volitional element, enabled by finding the point of reflexive negation (where the negation of the understanding meets the negation of passion), preserves the absolute in time. Construed as signs, especially as signs of an anonymous absolute sacred, I participate in the gathering of the world without characterizing the truth of any revelation relative to its concrete instantiation. Dickinson's awareness that God is everywhere and in all things, tempered with her awareness that this is not adequately comforting, points to a similar sense of the absolute.

To date, Jean-Yves Lacoste, in his *Experience and the Absolute*, has provided the most intriguing and comprehensive analysis of the potential of vigil relative to the absolute. Intended as a phenomenological analysis of liturgy, which he defines in a broad sense as the logic that governs encounters between humans and God, Lacoste's book provides a post-Heideggerean view of how vigil functions relative to a desire for an absolute God. For Lacoste, all divine-human relationships hinge on an uncertainty regarding God's parousical presence in spite of a conviction that this God might yet come. Defining the liturgical dimension in terms of what is excessive or not necessary to existence, Lacoste forges a connection between freedom and a skeptical faith. Put otherwise, Lacoste indicates that willing what I call a skeptical or vigilant faith, which grasps after a complex lifestyle indifferent to one's basic needs, is an act of freedom that removes the vigilant skeptic from the basic logic of mundane existence.

Vigil manifests through Lacoste's opposition of the liturgical (which locates the human relative to the absolute) and the necessary (which locates humans relative to earthly or worldly logics). His phenomenological analysis merits summarization, as he provides three useful ways of distinguishing vigil. First, based on his explanation of liturgy, he holds that vigil opposes what is merely necessary. This distinguishes vigil from staying awake out of hunger or fear. Arguing that vigils are dictated by a logic of "inoperativity," Lacoste distinguishes the vigil from work and other obligations— including ethics. Thus the daytime work of ethics is "necessary," and the nighttime inoperativity of prayer is "surplus," if one assumes the relative, human work of ethics has already been accomplished. Prayer, superfluous, unfolds as prayer, praise, and worship; these enable us to relate absolutely to the absolute in times of vigil (78–81).

Second, Lacoste contrasts vigil with revelry. Both vigil and revelry occur at night, free activities chosen beyond the requirements of work or existence. The similarity ends with the question of freedom and hours, however, as Lacoste uses the question of ethics to differentiate the two. A reveler, who holds vigil in a carefree way, affirms existence in a spirit of life; in contrast, a vigilant vigil affirms existence *in addition* to life. Put otherwise, a vigilant vigil requires that one have already met one's relative, ethical obligations and that the vigil operates in a repetition of care beyond obligation (79).

Finally, Lacoste discusses liturgical night. Enveloped within the liturgical night, humans are distant both from the "earth" that encompasses the cares and obligations of the widest community and from the "eschaton," or the ultimate end in the form of the unveilation of the absolute. Lacoste describes the liturgical night in this way: "If it had to close up on itself, the present of the liturgical night would actually be atheistic. Having yet to experience the definitive reign of God and no longer having experience of the earth and of the sacred immanent in it, we can do nothing but make ourselves present to the 'world' and in the 'world,' man lives without God" (147). Holding a vigilant vigil, one maintains the self in the gap between the world of the relative and the world of the absolute. Bereft of an unveiled language capable of uttering the absolute truth (or full presence of God), and lacking the sacred that manifests in the closed worlds offered by a worldly language, the sole experience left for the vigilant skeptic is a liturgical night. Examples of this godless night appear in moments of infinite longing, such as Dickinson's seeking revelations of the God that everybody knows.[15] A vigilant vigil stands between the world continually disclosed in revelations (through signs of the absolute) and the world of relative goods and cares, keeping watch over both, simultaneously. Lacoste's contrast of the lost sacred earth (hierophantic manifestations of the divine) and the *eschaton* (full unveilation) leaves humans in the anonymous dark spaces of a broken twenty-first century. Instead of despairing over the absence of God, however, a vigilant faith hesitates before claiming as God the presence of the anonymous that the goods of mass production indicate.

Lacoste's framework reveals the importance of skeptical and vigilant faiths. A skeptical faith, focused on the construction and maintenance of equipollent perspectives, allows humans to continue in the ongoing task of gathering two distinct worlds (that of *world* and *eschaton*, in Lacoste's lexicon). Gathered near and held in tension, humans live isolated from the divine as it manifests in both the relative and the absolute worlds. A vigilant faith adds to this an intentional and volitional orientation to the absolute, an imminent future that remains at hand where the *eschaton* as *eschaton* unveils in its transformative truth. Beyond trusting in either the untimely presence of the *eschaton* or the distractions of this world, beyond understanding the inadequacies of the appearances of each world, a volitional faith remains oriented to the time when the worlds merge. The absolute manifests in the unseen space in the gap between the two worlds that a vigilant faith embraces at arm's length.

6 Vigilance as the Work of Faith

The act of faith demanded in bearing witness exceeds, through its
structure, all intuition and all proof, all knowledge. . . . Even the slightest
testimony concerning the most plausible, ordinary or everyday thing
cannot do otherwise: it must still appeal to faith as would a miracle.
It offers itself like the miracle itself in a space that leaves no room for
disenchantment.

—JACQUES DERRIDA, "Faith and Knowledge"

A vigilant vigil straddles the shared world of calculating efficiency
and the approaching world of the *eschaton,* and I undertake it as an end in
itself. Maintaining a skeptical orientation, a vigilant faith holds both worlds
in tension as counter-appearances of a "truth," persisting in a third world
(relating to the nonsymbolically mediated absolute) produced through the
work of vigilant faith.

This chapter explores how a vigilant vigil concretizes itself in ways more
permanent than watching—in works of creativity, construction, and cultivation that, like Dickinson's poems, promote a doubled vision for others who dwell in only one world. Interpretations that reduce this world to
one truth lead to struggle and misery, whether these interpretations are
polarized political parties within a country or rival views of the good that
separate cultures. By embracing two contrary perspectives and persisting
in unknowing, a vigilant vigil defies the mind-set of reduction that permits
objective certainty and perpetuates factionalism.

To explore how vigilance as a work of faith surpasses keeping watch, I
disclose how vigilance works as a "spiritual practice" in spite of its skeptical
foundation. I begin by analyzing a parable, revealing how vigilant faith op-

erates within traditional religious texts and showing the value of returning to traditional religions even without desiring symbolic mediation. I then supply a brief history of the works of faith before examining the possibility of performing prayer and worship in a godless world. I conclude by examining the virtues of a vigilant faith: these virtues—patience, hospitality, and re-creation—go beyond a skeptical faith in allowing vigilant skeptics to recreate an unknown revelation. These activities exceed skeptical faith without violating skepticism: a type of repetition, the movement forward is constructed around and contextualized within a skeptic's specific uncertainty, permitting the passion of skepticism to manifest its orientation to a better future (that may or may not come).

"Do Not Know the Day or the Hour"

> At that time the kingdom of heaven will be like ten virgins who took their lamps and went out to meet the bridegroom. Five of them were foolish and five were wise. The foolish ones took their lamps but did not take any oil with them. The wise, however, took oil in jars along with their lamps. The bridegroom was a long time in coming, and they all became drowsy and fell asleep. At midnight the cry rang out: "Here's the bridegroom! Come out to meet him!" Then all the virgins woke up and trimmed their lamps. The foolish ones said to the wise, "Give us some of your oil; our lamps are going out." "No," they replied, "there may not be enough for both us and you. Instead, go to those who sell oil and buy some for yourselves." But while they were on their way to buy the oil, the bridegroom arrived. The virgins who were ready went in with him to the wedding banquet. And the door was shut. Later, the others also came. "Sir! Sir!" they said. "Open the door for us!" But he replied, "I tell you the truth, I don't know you." Therefore keep watch, for you do not know the day or the hour. (Matt. 25:1–13)

In the parable, Jesus divides the original group of ten virgins who share the same goal—to meet the bridegroom—into two equal groups: the *phronimoi* (prudent, wise, shrewd) and the *morai* (foolish, and the common contrast to the "wise" person in wisdom literature). Unlike the *morai*, the *phronimoi* had the foresight to bring not only a lamp but oil in a jar. When the bridegroom arrives, the foolish virgins ask the wise to share their oil, and the prudent refuse, calculating that there might not be enough to go around—sensibly acting in their own self-interest. The foolish virgins leave for the marketplace where, absent, they miss the bridegroom's arrival. The shrewd virgins attend the banquet; the bridegroom does not recognize the foolish virgins, who missed his initial arrival. The bridegroom's declaration that he does not know the foolish ones is either descriptive (he assumes that all his friends had greeted him, and therefore outsiders are strangers) or performative (in which case, enraged, he cannot see the foolish virgins as the friends he thought they were). The narrator frames the bridegroom as either naïve or merciless.

The import of the parable—its message—is to "keep watch" because "you do not know the day or the hour." This invokes the notion of "vigilance," appropriate because the virgins are forced to keep watch until midnight, long past the hours when the logic of work demands productivity. If watching for the bridegroom united the virgins, then the sensible virgins— prepared—should be commended for *keeping* watch. The notion of "keeping" watch implies preparation for ensuring the perpetuation of the vigil. Because it is a time of vigil, one can perhaps forgive—if not admire—the prudent virgins for choosing to keep their oil, ensuring that at least some might attend the bridegroom. Because they did not know if there would be enough oil for all, because they were not prepared to aid those less prepared, they prioritized the actual good of allowing some (themselves) to meet the bridegroom over a good that would risk the bridegroom's being missed. They kept watch in this way, and such, explains Matthew, is the Kingdom of Heaven.

Problematically, this interpretation of the parable does not recognize that these virgins were *not* vigilant. Lacking patience, the virgins—shrewd and foolish alike—are weary, sleeping, not keeping watch: the delights of dreams distract from the boredom that accompanies a vigil. Instead of keeping watch over the needy with an uncalculating hospitality, the sensible virgins send the foolish virgins away. In addition to a seeming lack of ethics, the self-interested (cunning) virgins demonstrate a persistence of the self, determining their superiority relative to their fellow sleepers. Nothing is re-created: the foolish do not sustain their lamps, the "intelligent" virgins lack faith to see enough oil for all. The conclusions are troubling: the wise virgins are no more vigilant than the foolish ones. Additionally, the Kingdom of Heaven—where a merciless bridegroom rewards calculations that sacrifice fellow humans—is undesirable. Such internal problems are common in parables, a genre typified by confusion and an ability to prompt critical reflection.

John Caputo resolves the parable's internal tension, arguing that the Kingdom of Heaven, whose economical system of "debt and sacrifice" seems in line with this world, is an *inferior* interpretation of the absolute and therefore at odds with a Kingdom of God structured around "giving and forgiving." Caputo explains that the most authentic sayings of Jesus claim the Kingdom of God is "at hand," now, not delayed until after death. Faith is linked "not with building credit but with trust," and the Kingdom of God roots itself in a regard for the outcast and overlooked in society: "The kingdom is not like a long-term bond, not a wise form of estate planning for a vault of heavenly virtues. The kingdom is the call of the other, and the kingdom is here and now" (235). The "wise" virgins *are* wise—given the perspective of the worldly logic that a calculating Kingdom of Heaven reflects and sublates. A God that rewards "wise" virgins for their prudence commands a kingdom that translates individual faith into an economic register.

The parable, however, does not end with a call to prudence or sensibility; instead, it summons the reader to *vigilance* in offering the imperative to "keep watch." Because the virgins—wise and foolish alike—failed to keep watch, I read vigilantly to find an example of keeping watch in the text. I discover it in verse 6: "At midnight the cry rang out: 'Here's the bridegroom! Come out to meet him!'" While the virgins slumbered (both those with and those lacking oil), at least one person, still awake at midnight, was able to alert others. The narrator focuses my attention on the event of the outcry, which awakens the virgins and reveals the bridegroom, but discloses nothing about the source of the cry. I know only that this one was awake, able to shout.

Interrogating the origin of this work, the outcry, exclusively reveals a hint of both vigilance and the Kingdom of God (which, as Caputo notes, resists the economics of the Kingdom of Heaven). The absence of "agency" or "self" as a source of work is intentional: the vigilant one, who waited in faith, has already gone through the process of self-excavation that faith demands. As such, there is no "self" able to "do" anything—only the voice manifests. The selfless voice thereby becomes an alternative to the prudent virgins, who were unwilling to share their oil—perhaps beset by doubts that the remaining oil would be enough for all.

With this interpretation in mind, the parable may be reread in a way that restores its internal tension. The parable is, in truth, far from being a celebration of the worldly logic of "prudence" or "sensibility," in which a merciless bridegroom rewards the cunning of wise virgins at the expense of the foolish. The final admonition to keep watch directs the vigilant reader back to the one who *does* keep watch, revealing a good beyond the logic of prudence, a Kingdom of God that the Kingdom of Heaven requires. Second, this figure shows that the bridegroom's acceptance of the "wise" was an act of mercy in itself, not a reward for a good or faithful servant. The inability to recognize the foolish virgins, the impious ones who were not steadfast in their commitment to the watch, was not a slight on the bridegroom's part but an honest assessment of the situation—the bridegroom spoke "in truth."

This parable confirms that the nonsymbolically mediated projections of a work of faith exist within the traditional text of the Christian canon—in other words, the work of vigilance applies to the sphere of Christian practice. The parable also reveals how the life of faith, developed on atheistic or agnostic grounds, translates into one particular religious tradition. If, as Tillich indicated, a discussion of faith cannot actually or legitimately take place absent some concrete religious framework, then the parable reveals how a vigilant faith both exists within and might enhance an understanding of one traditional religion.

The parable exemplifies how to hold vigil vigilantly, although more analysis is needed. If we assume that the source of the cry was not a messenger sent ahead to prepare the way, the vigilant voice—especially in contrast to the ten virgins—manifested a great deal of patience. Instead of feeling the need to shop or sleep, the nameless voice persisted in vigilantly remaining focused on a task that exceeded reasonable boundaries. The vigilant voice also embraced the virtue of hospitality: the purpose of announcing the bridegroom in a loud way was to ensure the bridegroom received a proper welcome. The choice to stir the sleeping virgins was a work of charity, one that worked toward the mutual benefit of both the virgins and the bridegroom. Finally, it is telling that the voice precedes the arrival of the bridegroom by a significant portion of time. The narrator allows the vigilant reader to understand that the cry announces the bridegroom before the bridegroom is seen. Understanding the voice as articulating and concretizing the desired reality reveals the work of vigilance in re-creating the world. In turn, re-creation discloses how maintaining a vigilant faith maximizes possibilities.

These qualities—patience, hospitality, and re-creation—are the works of vigilance that exceed the boundaries of a skeptical faith. Without moving beyond skepticism, the practice of skeptical faith risks inducing a sense of futility: humans are driven to put belief into practice. The accompanying despair would likely hasten the collapse of faith into a resigned movement to knowing. A lack of patience resembles the prudent virgins, unwilling to trust that the extant level of oil will suffice. One can practice a skeptical faith selfishly—like the wise virgins, perhaps—who, listening to doubts about adequate oil, eliminate the opportunity for hospitality in the name of a calculated self-preservation. It is also possible to maintain a skeptical faith without re-creation—like the other unnamed watchers in the background of the story, unwilling to speak forth a vision of the bridegroom's appearance. Through patience, hospitality, and re-creation, one with vigilant faith surpasses the limits of skepticism in concretizing the faith that a truth will be unveiled—even without a symbolic mediator.

A Brief History of the Works of Faith Prompted by Trusting

The work of faith complements faith's dynamic process: it requires the re-creation of the finite based on the revelation of an infinite truth. The work of faith produces an objectively certain correlate to that about which one remains subjectively convinced. The completion of the work of faith allows the full unveilation of the truth, when faith's role appropriately gives way to knowledge. In mythic-religious terms, this betokens the arrival of the Kingdom of God on earth. Recognizing the need for a subjective conviction that exists apart from objective certainty, but also the human need to bring about the changes one desires, the Christian scriptures offer different stances regarding the role of faith and work. Paul writes that we are saved by grace and through faith—and not by works—while James contends that faith without works is dead. Over the centuries theologians have wrestled with how to achieve the balance between these two perspectives.

In a faith grounded primarily in trusting, centered on God as an object, Martin Luther outlines the most vital works of faith. Despite his famous disdain for including "works" as part of faith, Luther acknowledged the importance of some work faith accomplishes in human lives. Each work of faith that Luther explores remains grounded on the principle that believers translate a higher spiritual work of faith into the lower, physical world, causing the earthly world to be re-created as a reflection of the Kingdom of Heaven. In *Concerning Christian Liberty*, Luther describes the work of liberation that occurs when faith undermines merely earthly restrictions and hierarchies to make the believer "a perfectly free lord of all, subject to none."[1] This freedom *from* restriction enables the second work of faith—the freedom *to* worship in a wholly self-sacrificial way that allows the physical self to act in accordance with a spiritual God. Luther writes, "In [worship] the soul shows itself prepared to do His whole will; in doing this it hallows His name, and gives itself up to be dealt with as it may please God."

The third work of faith, self-discipline, internalizes the process as individuals dematerialize faith in a translation of matter into spirit. Luther writes that a believer motivated by a disinterested love of God should "easily instruct himself in what measure, and with what distinctions, he ought to chasten his own body. He will fast, watch, and labour, just as much as he sees to suffice for keeping down the wantonness and concupiscence of the body." The incorporation of physical disciplines at the behest of a spiritual principle that urges the practices of fasting and watchfulness in order to "keep down" bodily desires literally manifests the transformative power of faith within and as the body itself.

The final work of faith involves the creation of a community based on love for the neighbor; just as the believer is "subject to none," so also ought the Christian to be "servant to all." Luther indicates that Christians should live "in Christ, and in his neighbor, or else is no Christian; in Christ by faith, in his neighbor by love." A Christian's joint position in the spiritual and material allows him or her to serve as a transformative bridge. Luther adds, later, "And as our heavenly Father has freely helped us in Christ, so ought we freely to help our neighbor by our body and works, and each should become to other a sort of Christ, so that we may be mutually Christs, and that the same Christ may be in all of us; that is, that we may be truly Christians." This defines the work of faith for Luther, made in the movement to God and back to the world again—the first movement grants freedom, the second demands servitude. The primary order of works define what it means to have faith, and the secondary order thus constitutes that which is seen as useful to living a Christlike existence.

Combined, these works of faith replace external delineations of community with an internal and invisible community, where all are Christ to each other in a universal priesthood. Luther reasons that this happens because all souls unite with Christ, which results in our sharing the joint status of "free lord" and "dutiful servant." As humans are allowed to be "brethren" and "co-heirs" with Christ, so also are they allowed to "to pray for one another, and to do all things which we see done and figured in the visible and corporeal office of priesthood," which makes priestly activities and habits a requirement of all believers. With this, Luther stresses a radical equalization of humans among each other, while simultaneously transforming the work of priests from an external (visible) office to an internal (invisible) one. Through the freedom from the law and the union to Christ, faith works to create a voluntary community of equalized believers in which nobody has power or authority over another, re-creating the Kingdom of God on earth.

In this paradigm of faith, the self performs the work of faith—righteousness—through a union of a finite self with an infinite God manifest through works of love intended to help the finite community that surrounds the individual. Problematically, this creates a static model in which the Spirit of God gives glory to Godself through the permission of the human being. Finite elements—concrete reality, fleshly materiality—are illusory or worthless. Even Luther's works of love are for "other Christs" in the community of co-heirs. The second model of faith offers a corrective in extending works of faith to what seems apart from God: in the post-Kantian model, I perform the work of faith—worship—through the union of my self with itself (blending its poles of the finite and infinite), which enables me to perform concrete acts formed and informed by love. The existential act of faith reaches from the abstract into the concrete, empowered by the presence of the infinite: both Kierkegaard and Tillich emphasize the value of finite and concrete elements of the work of faith. Attending to finite existence affirms being despite nonbeing: the human—merging finite and infinite elements—participates in this cosmic work.

If the first work of faith in the Kantian paradigm involves the unification of the self with the self, the second work of faith comes through existential individualization, as the finite human moves into an absolute relation with a nonfinite absolute. Kierkegaard develops this point in *Fear and Trembling*, as individualization becomes the process by which the individual is able to develop an absolute relation with the absolute, one no longer mediated by the universal. Kierkegaard signifies absolute individualization by defining faith as the "teleological suspension of the ethical" or "the paradox . . . that the single individual as the single individual is higher than the universal and as the single individual stands in an absolute relation to the absolute."[2] One additional consequence of becoming individuated by an absence of the universal is a loss of language: Kierkegaard emphasizes Abraham's silence for this reason.

The third work of faith involves passivity, revealed through Anti-Climacus's describing the self in faith as resting transparently in the power that established it. This work replicates the process of finding the finite through the infinite—differing with respect to the object. Kierkegaard makes it clear that the work of faith leads to concretization and finitization as an end in itself. "To become oneself is to become concrete . . . the progress of the becoming must be an infinite moving away from itself in the infinitizing of the self, and an infinite coming back to itself in the finitizing process. But if the self does not become itself, it is in despair, whether it knows it or not."[3] The work of becoming a self completes and refines the process of individualization begun in the first work of faith.

The next work of faith in this domain involves faith's self-constitution in terms of an infinite passion, held as a contradiction against objective uncertainty and the boundaries of the finite. Faith is thus defined as a passion that, with the terms "infinite passion" and "inwardness," allows for the absolute relation to the absolute. Climacus argues in his *Concluding Unscientific Postscript* that "true inwardness does not demand any sign at all in externals" and that "it does not want to disturb the finite, but neither does it want to mediate. In the midst of the finite and finitude's multiple occasions for the existing person to forget the absolute distinction, it only wants to be the absolute inwardness for him" such that "the maximum of the task is to be able simultaneously to relate oneself absolutely to the absolute *telos* and relatively to the relative ends, or at all times to have the absolute *telos* with oneself."[4] Neglecting externals and maintaining a focus on the concrete self as the absolute telos enables us to relate absolutely to the absolute—and only thereby can one relate relatively to relative ends.

The emphasis on inwardness leads to a final work of faith, the preservation of hiddenness, which serves as an existential correlate to Luther's emphasis on the equality of all believers. Kierkegaard features hiddenness as a theme throughout most of his pseudonymous literature: for example, understanding the centrality of hiddenness to faith means that Johannes de Silentio is unable to find a Knight of Faith but also cannot deny that each person he sees may be one. In the *Postscript*, Johannes Climacus finds that hiding the infinite within the finite is a key element of the *paradoxical-religious* Religiousness B that causes the individual, in time, to relate to the eternal in time. Religiousness B provides the ultimate repetition of the movement from the infinite to the finite as it both makes the infinite movement to grasp the hidden immanence of the eternal and also the infinite movement back seeing that the eternal is omnipresent, for "in immanence God is neither a something, but everything, and is infinitely everything, nor outside the individual, because the upbuilding consists in his being within the individual" (561). With Religiousness B, the individual knowingly sees that God is within the self in the same way that God is outside of the self. Like the Knight of Faith, the hiddenness of God manifests in a kenotic movement that allows the inwardness to hide so completely that it becomes external. Anti-Climacus discloses the relevance of hiddenness as an act of imitating Christ, also necessarily incognito, representing the unknowability of God in a knowable form.

The hiddenness of faith ultimately allows the faithful individual to reclaim the finite world; this is, perhaps, the strongest work of faith as it translates the infinite passion into a finite world. Kierkegaard's writing is full of a desire for the faithful to fully enjoy the pleasures of the finite world as an end in itself. Abraham gains the finite world as an intact whole, and the Knight of Faith belongs to the world even more than the bourgeois philistine (whom the Knight of Faith otherwise resembles). In *Fear and Trembling,* De Silentio offers, "Nothing is detectable of that distant and aristocratic nature by which one recognizes the knight of the infinite. He finds pleasure in everything, takes part in everything, and every time one sees him participating in something particular, he does it with an assiduousness that marks the worldly man who is attached to such things" (39). Johannes Climacus echoes this notion of taking pleasure in the *Concluding Unscientific Postscript.* Writing against the notion of monasticism (in which one attempts to flee the finite world), he writes: "The humblest expression for the relationship with God is to acknowledge one's humanness, and it is human to enjoy oneself" (493). Learning to grasp the pleasures of the finite world, re-creating, reveals one's relation with the infinite. Kierkegaard thus expands the relation of the infinite to the finite by attending to a broader sense of the finite world than Luther had done. Tillich also depicts faith as ending with the finite world; however, in a world stained and scarred by evil, he posits responsibilities for faith beyond enjoyment—one must use the power of faith and love to defend goods for others. Ultimately, what differentiates the second paradigm of works from the first is its basic orientation. While the works in the first model express one's unity with God, the works in the second model move out from the self and into an improvement of the world surrounding the self. Rather than remaining content with storing up treasures in heaven, the orientation of faith works to construct the Kingdom of God on earth.

The history of works of faith frames what seems most necessary to works of faith. Understanding this history as a type of heuristic, one can look to the pre-Kantian model as identifying *which* activities are works of faith. The following formula will suffice: *works of faith are free acts of charity and creativity that reorient the finite world in terms of a revealed, infinite truth.* The emphasis provided by Tillich and Kierkegaard both deepens the understanding of *how* one should perform an act of faith and expands the sphere in which humans undertake acts of faith. The summarized formula relating to the post-Kantian understanding of faith is as follows: *acts of faith are undertaken by a self who relates absolutely to the absolute and relatively to relative ends so as to belong entirely to the world.* Although the incorporation of "relative ends" that allow the individual to belong entirely to the world and find pleasure within it might contradict the earlier ascetic model, it is a contradiction consistent with the hiddenness of faith belonging to the Christian revelation of God in the lowly figure of Jesus. A successful explanation of vigilant faith as the work of a skeptical faith must be able to account for these two prior understandings of works in addition to expanding the work of faith to motivate even those who are unable to hold to a coherent understanding of what "world" might involve.

The movement from Luther to Kierkegaard and Tillich indicates the increasing importance of allowing works of faith to focus on the present. On an ethical level, works of faith move from a community of undifferentiated believers to a community in which the truly faithful indistinguishably resemble everyone else. Relative to the parable, this gestures to the fact that any member of the community may have been the voice who spoke. Additionally, the finite goods of the world—ours to protect, preserve, and enjoy—are seen as goods in themselves. Understanding the finite world as filled with sites where God might manifest, a vigilant faith expands beyond goods to remain watchful even over that which is commonly derided or ignored.

The Worship and Prayer of a Vigilant Faith

Lacoste's phenomenological terms clarify the distinction between a vigilant skepticism and a vigilant faith and thus also testify to the unique work of faith vigilance enables. While vigilance clearly is a type of work, it has not yet been presented as a work *of* faith. In order to counter the charges of inertia that long attached to skepticism and also articulate how a vigilant faith manifests as a positive movement between the equipollent options of a skeptical vigilance, I argue how vigilant faith worships an absolute, unpresentable god, and how a vigilant faith transforms the world without violating its skeptical foundation.

Before understanding the particular kind of worship vigilant faith permits, it is first necessary to recall that language systems exclusively manifest through worlds known to symbolically mediated communities. This is the truth presented both in Heidegger's awareness of a "projective sketch" that serves as the backbone of a localized poetic world (which ranges in size from the idioms of an individual household to the common parlance of a nation) and also in Kierkegaard's recognition of the importance of Abraham's silence (having received the revelation of a truth that lacked a symbolic anchor in this world, Abraham lacked language to say it). The truth of revelations lingers more in the unsaid than the uttered. Awareness of the poverty of the shared world's languages occurs when one experiences a passionate revelation of the infinite. Thus Christianity, a faith based in trusting, depends on a Holy Spirit who intercedes for the faithful in prayer and worship, a Spirit who breathes the words that I cannot utter in a communication to Godself. Philosophers also connect the failure of language relative to faith: faith pushes against the limits of language and donates what we intuit without complete understanding. Kierkegaard defines this donation as the gift of the paradox. One worships with words only when a community migrates to a symbolically mediated world that renders a symbolic truth as knowable within its closed or localized center; departing from Kant, I argue that language generates pools of objective certainty relative to an idiomatic collective. The universal tongue of a faithful worship, which desires the God beyond the God of theism provided by the failure of understanding and trusting, necessarily slumbers with words unspoken.

A vigilant faith seizes on this unavoidable silence as an opportunity, prizing it as a good instead of despairing over its inadequacies. One vigilantly reserves one's silences as a mode of addressing the absolute God in a prayer characterized by a humility that goes beyond merely not uttering God's name. A vigilant silence is as filled with meaning as idle talk is void of it. Endowing a time with this silence, opposed to the flurry of words that often fill our interactions, is a performance that localizes a gathering of what remains necessarily unspoken. Instead of exercising the human capacity for naming, one with vigilant faith operates like a thing, in a silent witnessing that testifies to letting be.

Jean-Luc Nancy's *Dis-Enclosure: The Deconstruction of Christianity,* which examines the remains of Christianity after appropriating the critiques of atheism, focuses in part on the potential of a prayer that does not require a symbolically mediated God. Nancy starts with a vulgar, ordinary sense of prayer, perhaps more common in the French, appearing when one says, "I pray of you." Analogous to Scharlemann's depiction of trusting others, Nancy argues that the incorporation of language in such requests incorporates a third party, meaning the vulgar work of prayer has a twofold relationship with the letting be of openness. On the one hand, prayer allows this third to remain distanced, neither signifying nor conceiving it. On the other hand, the prayer nonetheless addresses the letting be that constitutes the other party; in Nancy's language, the prayer "*adores* this letting be" (135–36) as it either invokes or evokes it. If the "visual" act of vigilance, the passive mode of hearkening to the testimony of things, could be understood as "letting be," then the act of prayer is a way of relating reverently and reflexively toward this primary activity. The unspoken words remain unsaid and thereby greet the unsayable within the horizon of language.

Nancy describes how demythologized prayer compares to regular prayer, justifying how a vigilant silence expresses an absolute act of worship. First, Nancy argues that a demythologized prayer lacks the supplication common in regular prayers. Free from requiring results, demythologized prayer allows the person praying to experience the effect of the prayer in the act of praying. Nancy refers to this as the act of passing to the outside, through the other, in a transcendence that lacks verticality. Second, like all prayer, demythologized prayer maintains a difference from other modes of discourse through ritualized physical markers. Nancy characterizes the ritual of demythologized prayer as incorporating an openness to what is outside, including the way one holds one's body or inflects one's voice. Excepting intonation, a vigilant silence as an act of adoration or worship might include this same practice of an open posture or ritualized experience.

The final attribute of a demythologized prayer allows it to be a work of vigilant faith consistent with its skeptical roots. Nancy argues not only that prayers should not focus on answers but also that prayers should never end. He therefore urges his readers to pray for a lack of resolution, which remains an ingredient of an attitude of skeptical faith. This type of prayer for a lack of closure becomes a prayer to remain vigilant, to extend the time of one's vigil. Nancy writes,

> One thing, ultimately, is indubitable: we must concern ourselves with this emptied remnant of prayer, remain faithful to this obligation. For us it has the force of a categorical imperative, for nothing today is more important than this: to empty and let be emptied out all prayers that negotiate a sense, an issue, or a repatriation of the real within the narrow confines of our faded humanisms and clenched religiosities, in order that we may merely open speech once again to its most proper possibility of address, which also makes up all its sense and all its truth. (138)

A vigilant faith prays without concern that it communicate meaningfully with a larger world, seizing on the potential that silence offers for indirect worship. Knowing neither entity nor telos as object, and in opposition to the philosophies and religions that often incorporate the form of decayed words for the sake of tradition, a demythologized prayer enables those with vigilant faith to worship. In our silences, we worship the absolute we refuse to find. In our daily conversation, we speak in adoration, vigilantly attending to the sound our words make and to the unspeakable at the depth of each utterance.

The Virtues of Vigilant Faith

Avoiding the term "work," Luther used "virtue," to reference the quality that defines how faith interacts with the life of the faithful. Following Luther, I argue that vigilant faith comes with three virtues that define when faith and vigilance reach their highest point in relation with the other. These virtues—patience, hospitality, and re-creation—emerged in the parable of the wise and foolish virgins as important spiritual practices. Relating to the absolute in vigilant faith occurs through these virtues. Each enables me to overcome an element of the world that hinders my relating absolutely to the absolute while conforming to the necessary relative ends that come with the world.

The production of godless spaces, divine remnants akin to Sartre's pools of nothingness that we project in our anticipation, represents the background for how one's vigil constitutes a work of faith although, in faith, one avoids becoming objectively certain about the truth of any one given revelation of the infinite. Demythologized prayer outlines how humans can worship without a symbolically mediated sense of the divine and shows the importance of vigilance in maintaining this habit of praying. Problematically, however, producing godlessness and maintaining a vigilant silence are acts that fall short of the standard of a concretization of the infinite truth that the historical discussion of works of faith would lead us to expect. Completing the positive axis of a vigilant faith, I describe the virtues of a vigilant faith from abstract work to concrete task, focusing first on patience, then hospitality, and finally re-creation.

The first virtue of a vigilant faith is patience, which overcomes the threat of boredom and indirectly affirms a nonworldly temporality. The need for patience arises initially because of the duration of time that falls between a revelation and its unveilation. Humans generally avoid patience, defaulting into other behaviors during times of anticipation. The first alternative is waiting, but when we merely wait for something, we tend to become like objects (instead of the more vibrant things). We mark time idly, shutting down internally, filling space with our bodies in a way undifferentiated from the chairs and others in them. A second alternative is restlessness: the restless person does not submit to objectification but moves frenetically, defying the future to arrive. Problematically, of course, restless people have no outlet for their energy: the uncertain arrival of the anticipated event may be near enough that another project would be interrupted at any moment, and they must stay nearby. Therefore, the restless pace.

Patience works internally rather than externally and thus resembles waiting from external perspectives. The work of patience maintains a vigil in the gap between world and *eschaton* within the space of earth, without knowing when the need for patience will end. Patience feeds on the self-sufficiency of faith; Nancy describes faith as having an *"adhesion to itself of an aim without other"* to the extent that "faith is pure intentionality" (152). The life of faith (in general) requires patience, as there is no other end toward which this work would seem to be working. While other activities of thinking—trusting or understanding—engage in modes of production (sacrificial actions, conclusions), the intentionality of a vigilant faith patiently and quietly attends to itself.

Because those undergoing a vigilant faith do nothing, however, it is possible—and tempting—to experience the time between the shared cultural world and the world of the *eschaton* as boredom. Boredom occurs as one interprets the time as wasted or unprofitably used: it overleaps the quiet potential of patience and exchanges the virtue for more interesting distractions. Even as Lacoste identifies the possibility that the boredom felt before God is part of nocturnal experience, he also admits that one can "attempt to overcome boredom by intensifying its vigil" and believing that "the night is perhaps at its end and God will perhaps bring it to a close soon" (149). Because a sustained and endured nonproductivity runs counter to the logic of this world, the virtue of a patience that overcomes the boredom that negatively adheres to this mind-set is its ability to overcome the impoverished logic of the relative world in favor of an absolute world. This virtue of vigilant faith most closely corresponds to the form of reason, as one must critically think to reject alternatives; patience, in this sense, can be a universal form and explained to others.

The second virtue of a vigilant faith is hospitality, which enables those with vigilant faith to manifest a love for the neighbor while overcoming the worldly economic logic of zero-sum appropriation and gain. Unlike ethics, which declares a duty to aid the other in need, hospitality is an absolute standard: one offers hospitality to all, whether or not it is needed. This quality allows Lacoste to understand hospitality as being appropriable by the absolute,[5] allowing one to host the absolute in anonymous forms—feeding, clothing, or visiting others without knowing that it was the absolute. Absent an ethical mandate, hospitality is not a responsibility; its superfluous generosity allows it to be a virtue of vigilant faith.

Although hospitality is a virtue of vigilant faith, it is also a work of faith more broadly construed. Jean-Luc Nancy, in his analysis of the book of James, interprets the work of faith as the *"poisesi-praxis* of *pistis,"* which "presents itself in the letter under three aspects: the love of the neighbor, the discrediting of wealth, and the truthful and decided word." He then argues that hospitality, as a virtue, comprises all of these: it loves the neighbor in offering what goes beyond ethics; its psychology of giving reveals a disdain for worldly economics; its word of welcome makes good on what it pledges (55). True hospitality is not limited to humans: we practice hospitality toward animals, plants, and natural goods by acknowledging the integrity of life,[6] preserving an environment that maximizes the universal possibility of the flourishing.

In an extreme that perhaps only Derrida could deconstruct, hospitality is that which goes beyond either host or guest, inasmuch as the French *hôte* suggests both terms—and therefore neither.[7] Hospitality is related to patience because patience is required for hospitality (as one awaits the opportunity to be hospitable, not knowing how long this wait must be endured), and, as hospitality, this type of patience exceeds ethics. This virtue of faith manifests the form of passion: hospitality is an anticipation that demands the self as a whole self, giving and accepting the occasion of hospitality as it manifests in a moment-by-moment and often physical manner.

The third virtue of a vigilant faith is re-creation, which overcomes moral fatalism and manifests in a creative play with the finite world. This creative engagement allows us to relate to a world uncontaminated by evil or fallenness: the finite interaction with finitude allows us to configure the world in light of the revealed truth. This virtue of faith assumes that faith—far from "weak knowledge"—has a potency in its re-creative abilities. As Nancy puts it (in reference to Jean-Luc Marion), it is the possibility that faith exists as a "saturated phenomenon," or even, "perhaps, saturation itself" (153). Put otherwise, the creativity of faith allows Nancy to see faith as "the birthplace or the creative event," claiming "'God' himself may be the fruit of faith, which at the same time depends only on his grace (that is, exempts itself from necessity and obligation)" (26).

In part, this re-creative dimension of faith reveals how the work of vigilant faith can move beyond the pools of godlessness created through an anticipation for revelation that one refuses steadfastly to affirm as absolute. These pools gather, bestow, and donate a divine depth to the world that the individual hesitates before affirming absolutely. Beyond this work (which remains a work of skepticism), the notion of re-creation resembles Kierke-gaard's image of the joyful and playful embrace of the finite world as a good in its own right. Language cannot be fashioned in a way that captures and reflects the infinite truth that has been revealed without entering into a symbolic format that constitutes knowledge; however, we can create new things that provoke an unwillingness to be ready to hand, a moment of suspicion or hesitation, a glorious mystery that enables others to see the potential of faith outside the limits of reason alone.

Put otherwise, in acts of creation (art, goods, friendships), our making should intentionally incorporate our willingness to remake *this* world into one conducive to the time between worlds. Our homes, spaces of hospital-ity, should allow us to dwell patiently in active opposition to the Enframed frenzy that fills houses with goods of distraction. Remaining vigilantly con-cerned about the integrity of *all* life allows us to re-create the world slowly and patiently, against forces of that call for a violent re-creation of the world that conforms to their sense of objective certainty.[8] In this context, a vigilant and joyful re-creation of the world stands between two more serious trans-formations that currently threaten the world. On the one hand is an apoca-lyptic end, demanded by hypertheists whose certainty (framed by trusting) demands that they assert the coming of the end out of impatience or rest-lessness. On the other hand, a rival danger emerges in the visions of a tech-nological utopia framed by more roads, chemicals, and a techno-scientific understanding that re-creates through statistical reduction. A vigilant faith re-creates the world by holding the extremes in tension, denying neither the possibility of the *eschaton* nor the power of techno-science, but instead gathering uncertainty and questions into both frameworks. Those with a vigilant faith create a world providentially imbued with hesitation through pious acts of questioning and projections of a certain kind of godlessness. The virtue of re-creation and the delight in simultaneously accepting and transforming the givenness of world and worth comes through the form of volition, as one wills the realization of truth that one has been given.

It is possible to test these virtues of vigilant faith against the parable examined earlier in this chapter. The character who cries out does so as a clear work of faith, whether the cry originates from a group of those waiting to celebrate or from a messenger who has raced joyfully ahead of the bride-groom. The outburst is a work of creativity and charity (a selfless summons) that reconstitutes the finite world of the sleepers in terms of the revelation of the bridegroom's arrival. The efficacy of this work of faith manifests as relative ends that had become important (sleep or reprieve from boredom) are undone in light of the new work of readying a greeting for the bridegroom. Additionally, the watcher—already shown to have excavated the self—related absolutely to the absolute end of welcoming the bridegroom as well as relatively to the relative (ethical) ends of ensuring that others were able to perform their duties as well.

Unlike the slumbering virgins, the originator of the outcry maintained *patience* (especially if the source was near the virgins) and kept vigil vigilantly despite the fact that the bridegroom was "a long time in coming." However, the loneliness of the proclamation implies that the one keeping watch did so without company. The voice also manifested *hospitality*: in a superficial sense, the voice spoke out to ensure the bridegroom received a proper arrival, shouting forth selflessly to alert others from their slumber. Were it not for this cry, none of the virgins (the only group identified as awaiting the bridegroom) would have been there to greet or receive him. The pleas of hospitality ensured that at least *some* more be awake to welcome the bridegroom. On a second level, the sheer equality of the act of crying out shows *hospitality*: all benefit equally from the watcher's vigilance, although the watcher gains no personal reward.

The final virtue of faith, *re-creation,* emerges in the watcher's twofold outcry—simultaneously an observation and an exhortation. The narrator leaves unclear whether the bridegroom's coming was described or invoked: in other words, although it is possible that the watcher witnessed the coming of the bridegroom through the darkness of midnight, recognizing his features in an act of vigilance, it is also possible (and perhaps no more unlikely) that the watcher *performed* the coming of the bridegroom. If the bridegroom, expecting a reception of friends, came to a place dark with sleep or boredom, he may have become dismayed. Frustrated, he was awaiting the invocation, the announcement of coming, in order at last to arrive. In other words, perhaps the watcher sensed that the bridegroom was at hand, that the arrival was imminent and announced the arrival before it actually occurred. There was time enough, after all, for the foolish virgins to have left before the bridegroom materialized (unless the foolish virgins failed to recognize the very one for whom they had gone to watch, which was equally possible, even if the watch was idly undertaken). In expectation, heightened by each prior moment of incomplete fulfillment, perhaps the watcher had seen in the things around a joyful anticipation of the bridegroom's coming: perhaps a familiar odor wafted in the breeze or the stones sang with a familiar cadence.

In adoration, the watcher transformed watching into rejoicing: "Here comes the bridegroom!" Unable to contain the joy or passion, the watcher also cries, "Come out to meet him!" This outcry issues forth with urgency, but as an invitation and not an ultimatum: the watcher desires others to partake in the joyful reunion as well. The vigil has ended; the celebration can begin! A community forms, summoned by the words, other voices echoing the refrain to one still unseen: "Here comes the bridegroom! Come out to meet him!" Bodies gather near as the excitement builds, voices come together, blending and overlapping. Witnesses emerge, each wanting to be close to the middle. The passionate desire to greet the bridegroom calls everyone out from the warm places into the cooler darkness that has suddenly exploded with light, expanding the sphere of celebration into the world. Thus, even if the advent of the bridegroom was discovered instead of performed, the work of adoration nonetheless successfully creates a community predicated on an imminent (not actual) presence.

Although patience, hospitality, and re-creation are works and manifest the virtues of a vigilant faith in a concrete fashion, they nonetheless do not require that one sacrifice one's skepticism. Like the skeptic's embrace of the "ordinary regimen" that would not violate the principle of *ataraxia,* the virtues of a vigilant faith do not require certainty before acting. Instead, the works of a vigilant faith—visible in the production of the pools of godlessness throughout the world—inspire uncertainty that disrupts the casual lives of naïve skeptics and the knowledgeable. Rather than accelerating toward a final unveilation, the work of a vigilant faith struggles to enlarge the space between world and *eschaton* and thereby maintain an absolute faith in relation with an undefined god.

The End of Faith

The end of faith, its telos, arises in its perpetuation. The work of a vigilant vigil goes this far and not a step farther. Nothing more can be done, in faith, without departing from faith and into a community of believers who concretize a revelation into something more objectively certain. Such certainty is desirable for humans; however, with the birth of knowledge through the making-certain of a revelation, faith itself comes to an end.

In sum, this book has defined and articulated the domain of prebelief, the faith that arises *prior* to the affirmation of a particular revelation or symbol of God. This domain is populated by a variety of skeptics, ranging from the naïve skeptics, who lack the initial willingness to suspend disbelief necessary for faith, to vigilant skeptics, who volitionally suspend objective certainty in favor of faith. A skeptical faith that promotes the perpetuation of faith as faith into the future, while searching the world for possibilities of God (which are then suspended and not resolved), requires vigilance. A vigilant faith moves beyond hesitation to build uncertainty and godlessness into the present and future as a positive work. Unlike a faith predicated on the initial impulse of trusting or the moment of the failure of the understanding, a vigilant faith uses the human capacities of passion, reason, and volition to maintain the conflict between a mundane world and the world of the *eschaton*. By enduring this conflict, humans maintain an absolute relation with the absolute and still enjoy the pleasures of relative goods. Thus a vigilant faith is set apart from a skeptical faith, becoming a normative model of faith, able to account for the phenomena identified by previous models as well as skeptical outliers.

Vigilantly Undergoing Faith

I feel now
The future in the instant.
—*Macbeth*, act 1, scene 5

Heidegger's theory that truth emerges in the event of revealing and concealing implies that truth occurs through a dynamic tension instead of "existing" in an independent, abstracted way. The truth of faith, disclosed in full with an initial revelation, becomes hidden in and by the symbolic world. Things *preserve* truth as a gathering potential, activated (occurring) when I participate in its gathering. In addition to preserving truth, I must *perform* it in my re-creation of the world. The human preservation of truth requires activity—shifting from the absolute future into the future present, shifting from the infinite into the finite.

Preparation

Without warning, events precipitate my being displaced into a passionate state of *trusting* faith relative to a truth unexpectedly revealed. Because an outside source enables *trusting*, I can only prepare for a faith formed by the labor of pure reason. Even if I am prepared to enter into a state of faith, I cannot force a truth to reveal itself to me or compel my own displacement.

Prior to revelation, I dwell in the domain of prebelief. This world is godless and filled with nothing; at most, the spirit of anonymity hovers behind the things of the world in a mass-produced perfection. Because of this, my initial preparations for faith are made in a nihilistic and atheistic sense: I decide that *faith* is different from *knowing* and worthy of being prized, and therefore that it is desirable to be *subjectively convinced of the uncertainty of subjective conviction* (or *subjectively convinced of the uncertainty of objective certainty*) in order to increase the possibilities for faith to manifest, because this mind-set negates the *understanding* and permits faith to occur in relation to all things. This rational form of faith requires that I begin developing an attitude of vigilance directed both internally (as I watch over how I watch) and externally (toward the world of things) through a skeptical mind-set. Because the possibility of uncertainty is uncomfortable, this *rational* form of faith demands the form of *volition*, which allows me to make this decision in each consecutively occurring moment despite my discomfort.

The discipline gained by maintaining a willed state of vigilance, where I make belief through attempting to find multiple viable explanations for events as they occur, translates into the preparatory stage of *ethics*, also demanded by reason. Although ethics is an important end in itself, from the perspective of faith, ethics is merely necessary (the work of the day, in Lacoste's terminology [263]), a work of knowing what I *must* do at odds with faith's uncertainty. Ethics thus is necessary but not sufficient for faith. Successful preparation enables me to be in a *state of faith* relative to my existence but not relative to any truth or meaning. The state of faith formed by reason and volition is empty, useless. The abstracted nature of this impersonal faith confirms that nothing grounds it: it remains an unwarranted and unnecessary leap into unknowing. Faith works through *hesitation,* tarrying at the reflexive level as demanded by a rationally formed faith.

Excavation

Faith traditionally requires a negation of the self. The excavation of the self occurs through encounters with nothingness; the nature of the encounter varies depending on the model of truth I embrace. In a pre-Kantian framework, the excavation comes atheistically when I realize that the finite world is illusory and spiritually as I ascetically deprive my flesh, conforming physically to the revealed truth. In a Kantian (existential)[1] framework, the excavation comes atheistically as I realize that my inability to be myself means I can do nothing and, thus, that nothing is possible. The spiritual dimension occurs as I realize it is impossible to do the work of the law myself, that I cannot be justified by my actions, that nothing I do "counts" in an important sense. In a post-Heideggerean framework, excavation occurs as I embrace the task of doing nothing as a positive capacity: nothing is a *human* possibility, and I therefore engage in continual acts of deconstruction, an activity that requires its own vigilance. This type of activity led to the "death of the author" and "death of the subject" and emphasized the notion that a self is a construction of disparate and conflicting identities. In all cases, the excavation of the self requires an encounter with, acceptance of, and movement through nothingness. This encounter results in humbling myself and realizing my interdependence with others. Humility and letting go of an illusion of independence are necessary preconditions for the letting-be concomitant with a vigilant faith, and both attend the actualization of faith in a more traditional religious sense. In the humbled continuation of a faith, which one enacts even as it is impossible, *faith* becomes the ground of faith. In other words, I remain uncertain about the impossibility of continuing because I have experienced its possibility, moment after moment. The work of faith in this stage is *self-negating*. I refuse to accept the illusion of independence or isolation, enabling an entry into or appreciation of a world shared with others—but I continually mediate my relation with this shared world through my insistence on uncertainty.

Anticipation

In an undefined and abstract state of faith, I move through my world attending to things and that to which things testify, embedded in a skepticism that withholds assent to appearances. Things testify to the world, to the importance of politics and labor, to the need for wealth and insurance and retirement portfolios. Aesthetic goods testify to the truths of this world—to minor victories and minor successes, heartache and tragedy, joy and forgiveness. The ink on newspapers and the blend of skin tones and languages on the flickering of television screens reflect the nature of the world as a globalized and postindustrial unit. This world is a certain world, yet because I have chosen to *make belief*, I avoid this certainty and anticipate a truth that could render this world less certain. In a pre-Kantian framework, this truth reveals that materiality is illusory and that true reality persists beyond this world. In a Kantian framework, this truth reveals the limits of reason and rationality and the ultimately subjective nature of truth. The post-Kantian framework, which understands truth as a dynamic event, posits truth is unattainable. I expect, perhaps, that something awaits me "beyond" or "other than" this world, but as yet, no such truth has occurred. I merely believe that, in faith, the revelation will provide something that counters the world as I know it: anxious, I desire revelations of comfort; weak, I seek revelations of strength; hungry, I crave a revelation of nourishment. This anticipation, in a mode of prehending the truth, allows me to recognize the revelation as it manifests. The work of faith at this level is *meditating*, defining a space opposed to my world where a revelation could fit, and *hearkening* to the testimony of the surrounding world, unknowing my certain experience of it in a hesitation that implicitly asks: "Is this all?"

Revelation

Suddenly, and seemingly from nowhere, I receive an intimation of the absolute reflected in a gathering of the thing. The object—a paper container whose contents an anonymous person consumed long ago, and whose logo breaks through from beneath the grime of a tread mark—comes into focus. The cup is disposable and is meant to be disposed of, although perhaps in not such an offhanded manner as would cause it to move leaflike down the sidewalk. It gives itself obviously as a thing, an unwanted thing, a thing about which nobody even cares enough to eliminate. I am tempted to be certain of this experience, an experience I have had hundreds of times. I have walked past plastic lids and straws, wrappers from sandwiches and chips, shoelaces and hubcaps, receipts for food and new books, letters from lost loves and notices of missing pets, advertisements for past events and announcements for future political rallies. Yet, vigilantly, I perform the skeptical work of *hearkening* to *this* cup, *this* thing, attending to it.

The cup signifies a world where everything is mass produced and custom made. I attend to a name: this cup held *David's* drink. Marked boxes specify the exact drink that David desired, markings made after its factory-standard perfection. I see that *this* thing is handy in a world where time is short: one receives too little sleep and thus requires caffeine to stay awake. One cannot sit and enjoy a coffee in a café with a friend but instead must get it to go. The large size of the cup reveals the desire for value and quantity: a cardboard band allows one to transport it with ease, so that one can get a cup and consume its contents as one walks. Because this cup is identical to billions around the world, it reflects a world that values consistency over individuality, reliability over chance. The disposable nature of the cup—and the fact that it persists now as refuse—reveals that this is a world, too, consumed more with convenience than responsibility. I am not surprised when, continuing to stay with the cup, allowing myself to be gathered by it, I see that the coloring of the cup was once white, a green logo upon it. The logo, the shade of tree and grass, gathers also the form of a mermaid or siren whose bared breasts nourish no human life, encircled by the language of mortals and stars from the sky. It meaninglessly mentions a Melvillean character no more worthy of attention than Ishmael or Ahab. It gathers earth and sky, gods and humans, but does so with no seeming purpose—no meaning, no significance except to refer to itself. It symbolizes only itself—or, I realize—it negates itself and its own individuality in gesturing toward a larger company that bears no necessary relation to these markings. The company employs thousands as a faceless mass, disconnected from the cup although referenced by it. The cup is an alien thing, and alienating.

The cup itself is anonymous, worthless, empty, used up: sheer refuse. The warmed combination of earth's bean and sky's water vanished long ago from the holey cup that can gather these elements no longer. And yet, although evacuated and despite the fact that the recycled paper mass that constitutes the cup only faintly echoes earth or sky, I witness how the cup has *gathered* these very elements to itself as it has rolled about on the ground. Although intended for a brief life, and having outlasted its function, it endures. Its persistence clamors for my attention. It resists the power of the ground to swallow it up and decompose it back into earth. It resists the power of sky to wash it away. It resists the power of humans, who prefer living in an orderly world where such trash remains unseen. It is omnipresent and indestructible like gods in stories, but it resists their mythology and personalized nature. It gathers together that which it resists, connecting those things with its sense of refusal[2] while remaining set apart from them, gathering without bringing them into focus.

I hearken to it, staying within the truth it gathers: the truth of a ground filled with things that are not earth, a sky whose acid rains drip reminders of human negligence. It brings together a promise of comfort (to be found in a cup!) with humans desperate to believe marketing slogans. No gush or flow emanates from this container—its ability to give is spent. I persist, looking at the cup, no longer moving forward or rushing, *trusting* that the cup testifies to the ability to persist in a depersonalizing and empty world where symbols filled with sound and fury invoke a certain nothing, an *anonymous* nothing. I begin to refuse with the cup, refusing to move, refusing to hurry, *trusting* the value of persistence, *trusting* the possibilities within the anonymous, *trusting* the value of the artificial and the need to cherish what has been forgotten. As the wind blows, I follow the cup: past storefronts that are empty and others that show signs promising new possibilities for consumers.

Revelatory moments cannot be captured by clocks. The moment prior to death conveys a lifetime. The scent of a former lover's shampoo reminds a man that he had once been in love. A silk jacket reminds a woman of wearing her grandmother's nightgowns. A whistled tune awakens a man to a forgotten summer running through the trees. An apple pie returns a woman to a childhood filled with autumns. Sense impressions trigger bursts of emotions, swaths of conversations, impressions, reactions, deeds. These represent physical memories, tactile memories that communicate years of pasts. Revelatory moments share the intimate, corporeal nature of these communications and the passionate, identity-causing responses; they differ from these more common occurrences only by direction (it concerns a future) and potency (it is absolute, not relative). Each time, we undergo the experience with a prereflective consciousness, where not even the distance of a verb separates the self from the event: smell, taste, touch obliterate other concerns. At this point, one is *close* to the thing and the absolute.

At the prereflective level of consciousness, the shadow of the absolute lingers, overwhelming me: under its influence, I sense the futility of my previous efforts. My daily concerns are forgotten: my political viewpoints, errands, desires for lunch, pet peeves, career goals, economic problems, social standing, sports team—none of these matter. The book in my hand, the watch in my pocket, the phone in my bag reflect nothing of value. The weight of them has been removed: they have become *unbeings* in the light of the absolute. The relative goods seem trivial, mere childish things. The cup skates along; I pursue it as I chased friends in my youth. It has been crushed and drained, kicked and ignored, but it maintains its vitality, moving easily down the street, not worried about the opinions of others.

Other experiences filter ghostlike onto the horizon of consciousness, appearing briefly before disappearing again. I remember a Catholic Mass and the vast size of the cathedral. I recall a concert, and how sound filled the space and united the thousands of voices together into a massive wall of joy. A quiet art museum flickers into mind. A hike in the mountains. A kiss. Images multiply: the birth of a child, a broken heart, a sunset, the flight of a lonely crow, a moonrise. Filled with the encounter with the absolute, I cannot attend to these images fully because each possesses the power to disrupt the revelation as it summons me. Nonetheless, as a set of background images, they offer a preunderstanding, of sorts, of what is happening. Unable to grasp or have the moment, I fall into its power, accepting it, *trusting,* assenting to the possibilities of the truth opened by the cup. Still, contrary to my desire to embrace this revelation, I hesitate and neither confirm nor deny the truth of the cup's testimony to the power of refusal and the power of its witness to an anonymous sacred.

Preservation

Maintaining my *conscious* assent to the truths of refusal and the anonymous I received (*trusting*), and ensuring that I maintain a skeptical stance of hesitation relative to them (*understanding*), requires vigilance. This letting the truth be the truth that it is *preserves* the truth within the revelation, cradling it within a dynamic of conflicting interpretations that prevents it from atrophying into an idol. Once I begin to consciously *interpret* what I witnessed, I leave the initial proximity of the event accomplished through *hearkening* as various levels of my consciousness vigilantly filter the data of naïve experience that allowed *trusting* to occur. Interpreting is necessary given the nature of the thing as a *sign,* which demands my impassioned response, the disclosure of the thoughts of my heart. The first level of distance, which simultaneously enables interpretation and misunderstanding, comes at the subject-object relational level; this occurs as the revelatory moment begins to recede. When I attempt to formulate the experience in language, failure results, for the potency of the revelation cannot be located in the subject, the object, or the verb. The absolute, indivisible, is lost when language wrests it from experience. Thus, to say, "I saw a cup," an objectively or relatively certain evaluation, is absolutely inaccurate—even when I am tempted to make the experience certain, claiming that such a mundane artifact should not have that kind of power, stating that the whole notion was an idle daydream, if not just silly. I had an experience where it *seemed,* at least, that the absolute manifested in a totalizing way that incorporated sight, smell, sound, taste, touch, and memory. While the event may have been grounded in the cup, the experience itself was of the absolute, that which the cup referenced, and not the cup at all. The absolute was cocreated and thus exists neither in the cup nor in me as witness. I am forced to accept the failure of this level of consciousness to mediate this event.

One can only understand the failure of the subject-object relational level of consciousness at the *reflective* level of consciousness. Nonetheless, even reflective statements of knowledge have difficulties grasping the event: claiming "It is true that I saw a cup" oversimplifies the experience, as does stating "It is true that I witnessed God." This is especially true as my experiences with God have come emptily: the feeling that my prayers have not been heard, an apathy toward the symbol of the Cross, a boredom with the overtold story of Christmas. The level of belief comes closer to a correct account of the experience, as I can claim, "I believe that I saw a cup," "I believe that I witnessed a new world," or "I believe that was an encounter with the holy" with more validity. Statements of belief manifest the subjective conviction in the uncertainty of subjective conviction important to an experience of faith. Vigilance demands that I formulate coherent conflicting beliefs to ensure I maintain an attitude of uncertainty toward that which occurred.

The conflicting interpretations (objective, eschatological, numinous) pile against each other, however, making necessary a reflexive analysis of the interpretation. At the reflexive level, I appeal to a truth able to hold mutually exclusive reflective judgments in tension. I thus state, "I believe that the experience was neither wholly of the cup nor of God." This statement merges the rational and numinal interpretations and advocates (in terms of belief, not knowledge) thinking that both interpretations are incomplete. Statements that open the space between two interpretations provide the skeptical ground for hesitation and thus the grounds for faith. Because the event could have been illusory, I choose to look for further confirmation, keeping watch for a reemergence of the truth. The reflexive level also allows a positive assessment of the situation, a statement of belief that can guide future decisions.

After interpreting, I begin *acting* in light of the revelation in order to preserve what I experienced. The most basic action is *remembering*, keeping the belief spawned in the event of the revelation foremost in mind—in this case, remembering I believe that the experience was neither wholly of the cup nor of God. Staying within the truth of the revelation also compels me to reclaim the mind-set I had when I was displaced: letting go of my cares and concerns in a relentless drive to reorient the world (and myself) back toward what my witnessing impressed on me. The major difference between this and the abstracted state of a rationally formed belief (which guided my vigilance in *anticipation*) is that my faith now has a passionate form as well as a rational and volitional one. The event of the revelation, all-consuming and absolute, allows me to reinterpret my self in light of what was given and thus allows me through my actions to reproduce elements of what occurred. For example, in a globalized world with an increasing drive toward homogenization, I can refuse natural and mechanized powers bent on my depersonalization. I base my resistance neither on "courage," nor any consolation, nor hope of a tragic life, but in a *trusting/understanding* of the power of fleshly, finite persistence. The more often I filter my activities through my reflexive belief about the event, and the more frequently my actions intentionally conform with this truth, the more I have *appropriated* the truth of the event. This allows me to remain steadfast in my orientation toward the revealed truth, even as I persist in relating to the truth as a belief instead of knowledge.

Throughout the activities of hearkening, interpreting, and acting, I still engage in *hesitating*. The *certain* explanations are ready at hand and serve as a ready defense against faith: I experienced *nothing*, a flight of fancy sparked by boredom. Desiring certainty, I recall litter on the ground that I was disinclined to retrieve. I can be subjectively convinced of this—and then, with vigilant skepticism, refuse (like the cup, perhaps) this certainty and instead keep open to the possibility (only a possibility) that this experience, the chasing after the cup, was more than a futile exercise of an underworked mind. There are two possible explanations for what occurred, and I cannot be certain that the uncertain explanation is true.

One preserves revealed truths by being transformed and acting in light of them. Vigilance ensures that my thoughts and actions still attend to my truth as belief, because the calcification of such a revealed truth into a knowledge claim transforms the cup into an idol. Retaining the subjective conviction concerning the uncertainty of objective certainty in relation to a truth to which I have assented is crucial, as *this* truth concerns my identity from the perspective of eternity, manifest in a vision of an absolute future, or God. Problematically, postrevelation, I am denied the foundation of a world. The things that reflected my former world, the once important things, have become *unbeings,* worthless currency minted by a toy bank. These serve as signs of old understandings and, as obsolete equipment, become uncanny reminders that I am not *of* the world that I still dwell within.

No other persons inhabit my revealed world, as this world exists only as a projected sketch, a reflection of an absolute future potentially gathered in this thing, that thing. Because this world is not uniformly reflected, however, not yet concretely anchored to the present, I cannot communicate the nature of this truth, this revealed world, to others. I am reduced to a silence, my faith—relative to the absolute truth—is my own, appropriated, incarnated only within myself. Externally, in the world of objective certainty, nothing has changed: I still have bills to pay, friends to visit, family to care for. I must relate relatively to these relative ends, as it is possible that the projected sketch that I witnessed was a false world, a vision that fell short of being truly absolute. I therefore remain constrained to deal with those things that populate the former world, things on the edge of becoming unbeings: the temptation to simply forget the event or to dismiss it as a way of returning to my former world is ever present. Because language is universal and abstract, and my faith involves an impassioned dynamic, I can only communicate about this absolute future indirectly.

Although remembering the event in the background of my conscious thoughts is a useful mode of preservation, such mental activities cannot preserve the truth in light of the struggle to stay apart from the world at large. Memory is a weak and unreliable light, and each time I recall the event, its truth is less crisp, less stark, reflective more of consciousness than the absolute. Because of this, proper preservation requires *building, dwelling,* and *communing.* Building comprises the activities of *cultivating* natural goods and *constructing* equipment and reflective goods that serve as signs to reflect the truth from which I remain slightly distant, hesitant. Building requires vigilance: in cultivating, I must be responsible to both the plants and the land in which they are sown. I am *co-responsible* for the plants, working with earth and sky as a mortal who watches providentially over these living things before divinities, maintaining them. In my constructions, I work to enable the possibility for the fourfold's installing itself in that which I alter: places and goods in this way intentionally exist as gathering points for the possibility of the absolute's manifestation. In this way, I engage in efforts of *hospitality* relative to the absolute, preparing the way for its arrival. The work of building is not limited to the erection of structures or the manipulation of tools. I also build with other types of goods: stories, songs, and prayers all open locations able to unconceal the absolute and allow it to manifest. These works of faith are necessarily signs, as the uncertainty that goes into their construction forbids any direct or necessary (symbolic) participation with the absolute. In this way, the event of revelation transforms my way of being in the world in an ontic way that still allows me to engage the world in an ontologically determined fashion.

The second type of work is dwelling. If the efforts of building involve the development of that which does not exist prior to the revelation, then the work of dwelling is to invest myself with what is present, in a way that frees things to be the things that they are. Dwelling is a "sparing" and a "preserving" and, as such, comes into conflict with the task of keeping the new world at bay and delaying the moment that will permanently transform the equipment of the present world into unbeings. In the absence of the divinities, I take their place in providentially watching over and gathering this thing, that thing. I watch over natural goods—trees, rivers, plants—to ensure that they are nourished; I make art and enjoy reading, writing, and viewing gifts of culture.

Most urgently, dwelling and preserving the equipmental things of this world requires that I stave off the advent of the absolute future. The gap between the activities of building and dwelling requires the uncertainty manifest in a vigilant faith: tarrying between the absolute future and the recent past, I attempt to *build* something capable of welcoming the future while *dwelling* with that equipment rooted in the past. I *have* neither the past world nor the future one; stuck in the space opened between worlds, I require a faith that this situation will not last forever and a vigilance to ensure that the two worlds (the one that I *trust* and the one I *understand*) are held in tension through *volition*. Dwelling in the former world requires that I still attend to those goals and cares relative to that world: the nature of building hospitably for the absolute—that toward which I am directed passionately and volitionally (although with trepidation)—requires an absolute relation.

The third type of work is communing. I cannot cultivate or construct a human being, and I cannot build a world alone. Humans are social beings and companionship and coexistence is important, even if one shares silences concerning those matters that cannot be spoken. A community is especially important in terms of *faith,* which historically has unified humans into groups willing to share with each other. In religious settings, such communities gather by creeds and exclude those who are not willing to assent to its truth. A vigilant faith, based on a personal (and not universal) experience, lacks a creed or anything that would violate the main precept that one remain *subjectively convinced of the uncertainty of subjective conviction.* Based on this supposition, it becomes necessary to accept all individuals whom I meet as members of my community, in spite of any appearance or inclination that the other individual might present. I cannot be certain that others are how they appear, especially as those with vigilant faith appear to dwell in the world as fully as those who are not aware of the absolute.[3] Accepting others as though they also undergo a vigilant faith without requiring certainty about this, and communing with them in silent adoration, preserves the revelation in communion with others.

Throughout, I remain steadfastly oriented toward two divergent truths that cause me to orbit about both elliptically instead of grasping one absolutely. The first truth, rational, is that I am subjectively convinced only of the uncertainty of subjective conviction. The second truth is the passionate truth, too mammoth to fit into anything as abstract and empty as language: this is the truth of the vision that I received, mediated by the empty cup. Both truths require *volition* in order to maintain an orientation toward them, as both are arduous in nature. Either may end up falling short of an absolute truth—even as I am oriented toward these truths, staying close to them, I do not embrace them or hold them. The *rational* and the *passionate* truths are in this way kept apart, testing each other and providing a dynamic movement that preserves the truth of both in every moment. I continue forward in *making* these truths real, vigilantly maintaining my subjective certainty in the uncertainty of objective certainty while simultaneously also acting to realize the truth of my vision through the patient, hospitable and re-creative acts of preserving preparation found in building, dwelling, and communing.

Expectation

Although I must recommit to it with each new present, the dynamic of faith pushes me toward the future when the truth can be fully unveiled, reflected fully within the things of this world. In expectation, I begin the work of hospitality that prepares the way for the arrival of the absolute. There are four stages of expectation, but although they are arranged in a direction, there is no force that necessarily propels one from a certain position onward to the next. The first stage of expectation is *patience,* which begins all stages of faith. I receive the revelation in its overwhelming abundance; as the vision fades and effort is required to preserve the revelation as it was given, I yearn for the conjunction of the absolute future and the present world, which concludes the work of faith. I anticipate the end of faith in unveilation. Time passes, and I remain patient. More time goes by, and I stay busy with the work of building for the new world; that which is engineered is internal, a reorientation of the self. Values, ideas, desires begin to shift as I build a self appropriate to that future while remaining with that which has always been factually true of myself: I build, I dwell. Time passes. I continue in my labors, attempting to recall and remember the revelation as it was presented, repeating it to myself. I remain focused on the task of building and dwelling within myself, watching for the absolute.

Some have the stamina to stay, to wait, to build, to dwell, to persist within the self; many do not. Some grow weary of dwelling in the same place; some desire to move out of the self and into the world. The external manifestation of patience is searching, when, wearied of my surroundings, I seek places where the things reflect the absolute with the clarity I find within myself. Knowing that all places are as one for the absolute is no deterrent: I go outside to find and learn, searching for a sign that my vigil might come to an end. *Searching* is the second stage of expectation. My heart anticipates the apocalypse, an echo of the anticipation that I had possessed for the initial revelation. I look for more information, some new word, another revelation; I search for sites where the absolute is known, for people who certainly belong to my community. I go into the world, even though I still adhere to my original credo: to be subjectively convinced of the uncertainty of subjective conviction. I find signs, see wonders, meet prophets—and I hearken to and delight in them but cannot embrace them, subjectively convinced of the uncertainty of subjective conviction.

Although some have the strength to wander for a lifetime, others weary of travels and desire a home once again. This leads one to *dwell,* although now, to one more comfortable with the world, dwelling occurs in the world and as a part of it. Sites that had seemed alien before, devoid of a manifestation of the absolute, perhaps rooted in the nothingness I felt at the core of my being before—churches, mosques, museums—now reveal themselves as possible homes for the absolute as well. The darkness and space of the cathedral, the identical folding chairs of a Baptist megachurch, the smiling yellow face of a discount store: all things point to the total presence of the anonymous. Parking lots filled with SUVs, rows of houses in suburban real estate developments, strip malls featuring more of the same: these things, too, gather the absolute. The absolute is concealed again as soon it is revealed within these things: I sense the presence of the absolute everywhere and yet hesitate to name any one thing as presenting it fully. The time is not yet come, the absolute future remains at hand; vigilantly, I continue to search, to build, to dwell. The vigil for the absolute is performed in addition to my other labors; the work of caring for friends and family, earning pay for needs or luxuries constitute *relative* goods that do not affect my absolute relation to the absolute.

Individuals enjoy dwelling, and once the world has been opened and the urge to travel has been sated, I find myself contentedly among things that at one time were foreign and strange. Some individuals move from this comfort, disquieted, and attempt to preserve the truth more actively than through an observant and vigilant gathering. I visit poor places to bring food or clothing to the hungry and cold; I find the ignorant and provide instruction; I notice the oppressed and speak to power on their behalf. The sick are medicated, the elderly visited. I enter the stage of *transformation* and refuse to succumb to injustice. Self-determined, autonomous, and anonymous, I persist in and through the world, fixing and healing in an attempt to bring forth the absolute. I build in ways more conducive to the absolute future, willing *that* world into existence with each and every interaction that I have.

Adoration

During the day, I work to attain my relative needs, having conversations with my friends and family and sustaining myself against the inevitability of death or old age. Those loves are relative goods, toward which the absolute is indifferent. I make the decision to keep watch over natural things, equipmental things, reflective things, and the social world during what Lacoste refers to as a "liturgical night"; these are actions performed when others are at leisure or sleeping. I spend my vigil vigilantly, patiently, hospitably. Time passes, and the revelation of my youth still seems no closer. I have gathered, I have built, I have dwelt: the absolute future remains at hand. It, like the coffee cup, refuses. Praying, I begin to ask "Is this all?" as I dwell, build, watch. "Is this all?" I cannot supplicate for the absolute to be fully unveiled: it has no reason to come sooner or later based on my request. With every step and every action, I examine what appears, my breaths asking: Is this all? I am still between worlds, learning to dwell in the space between, hesitating eternally. Is this all? I am weary and require rest, and I ask of the things and of those around: Is this all? I wait. There is patience, there is hospitality. I re-create the world, each construction and cultivation a prayer. "Is this all?" The expectation builds, and I summon others, awakening them, anxious to transform the need for a vigilant vigil, a work, to a vigil that allows one to relax. Is this all?

Anticipation II

Before, I had anxiously searched for a revelation to provide content for my vigilant faith. Anchored passionately in my refusal, I now anticipate the time of unveilation, when my tongue may be loosened and I can speak the fullness of my truth. I anticipate the fleshing out of the projective sketch gathered by the cup, seeing it manifest across the world. I anticipate the elimination of tension between this world and the future, when the absolute becomes presence. I anticipate a communion with others who can understand and speak my new words, the end of my solitude. The vigil will end, the bridegroom arrive. I anticipate the culmination of the dynamic of faith, my incorporation into the absolute, the gift of full knowledge. Vigilantly, I search; vigilantly, I continue to tarry in faith.

Unveilation

Notes

Introduction

1. Bob Dylan, "Everything Is Broken," *Tell Tale Signs*, Sony, 2008.
2. C. Taylor, *A Secular Age*, 20–21.
3. W. Smith, *Faith and Belief*. See especially 105–72.
4. Klemm and Klink, "Constructing and Testing Theological Models."
5. Heidegger, *Phenomenology*, 19. In his critique of Troelsch, Heidegger asserts that faith in the existence of God, not God as an object of faith, is the primal religious phenomenon.

1. The Model of Absolute Faith

1. Klemm and Klink, "Constructing and Testing Theological Models."
2. Tillich discusses this at length in his *Biblical Religion and the Search for Ultimate Reality*.
3. See Scharlemann, "The Question of Philosophical Theology"; and Scharlemann, *The Reason of Following*, 63.
4. Kant, *Critique of Pure Reason*, 645–52.
5. Aquinas, *Summa Theologica*, II-II, questions 1–10.
6. See Hay, "*Pistis* as 'Ground of Faith.'"
7. See Williams's introduction to Anselm, *Proslogion*.
8. Allison, *Kant's Transcendental Idealism*, 413.
9. Malantschuk, *Kierkegaard's Thought*, 208–11. Malantschuk argues that Climacus sketches "the way from the lowest stage to man's encounter with Christianity" (210), which is based "primarily on the idea of man as a potential possibility consisting of two opposites which are separated by reflection but which can ultimately achieve immediacy on a qualitatively new plane" (211). Malantschuk further argues that the internal paradox is reflected in Climacus's understanding that Christianity increases the tension between the ideal and the actual, leading to a despair resolved only by faith.
10. Kierkegaard, *Fragments*, 59. One of several points where Kierkegaard makes this plain is in his discussion of the contemporary follower, whom he argues requires

the same amount of faith as the follower at second hand. Both rely on historical facts that were not witnessed firsthand.

11. Kierkegaard, *Postscript*, 461–86. Here, Climacus shows the difficulty of even being capable of nothing at all.

12. Kierkegaard, *Sickness*, 82. Kierkegaard provides his famous definition of faith as occurring when "the self in being itself and in willing to be itself rests transparently in God."

13. Kierkegaard, *Practice*, 24–25. Writing that "one cannot become a believer except by coming to him in his state of abasement, to him, the sign of offense and the object of faith" (24) and that "one cannot *know* anything at all about *Christ;* he is the paradox, the object of faith, exists only for faith" (25), Kierkegaard weaves together notions of abasement, paradox, offense, and faith such that faith follows the more intense subjective experience of having been repulsed (offended) by an interaction with a paradox (which, in itself, offends only one's objective, rational thought).

14. Kierkegaard, *Postscript*, 499.

15. Kierkegaard, *Fragments*, 83.

16. Tillich, *Dynamics*, 46.

17. Ibid., 20.

18. Klemm and Schweiker, *Religion and the Human Future*.

2. Skepticism as a Ground of Faith

1. Heidegger, "The Origin of the Work of Art," in *Poetry, Language, Thought*, 52. "With all our correct representations we would get nowhere, we could not even presuppose that there already is manifest something to which we can conform ourselves, unless the unconcealedness of beings had already exposed us to, placed us in that lighted realm in which every being stands for us and from which it withdraws."

2. Ibid., 61–62. Heidegger here lists other actions that embody the occurrence of truth that his model can uniquely account for: (1) the act that founds a political state, (2) the essential sacrifice, and (3) a thinker's questioning.

3. Johnsen, "On the Coherence of Pyrrhonian Skepticism," 529.

4. See Scharlemann, *The Reason of Following*.

5. Breuer and Freud, *Studies on Hysteria*, 283.

6. Freud, *Three Case Histories*: "It is also a matter of indifference in this connection whether we choose to regard it as a primal scene or as a primal phantasy" (279n5).

7. The *passionate* element is attested to not only by the emotional affect with which the proposition is uttered but also in terms of the two physical elements that Freud lists: first, the early technique of applying the physical pressure of his hand on the patient's forehead during a therapy session (*Studies on Hysteria*, 281–82, 289). While he later opts for alternate methods, it nonetheless shows the *physical* dimension of the patient's diagnostic utterance. Second, of course, is the matter of the cure: the utterance yields a desired physiological change within the patient's body and eliminates a degree of suffering in which the physical and psychical were merged indistinguishably.

3. Skeptical Consciousness and the Dynamic of Faith

1. See Olson, "Postmodernity and Faith." Part of my task in this chapter is to work substantially through Olson's suggestion that theologians should ground a definition of faith in terms of consciousness.

2. Hawthorne, *Young Goodman Brown and Other Tales*, 111–24. Although as a name "Faith" works particularly well for Hawthorne, in terms of the model of faith established in chapter 1, Brown, at most, experiences the world through a *trusting* that has yet to be negated and become faith. "Faith" expresses the domain of Hawthorne's topic, but it differs from what I call "faith." Confusing *faith* with *trusting* leads to Brown's unhappy end.

3. Hawthorne states that Brown would shrink "from the bosom of Faith" and gaze "sternly at his wife" (124).

4. This is, of course, a rather broad generalization. Nicholas of Cusa both works through Platonic conceptions of truth and emphasizes the role that the failure of the understanding plays in allowing faith through a coincidence of opposites.

5. Aquinas, *Summa Theologica*, II-II, 4. 1.

6. Ibid., 1–8.

7. See Augustine, "On the Spirit and the Letter," chapter 9.

8. Ibid., chapter 51.

9. Theunissen, *Kierkegaard's Concept of Despair*, 83–87.

10. Derrida, "Faith and Knowledge: The Two Sources of 'Religion' at the Limits of Reason Alone," in *Acts of Religion*, 42–191.

11. Derrida, "Force of Law," in *Acts of Religion*, 230–98.

12. Kant, *Critique of Pure Reason*, 645–52, especially 646.

13. Cupitt, *Is Nothing Sacred?*, 32–38.

14. As indicated in chapter 2, there is no pure form of faith. All forms require the other two, although one may not always be conscious that this is the case. The highest form of faith is one in which all three forms are affirmed in consciousness.

15. Schleiermacher's *Psychologische* is not yet available in an English translation. My thanks to David Klemm for alerting me to this distinction.

16. Olson, "Postmodernity and Faith," 50.

17. Scharlemann, *The Being of God*, 178.

18. Ibid., 179.

19. Tillich, *Dynamics*, 98. Emphasis added.

20. Tillich welcomes this possibility, arguing for the superiority of Protestant Christianity because he felt that writing successfully about faith required a particular tradition.

21. Tillich, *Dynamics*, 96.

22. Ibid., 97.

4. Anonymous Hierophanies and the Mundane Possibilities of God

1. Derrida, "Faith and Knowledge," in *Acts of Religion*, 57.

2. Olson, "Postmodernity and Faith," 50.

3. Ricoeur, *The Symbolism of Evil*, 15.

4. Heidegger, "Origin of the Work of Art," in *Poetry, Language, Thought*, 21–22.

5. Ibid., 41.

6. Ibid., 49.

7. Ibid., 44.

8. Ibid., 42.

9. Ibid., 43.

10. Ibid., 72.

11. Ibid., 75.

12. Tillich, *Dynamics*, 42.
13. Heidegger, "The Thing," in *Poetry, Language, Thought*, 166.
14. Heidegger, "Building, Dwelling, Thinking," in *Poetry, Language, Thought*, 152–53.
15. Cupitt, *Is Nothing Sacred?*, 65–67.
16. Ibid., 74. While Cupitt's example is helpful here, it no longer seems as important to cling to the "Christianness" of this declaration so much as its potential to add to an atheist theology.
17. Altizer, *Total Presence*, 35–36.
18. M. Taylor, *Disfiguring*, 230–35.

5. The Work of Vigilance

1. Heidegger, "Origin of the Work of Art," in *Poetry, Language, Thought*, 66.
2. Heidegger, *The Question Concerning Technology*, 13–14.
3. Ibid., 35.
4. Ibid., 18.
5. Ibid., 18–19.
6. Ibid., 24.
7. Ibid., 25.
8. Ibid., 26.
9. Heidegger, "Origin of the Work of Art," in *Poetry, Language, Thought*, 72.
10. Heidegger, *The Question Concerning Technology*, 32.
11. Ibid., 8–9.
12. Hemming, *Heidegger's Atheism*, 212.
13. Heidegger, "Origin of the Work of Art," in *Poetry, Language, Thought*, 66.
14. Sartre, *Being and Nothingness*, 59–64.
15. As examples, see Fr. 377: "Say, Jesus Christ of Nazareth— / Hast thou no arm for Me?" and Fr525, "Infinitude—Had'st Thou no Face / That I might look on Thee?"

6. Vigilance as the Work of Faith

1. Luther, *Concerning Christian Liberty*.
2. Kierkegaard, *Fear*, 81. This absolute relation *to* the absolute is not an absolute relation *with* the absolute: rather than participating *in* the absolute, which would make the relationship one of a part to a whole (where the part is *relative* to the whole), the absolute relation is one in which two things are related by being gathered close to each other without direct contact.
3. Kierkegaard, *Sickness*, 30.
4. Kierkegaard, *Postscript*, 414.
5. Lacoste, *Experience and the Absolute*, 93: "We are free to open ourselves up to the Absolute's design. We are free to offer him our hospitality. But this hospitality can be accepted unbeknownst to us, on the one hand, and history maintains us far from the eschatological reversal by which the Absolute will offer us definitive hospitality, on the other. Our time must thus be lived in patience."
6. See Klemm and Schweiker, *Religion and the Human Future*, 73–93.
7. See Derrida, "Hostipitality," in *Acts of Religion*, 356. The essay weaves in and around a discussion of hospitality that further reinforce its connection to a vigilant faith, discussing the need for waiting in a state of readiness that goes beyond an ethical mandate (one cannot welcome a guest whom one *must* welcome: the lack of

smile would not be a welcome) for a guest whom one may or may not expect. See also Jean-Luc Nancy's interview with Derrida published as "'Eating Well,' or the Calculation of the Subject: An Interview with Jacques Derrida."

8. See Klemm and Schweiker, *Religion and the Human Future;* and Egginton, *In Defense of Religious Moderation.* Both give excellent accounts of the need for third-way thinking between extremist positions.

Conclusion

1. The term "existential" is used here in a broad sense, reading Augustine and Luther's psychologization of the event of excavation as an *existentially* relevant moment, even though "existentialism" did not come into use before Kant.

2. Theodore Adorno, commenting on Kant, wrote the following in a strikingly direct fashion: "The single genuine power standing against the principle of Auschwitz is autonomy, if I might use the Kantian expression: the power of reflection, of self-determination, of not cooperating." In some ways, perhaps, one might see the cup's refusal as providing the ground for an individual to cocreate a similar notion of autonomy, where the vigilant individual shares a power of reflection and self-determination and partakes of the cup's offering of not cooperating. See Adorno, "Education after Auschwitz," 195.

3. If one could know, with certainty, that the individuals one encounters are in fact part of one's community, then one might be said to have a duty to assist those who come for help, as they would no longer be strangers. Because one does not know for sure whether individuals are a part of one's community, one's endeavors to help them cannot be reckoned fully under the auspices of ethics, and such actions thus involve hospitality.

Bibliography

Adorno, Theodor W. "Education after Auschwitz." In *Critical Models: Interventions and Catchwords,* translated by H. W. Pickford. New York: Columbia University Press, 1988.

Allison, Henry E. *Kant's Transcendental Idealism: An Interpretation and Defense.* New Haven, CT: Yale University Press, 2004.

Althaus, Paul. *The Ethics of Martin Luther.* Philadelphia: Fortress, 1965.

Altizer, Thomas J. J. *The Gospel of Christian Atheism.* Philadelphia: Westminster, 1966.

———. *Total Presence: The Language of Jesus and the Language of Today.* New York: Seabury, 1980.

Aquinas, Thomas. *The Summa Theologica of St. Thomas Aquinas.* 2nd and rev. ed. 1920. Literally translated by Fathers of the English Dominican Province. Online edition copyright © 2008 by Kevin Knight. http://www.newadvent.org/summa/. Accessed 19 July 2012.

Augustine. "On the Spirit and the Letter." http://www.newadvent.org/fathers/1502 .htm. Accessed 19 July 2012.

Ball, Alan. *American Beauty.* Screenplay. Quoted from The Daily Script. http://www .dailyscript.com/index.

Breuer, Josef, and Sigmund Freud. *Studies on Hysteria.* Translated and edited by James Strachey. 1957. Reprint, New York: Basic Books, 2000.

Bultmann, Rudolf. *New Testament and Mythology and Other Basic Writings.* Edited and translated by Schubert M. Ogden. Minneapolis: Fortress, 1984.

Caputo, John D. "Instants, Secrets, and Singularities: Dealing Death in Kierkegaard and Derrida." In *Kierkegaard in Post/Modernity,* edited by M Matuštik and M. Westphal, 216–38. Bloomington: Indiana University Press, 1995.

———. *On Religion.* New York: Routledge, 2001.

———. *The Prayers and Tears of Jacques Derrida: Religion without Religion.* Bloomington: Indiana University Press, 1997.

Cary, Philip. *Inner Grace: Augustine in the Traditions of Plato and Paul.* New York: Oxford University Press, 2008.

Cupitt, Don. *Is Nothing Sacred? The Non-realist Philosophy of Religion: Selected Essays.* New York: Fordham University Press, 2002.

———. *Taking Leave of God*. New York: Crossroad, 1981.

Derrida, Jacques. *Acts of Religion*. Edited by Gil Anidjar. Translated by S. Weber. New York: Routledge, 2002.

———. "'Eating Well,' or the Calculation of the Subject: An Interview with Jacques Derrida." By Jean-Luc Nancy. In *Who Comes after the Subject?* edited by Eduardo Cadava, Peter Connor, and Jean-Luc Nancy. New York: Routledge, 1992.

Dickinson, Emily. *The Poems of Emily Dickinson*. Edited by Ralph William Franklin. Cambridge, MA: Belknap Press of Harvard University, 1998.

Eagleton, Terry. *Reason, Faith & Revolution: Reflections on the God Debate*. New Haven, CT: Yale University Press, 2009.

Edwards, James C. *The Plain Sense of Things: The Fate of Religion in an Age of Normal Nihilism*. University Park: Pennsylvania State University Press, 1997.

Egginton, William. *In Defense of Religious Moderation*. New York: Columbia University Press, 2011.

Eliade, Mircea. *Patterns in Comparative Religion*. Translated by Rosemary Sheed. Lincoln: University of Nebraska Press, 1996.

Fichte, Johann. *The Vocation of Man*. Translated by P. Pruess. Indianapolis: Hackett, 1987.

Freud, Sigmund. *Three Case Histories*. Edited by Philip Rieff. New York: Touchstone Books, 1996.

Gilson, Etienne. *Elements of Christian Philosophy*. New York: Doubleday, 1960.

———. *The Spirit of Thomism*. New York: P. J. Kenedy & Sons, 1964.

Green, Ronald. *Kierkegaard and Kant: The Hidden Debt*. Albany: State University of New York Press, 1992.

Harris, Sam. *The End of Faith: Religion, Terror, and the Future of Reason*. New York: W. W. Norton, 2004.

Hart, Kevin. "The Experience of God." In *The Religious*, edited by John D. Caputo, 159–74. Malden, MA: Blackwell, 2001.

Hawthorne, Nathaniel. *Young Goodman Brown and Other Tales*. New York: Oxford University Press, 2009.

Hay, David M. "*Pistis* as 'Ground of Faith' in Hellenized Judaism and Paul." *Journal of Biblical Literature* 108, no. 3 (1989): 461–76.

Heidegger, Martin. *Being and Time*. Translated by Joan Stambaugh. Albany: State University of New York Press, 1996.

———. "The Memorial Address." In *Discourse on Thinking*, translated by John Anderson and E. Hans Freund, 43–57. New York: Harper & Row, 1969.

———. *The Phenomenology of Religious Life*. Bloomington: Indiana University Press, 2004.

———. *Poetry, Language, Thought*. Translated and edited by Albert Hofstader. New York: Harper & Row, 1975.

———. *The Question Concerning Technology*. Translated and edited by William Lovitt. New York: Harper & Row, 1977.

Hemming, Laurence Paul. *Heidegger's Atheism: The Refusal of a Theological Voice*. Notre Dame, IN: University of Notre Dame Press, 2002.

Johnsen, Bredo C. "On the Coherence of Pyrrhonian Skepticism." *Philosophical Review* 110, no. 4 (2001): 521–61.

Kant, Immanuel. *Critique of Pure Reason*. Translated by Norman Kemp Smith. New York: St. Martin's, 1965.

Kearney, Richard. *Anatheism: Returning to God after God.* New York: Columbia University Press, 2011.

———. "Eschatology of the Possible God." In *The Religious,* edited by John D. Caputo, 175–96. Malden, MA: Blackwell, 2002.

———. *The God Who May Be: The Hermeneutics of Religion.* Bloomington: Indiana University Press, 2002.

Kierkegaard, Søren. *Concluding Unscientific Postscript.* Translated by H. V. Hong. Princeton, NJ: Princeton University Press, 1992.

———. *Fear and Trembling.* Translated by H. V. Hong. Princeton, NJ: Princeton University Press, 1983.

———. *Philosophical Fragments.* Translated by H. V. Hong. Princeton, NJ: Princeton University Press, 1985.

———. *Practice in Christianity.* Translated by H. V. Hong. Princeton, NJ: Princeton University Press, 1991.

———. *The Sickness unto Death.* Translated by H. V. Hong. Princeton, NJ: Princeton University Press, 1989.

Klemm, David. *Hermeneutical Inquiry.* Vol. 1, *Interpretation of Texts.* Atlanta: Scholars, 1986.

Klemm, David, and William Klink. "Constructing and Testing Theological Models." *Zygon: A Journal for Religion and Science* 38, no. 3 (2003): 495–528.

Klemm, David, and William Schweiker. *Religion and the Human Future: An Essay on Theological Humanism.* Malden, MA: Blackwell, 2008.

Lacoste, Jean-Yves. *Experience and the Absolute: Disputed Questions on the Humanity of Man.* Translated by Mark Raferty-Skeha. New York: Fordham University Press, 2004.

Lundin, Roger. *Emily Dickinson and the Art of Belief.* Grand Rapids, MI: William B. Eerdmans, 1998.

Luther, Martin. *Concerning Christian Liberty.* New York: P. F. Collier & Son, 1909–14. Quotations from bartleby.com.

Lyotard, Jean-François. *The Postmodern Condition: A Report on Knowledge.* Translated by R. Durand. Minneapolis: University of Minnesota Press, 1984.

Malantschuk, Gregor. *Kierkegaard's Thought.* Edited and translated by H. V. Hong. Princeton, NJ: Princeton University Press, 1971.

Marion, Jean-Luc. *God without Being.* Translated by Thomas A. Carlson. Chicago: University of Chicago Press, 1991.

McGinn, Bernard. *The Mystical Thought of Meister Eckhart: The Man from Whom God Hid Nothing.* New York: Crossroad, 2001.

McIntosh, James. *Nimble Believing: Dickinson and the Unknown.* Ann Arbor: University of Michigan Press, 2000.

Nancy, Jean-Luc. *Dis-Enclosure: The Deconstruction of Christianity.* Translated by Bettina Bergo, Gabriel Malenfant, and Michael B. Smith. New York: Fordham University Press, 2008.

New, Elisa. *The Regenerate Lyric: Theology and Innovation in American Poetry.* New York: Press Syndicate of the University of Cambridge, 1993.

Olson, Alan M. "Postmodernity and Faith." *Journal of the American Academy of Religion* 58, no. 1 (1990): 37–53.

Ricoeur, Paul. *Fallible Man.* Translated by C. A. Kelbley. New York: Fordham University Press, 1986.

Sartre, Jean-Paul. *Being and Nothingness*. Translated by Hazel Barnes. New York: Washington Square Press, 1992.

———. *Freud and Philosophy*. Translated by D. Savage. New Haven, CT: Yale University Press, 1970.

———. "Religion, Atheism, and Faith." In *The Conflict of Interpretations*, translated by Charles Freilich, edited by Don Idhe, 440–67. Chicago: Northwestern University Press, 1974.

———. *The Symbolism of Evil*. Translated by E. Buchanan. New York: Harper & Row, 1967.

Scarry, Elaine. *The Body in Pain: The Making and Unmaking of the World*. New York: Oxford University Press, 1985.

Scharlemann, Robert P. *The Being of God: Theology and the Experience of Truth*. New York: Seabury, 1980.

———. "The Question of Philosophical Theology." In *Being and Truth: Essays in Honour of John Macquarrie*, edited by Alistair Kee and Eugene T. Long, 3–17. London: SCM, 1986.

———. *The Reason of Following: Christology and the Ecstatic I*. Chicago: University of Chicago Press, 1991.

Smith, J. K. A. *Introducing Radical Orthodoxy: Mapping a Post-secular Theology*. Grand Rapids, MI: Baker Academic, 2004.

Smith, Wilfred Cantwell. *Faith and Belief*. Princeton, NJ: Princeton University Press, 1979.

Taylor, Charles. *A Secular Age*. Cambridge, MA: Belknap Press of Harvard University Press, 2007.

Taylor, Mark C. *About Religion: Economies of Faith in Virtual Culture*. Chicago: University of Chicago Press, 1999.

———. *After God*. Chicago: University of Chicago Press, 2007.

———. *Disfiguring: Art, Architecture, Religion*. Chicago: University of Chicago Press, 1992.

Theunissen, Michael. *Kierkegaard's Concept of Despair*. Translated by Barbara Harshay and Hellmut Illbruk. Princeton, NJ: Princeton University Press, 2005.

Tillich, Paul. *Biblical Religion and the Search for Ultimate Reality*. Chicago: University of Chicago Press, 1955.

———. *The Courage to Be*. New Haven, CT: Yale University Press, 1952.

———. *Dynamics of Faith*. New York: Harper, 1958.

Todorov, Tzvetan. *The Fantastic: A Structural Approach to a Literary Genre*. Cleveland: Press of Case Western Reserve University, 1973.

Vattimo, Gianni. *After Christianity*. Translated by Luca D'Isanto. New York: Columbia University Press, 2002.

Williams, Thomas. Introduction to *Proslogion*, by Anselm. Edited by Thomas Williams. Indianapolis: Hackett, 2001.

Žižek, Slavoj. *The Fragile Absolute: Or Why Is the Christian Legacy Worth Fighting For?* New York: Verso, 2009.

———. *The Puppet and the Dwarf: The Perverse Core of Christianity*. Cambridge, MA: MIT Press, 2003.

Žižek, Slavoj, and John Milbank. *The Monstrosity of Christ: Paradox or Dialectic?* Edited by Creston Davis. Cambridge, MA: MIT Press, 2009.

Index

absolute, the, 15, 28, 39, 40, 45, 102, 127,
140, 157–60, 164, 174, 176, 184, 186,
187, 190, 191–94; and God, 36, 158,
172; relations, 15, 22, 37, 39, 40, 53,
64–65, 106, 157, 159, 168, 169, 170,
174, 180, 193; sacred, 130, 158; and time
(future), 101–2, 158, 181, 190, 192–94;
truth, 63, 65, 157, 159, 189; worlds, 160
aletheia, 53–54, 117, 148
Altizer, Thomas J. J., 11, 114, 129, 130–32,
134, 135
American Beauty, 111, 114, 116, 122, 201
anonymity, 110, 130, 131–35, 151, 181
anonymous, the, 130, 134, 135, 159,
185–86, 193; absolute, 158, 176, culture
as, 134; forms, 176; God or divine, 113,
129, 131, 140; grief, 157; hierophanies,
17, 49, 102, 106, 109, 116, 123, 124, 132,
133–35; nothing, 185; objects, 124, 132,
140, 151, 185; person, 184; presence,
132, 135; sacred, 158, 186; sign of, 132;
spaces, 159; vision, 131
anxiety, 43; crippling effects of, 43; and existential unity, 43; of meaninglessness,
60; and passion, 71; and skepticism,
58; and symbols, 43
appropriation, 74, 86, 126, 127, 141, 145,
151–53, 172, 175, 188–89
Aquinas. *See* Thomas Aquinas
artwork, 54, 125
ataraxia, 56, 57, 59, 179

atheism/atheist, 10–11, 14, 130, 155–57,
172; faith and, 16, 165, 181, 182; funda-
mentalism, 18; human, type of, 79–80;
new, 3; paradigms, 140; philosophies,
11; possibilities, 132; presymbolic and,
13; secular and, 5, 14; theology, 11, 14,
17, 27, 47, 111
Augustine, Saint, 6, 25, 66, 85, 107, 112,
136

belief: abandoning, 57; adhering to, 71;
analog of, 72; assenting to, 33, 34, 75;
attitude of, 96; avoiding, 56; beliefs
about, 87; bracketing, 59; certain, 34;
conflicting, 188; confirmed, 30; cost
of, 107; decline of, 2; desired, 22, 64;
disbelief, 6, 7, 52, 139, 180; dogmatic,
56, 96; doubt and, 90; etymology of, 3;
faith and, 33, 34, 87–88; individual, 34;
initial, 47; introductory, 9; knowledge
and, 33–34, 188; language and, 33, 87,
94; legitimation of, 115; level of, 187;
making, 66, 156, 182–83; mediations
of, 87, 105; memory and, 188; objective
uncertainty and, 61; passion and, 71,
73, 75; phenomenon of, 58; positivity of, 57; practice and, 165; problems
with, 28; proposition of, 33–34, 85;
reason and, 73–74, 188; reflexive, 188;
skepticism and, 56, 58–61, 68–69,
87, 91; statement of, 75, 87, 90, 188;

belief (*continued*)
suspension of, 57–58, 64; symbols and, 66, 156; thinking and, 90; truth and, 57, 135, 189; unbelief, 66, 134, 156; ultimacy of, 105; understanding and, 9; volition and, 75–76

Bewahren, 136, 145, 153

boredom, 163, 174–75, 178, 187, 189

bracketing: and existence of phenomena, 95; and faith, 75; and judgments, 150; and questions of existence of God, 5, 11, 14, 21, 52; skepticism and *epoche*, 56–57, 59, 61, 63; wholes, 13; world, 63, 139

brokenness, 1–6, 9, 14–16, 22, 30–31, 34, 45, 59, 66–67, 76, 82, 99, 105, 111, 116, 140

Bultmann, Rudolf, 10–11

Caputo, John, 11, 16, 163–64

Christianity/Christian: atheism, 11; Christendom, 2, 41–42; concepts of God, 25, 27, 132, 141, 155; *Concerning Christian Liberty*, 166–67; Don Cupitt and, 129–30; *Dis-Enclosure: The Deconstruction of Christianity*, 172; fundamentalists, 18; postreligious or postsecular, 15; *Practice in Christianity*, 38–39, 41; as religion, 23–24, 29, 31, 37, 85, 108, 172; revelations of God, 171; scriptures, 166; secularized, 11; symbols and, 46, 102; theological terminology, 135; Paul Tillich on, 103–4; tradition and, 11, 15, 22, 116, 165

coffee cup, 95, 106, 130, 134, 184–89, 191, 194

community: of agnostics, 34; contextualizing, 62; demonic, 83; distance from, 7, 9, 22, 35, 44–45; entering into, 34; external, 167; faith and, 13, 21, 167, 191; finite, 168; general or human, 7, 33, 34, 61, 62; hidden, 171; home in, 7; imminent, 179; internal, 167; language, 32–33; literal, 82; members of, 33; needs of, 29; and objective certainty, 33, 179; participation in, 7, 191–92; religious, 27, 168; and ritual, 21; skeptical faith and absence of, 49; smaller (restricted), 32–34, 62, 104; spiritual, 9,

179; and symbol, 6, 32, 34, 45, 61, 80, 105, 172; trusting, 62; voluntary, 167

consciousness: acts of, 97; elements of, 56; faith and, 14–15, 102, 107, 115–16; God and, 89; human, 11, 13, 56, 69, 79, 84; intentional, 88; knowledge and, 105; levels of, 91, 99, 187; limits of, 100; objects of, 88, 95, 99–100, 125, 135; prereflective, 186; reflexive, 17, 59, 99–100; Schleiermacher's forms of, 101; self, 97, 101; skeptical, 14, 17, 49, 53, 55, 59, 63, 64, 80, 99, 105; things and, 117; truth and, 88, 190; vigilance and, 15, 97, 99, 101, 106, 139; vigilant, 17 99, 100–102, 105–6

construction, 40, 43, 63, 67, 83, 127, 145, 159, 161, 183, 190, 194

co-responding, 125, 129, 135, 146–47

cross, 44, 46, 103–4, 123, 187

cultivation, 5, 127, 145, 147, 161, 190–91, 194

Cupitt, Don, 96, 129–30, 132

dancing, 112, 129–30, 133, 136

Derrida, Jacques, 53, 86, 161

despair: and atheism, 14; and existential doubt, 8; and faith, 14, 15, 48, 98, 107, 172; and Godlessness, 156, 159; Nathaniel Hawthorne and, 82–83, 91; and isolation, 9; Kierkegaardian, 2, 38, 60, 67–68, 107, 168; and knowledge, 73, 165; and meaningfulness, 11; and meaninglessness, 48; and nonbeing, 85; and paradox, 37; and passions, 71; salvation from, 43; and skepticism, 6, 8, 59, 67; and Paul Tillich, 47, 67

Dickinson, Emily, 140–45, 147, 150–52, 156, 158–59, 161

disclosure, 75, 79, 84, 112, 135, 161, 165, 169; divine, 62, 111, 157; equipmental, 125; of Faith, 181; human, 148; of new world, 32, 65, 89, 159; of outcry, 164; of plastic bag, 117; and poverty of language, 32; of prebelief, 155; of readers, 143; and relativism, 53; symbolic, 47; of thoughts, 187; of Truth, 55, 112, 114, 122, 136, 145

displacement, 2, 83, 121; Dickinsonian, 145; of faith, 41; of God, 36; Heideg-

faith (*continued*)
102, 139; skeptical, 14–18, 22, 27, 29,
42, 48–49, 52, 55–56, 59–60, 63–69,
76, 84, 87, 95, 98–99, 102–3, 105–7,
110–11, 116, 124, 130, 139–40, 145, 149,
151, 154–59, 162, 165–66, 173, 180;
state of, 24, 30–31, 33–34, 58, 74, 80,
85, 87, 89, 106, 111, 115–16, 154, 171,
182–83; static, 80; structure of, 14, 27,
40, 44, 48, 52; symbolic, 31, 42, 44–46,
48, 61, 105, 123; symbols of, 15, 103–5;
theological, 27, 35, 98; time of, 30, 74,
80, 103, 128; trusting, 17, 23, 26, 52,
61, 87, 166, 181; truth of, 46, 48, 103,
181; understanding, 85, 98; vigilant, 2,
13, 15–18, 35, 52, 102, 105–7, 113, 129,
140–41, 145, 147, 150, 155–61, 165–66,
171–77; virtue of, 18, 129, 174, 176,
178–80, 183, 190–91, 194; work of, 27,
30, 39, 42–43, 49, 67, 80, 82, 85, 114,
140–41, 144, 149, 153–56, 162, 165–67,
170–71, 173, 176–78, 183–84, 190, 192
fantastic, the, 92–97, 106, 204
Fichte, Johann, 73
fourfold, the, 126–27, 145–46, 151, 190
Freud, Sigmund, 10–11, 32, 72, 132

gathering: absolute, 193; by bag, 113, 128;
clouds, 110; communities, 6, 179, 191;
of cup, 184–85, 189, 194; of divinities,
131, 142–43, 152–53, 156–57, 177; dwelling as, 127; equipmental, 132; of faith,
75, 102; of fourfold, 126; meanings,
61; perspectives, 142; and revelations,
148, 157; as sign, 128; of things, 69,
125, 128, 133, 146, 157, 181, 184, 190;
of truth, 69, 144–45, 181; uncertainty,
177; of unspoken, 172; and vigilance,
150–53, 177, 193; words, 143, 147; of
worlds, 144, 147, 158, 160
God: as absolute, 13, 158, 171–72; as
anonymous, 113, 129, 131, 134–35,
139, 151; bracketing, 11, 14, 21, 52, 56;
Christian, 25, 28–29, 75, 82–85, 104,
108, 155, 168, 171; conception of, 24;
contingent, 36; critiques of, 10; death
of, 1, 11, 130–31; definitions of, 4, 16,
18; denial of, 10; dependence on, 40;
descriptions of, 9; existence of, 24, 42;

and faith, 3, 9–10, 45–46, 52, 66, 156;
God above God, 11–12, 17, 42–47, 63,
106, 115, 140, 157, 172; godless, 7, 11, 51,
69, 140–41, 153, 155–57, 159, 162, 174,
176–77, 179–81; God-Man, 38–39, 41,
44, 115, 124, 131, 134; God without God,
21; hand of God, 2, 39, 68; Kingdom
of, 29, 102, 116, 136, 152, 164, 166–67,
170; knowledge of, 3; model of, 4–5,
12–13; nature of, 21; nonsymbolically
mediated, 12, 67, 172, 180; as object, 15,
30, 42, 114–15, 144, 166; ontological,
35–36, 85; postmodern conceptions of,
86; as process, 102, 115; proofs of, 35;
questions of, 10–11, 24, 36, 52, 69, 155;
relationship with, 22, 30; revelations
from/of, 52, 62, 64, 74–75, 84, 111–12,
114, 124, 130–31, 155–56, 159; symbolic,
43, 45, 48, 67, 130; theistic, 5, 145, 153,
156; truth of, 75, 84, 111, 130, 156; visions of, 10

hand: at hand, 29, 73, 76, 102, 116, 118,
130–32, 136, 145, 152, 157, 160, 164,
177–78, 189, 193–94; of God, 2, 39, 68
Hawthorne, Nathaniel, 80–83, 92–94,
97, 107
Hegel, G. W. F., 11, 36, 132
Heidegger, Martin, 11–12, 17, 25, 29, 35,
52–56, 62–63, 86, 103, 114, 116–22,
124–31, 134, 135, 140, 171, 181; Heideggerean models, 29, 35, 62, 98, 114,
130, 144–51, 153; post-Heideggerean
models, 83–84, 158, 182
Herausforden, 147–50
Hervorbringen, 147–50
hospitality, 18, 162, 163, 165–66, 174–79,
190, 192, 194
Husserl, Edmund, 125

inwardness, 38–40, 42, 169

James, book of, 166, 176
Jesus, 31, 37–38, 44, 116, 151, 152, 162,
164, 171
Johnsen, Bredo C., 56–59

Kant, Immanuel, 23, 25–27, 34, 35–36,
42, 53, 55, 64, 85, 87–88, 90, 95, 158,

98; and truth, 189; and vigilance, 102, 106, 154, 188; and vigilant faith, 147, 179, 190–92; vulnerability to, 69; and the work of faith, 183, 188, 190

universal, the, 7, 41, 81, 152, 167, 176; and absolute, 40, 168; abstract, 135; accessibility, 130, 157; belief, 74; experience, 113; faith, 74; and language, 175, 189; model, 45; and particular, 104; and passion, 73; and personal, 191; rationality, 17, 74; sign, 129; symbol, 105; truth, 57, 70; unveilation, 35

unveilation, 194; of absolute, 159; of beatific vision, 85; deferred, 63; and end of faith, 192; final or full, 34–35, 84, 102, 107, 124, 139, 153, 174; of new world, 34; of nihilism, 130; of pos-

sible, 157; and revelation, 32, 71, 101, 174; time of, 194; of truth, 30, 59, 69, 96, 166

Van Gogh, Vincent, 120, 130
Vattimo, Gianni, 129
vigilant skeptics, 17, 99, 116–18, 124, 127–29, 132–36, 139–40, 156–59, 162, 171, 180, 189

worship, 17, 29, 39, 42, 47, 66, 155, 159, 162, 166

"Young Goodman Brown," 81, 89, 91–92, 97–98, 102

Žižek, Slavoj, 4, 11, 16

Recent Books in the Studies in Religion and Culture Series